"According to Lou Andreas-Salomé, Spinoza was the 'philosopher of psychoanalysis' who demonstrated that 'physical and mental manifestations are representations of one another', while Freud in a 1931 letter acknowledged his 'dependence on Spinoza's doctrine', although he did not 'expressly mention' Spinoza's name. In guiding the reader on what he calls a 'journey of actions and ideas across time', Ian Miller takes us backward to show how Freud found in Heine and Spinoza two 'fellow *un*-believers', and forward to link Spinoza's thought with that of Bion and Winnicott. Spinoza emerges from Miller's capacious study as the delineator of a '*practical* philosophy', which, like clinical psycho-analysis, is meant to point the way 'toward personal and societal betterment'".

Peter L. Rudnytsky, *University of Florida and Chicago Psychoanalytic Institute, author of* Mutual Analysis: Ferenczi, Severn, and the Origins of Trauma Theory

Clinical Spinoza

Discovering Spinoza's early modern psychology some 35 years into his own clinical practice, Ian Miller now gives shape to this connection through a close reading of Spinoza's key philosophical ideas.

With a rigorous and expansive analysis of Spinoza's *Ethics* in particular, Miller explores how Spinozan thought simultaneously empowered the original conceptual direction of psychoanalytic thinking, and anticipated the field's contemporary theoretical dimensions. Miller offers a detailed overview of the philosopher's psychoanalytic reception from the early work of German-language psychoanalytic thinkers, such as Freud and Lou Andreas-Salomé, forward into its Anglophone reception, influencing both mid-century humanistic American psychoanalysis as well as anticipating thinkers such as Bion and Winnicott.

Covering key concepts in psychoanalytic theory and clinical practice, this book demonstrates how knowledge of Spinoza's philosophical work can help to both illuminate and improve modern psychoanalytic therapies.

Ian S. Miller is a clinical psychologist/psychoanalyst and writer based in Dublin. He is the author of *Defining Psychoanalysis: Achieving a Vernacular Expression* (Karnac, 2016); *On Minding and Being Minded: Experiencing Bion & Beckett* (Karnac, 2015); and co-author of *Beckett and Bion: The (Im)patient Voice in Psychotherapy and Literature* (Karnac, 2013) as well as *On the Daily Work of Psychoanalytic Psychotherapy* (Routledge, 2018). He serves as Associate Editor on the *American Journal of Psychoanalysis*.

Psychoanalysis In A New Key Book Series

Donnel Stern
Series Editor

When music is played in a new key, the melody does not change, but the notes that make up the composition do: change in the context of continuity, continuity that perseveres through change. Psychoanalysis in a New Key publishes books that share the aims psychoanalysts have always had, but that approach them differently. The books in the series are not expected to advance any particular theoretical agenda, although to this date most have been written by analysts from the Interpersonal and Relational orientations.

The most important contribution of a psychoanalytic book is the communication of something that nudges the reader's grasp of clinical theory and practice in an unexpected direction. Psychoanalysis in a New Key creates a deliberate focus on innovative and unsettling clinical thinking. Because that kind of thinking is encouraged by exploration of the sometimes surprising contributions to psychoanalysis of ideas and findings from other fields, Psychoanalysis in a New Key particularly encourages interdisciplinary studies. Books in the series have married psychoanalysis with dissociation, trauma theory, sociology, and criminology. The series is open to the consideration of studies examining the relationship between psychoanalysis and any other field—for instance, biology, literary and art criticism, philosophy, systems theory, anthropology, and political theory.

But innovation also takes place within the boundaries of psychoanalysis, and Psychoanalysis in a New Key therefore also presents work that reformulates thought and practice without leaving the precincts of the field. Books in the series focus, for example, on the significance of personal values in psychoanalytic practice, on the complex interrelationship between the analyst's clinical work and personal life, on the consequences for the clinical situation when patient and analyst are from different cultures, and on the need for psychoanalysts to accept the degree to which they knowingly satisfy their own wishes during treatment hours, often to the patient's detriment.

A full list of all titles in this series is available at: https://www.routledge.com/Psychoanalysis-in-a-New-Key-Book-Series/book-series/LEAPNKBS

Clinical Spinoza

Integrating His Philosophy with Contemporary Therapeutic Practice

Ian S. Miller

Routledge
Taylor & Francis Group

LONDON AND NEW YORK

Cover image: © Ian S. Miller

First published 2022
by Routledge
4 Park Square, Milton Park, Abingdon, Oxon OX14 4RN

and by Routledge
605 Third Avenue, New York, NY 10158

Routledge is an imprint of the Taylor & Francis Group, an informa business

© 2022 Ian S. Miller

Library of Congress Cataloguing-in-Publication Data
Names: Miller, Ian S., author.
Title: Clinical Spinoza : integrating his philosophy with contemporary
therapeutic practice / Ian S. Miller.
Description: 1 Edition. | New York : Routledge, 2022. |
Includes bibliographical references and index.
Identifiers: LCCN 2021053427 (print) | LCCN 2021053428 (ebook) |
ISBN 9781032159409 (hardback) | ISBN 9781032159348 (paperback) |
ISBN 9781003246404 (ebook)
Subjects: LCSH: Psychoanalysis and philosophy. |
Psychology and philosophy. | Spinoza, Benedictus de, 1632-1677.
Classification: LCC BF175.4.P45 M548 2022 (print) |
LCC BF175.4.P45 (ebook) | DDC 150.19/5--dc23/eng/20220113
LC record available at https://lccn.loc.gov/2021053427
LC ebook record available at https://lccn.loc.gov/2021053428

ISBN: 978-1-032-15940-9 (hbk)
ISBN: 978-1-032-15934-8 (pbk)
ISBN: 978-1-003-24640-4 (ebk)

DOI: 10.4324/9781003246404

Typeset in Times New Roman
by MPS Limited, Dehradun

Contents

Acknowledgments

Psychoanalytic study, like Seneca's observations on philosophy two thousand years ago, requires daily practice; and the cumulative practice over a lifetime often results in surprise and joy. For me, this has been the case after thirty-five years of clinical practice, in pursuing Spinoza's thinking—which only occurred when my ignorance was tweaked by Freud's appropriation and defense of Heine's pointed humor, a story I relate in Chapter 3.

It would be unfair not to dedicate this work then, to that chain of Wisdom tradition including Aristotle and Seneca, al-Farabi and Maimonides, and Shmuel Ibn-Tibbon, Bacon, Descartes, and Spinoza, through to Heine and Freud and beyond to the 19th- and 20th-century readers of Spinoza I have encountered en route to our contemporary vernacular expressions of psychoanalysis.

I greatly value the encouragement and support of my New York colleagues and friends, Giselle Galdi and Robert Prince, throughout this passionate pursuit; and Donnel Stern for his willingness to include this *clinical Spinoza* in the "Psychoanalysis in a New Key" series.

The author also expresses his gratitude for permission to republish the following material in entirety or in part:

Miller, I. S. (2020) 'Spinoza: Multiple identities at the origins of psychoanalytic psychology', *International Forum of Psychoanalysis*, 29(4):

207–214. DOI: 10.1080/0803706X.2019.1634285 © The International Federation of Psychoanalytic Societies, reprinted by permission of Taylor & Francis Ltd., http://www.tandfonline.com on behalf of The International Federation of Psychoanalytic Societies.

Spinoza, B. (2002) *Spinoza Complete Works*, (Edited by Michael L. Morgan. Translated by Samuel Shirley). Reprinted by permission of Hackett Publishing Company, Inc. All rights reserved.

Reprinted by permission from Springer Nature Customer Service Centre GmbH: Springer AMERICAN JOURNAL OF PSYCHOANALYSIS Doublings between Bewilderment and Enlightenment: Reading Freud with Heine on the Troubled Identity of Hirsch-Hyacinth, Ian S. Miller, © 2019

Reprinted by permission from Springer Nature Customer Service Centre GmbH: Springer AMERICAN JOURNAL OF PSYCHOANALYSIS Spinoza's Announcement of Psychological Practice, Ian S. Miller, © 2020

Introduction

The present work, *Clinical Spinoza: Integrating His Philosophy with Contemporary Therapeutic Practice,* is rooted in overdetermination, a form familiar to psychoanalysts. On the one hand, the illuminative experience of a "flash", a common-enough experience in reading Spinoza (Andreas-Salomé, 1964; Deleuze, 1988; Wolstein, 1987, p. 635; Vermorel, 2009), linked directly to my intuition that Spinozan thought showed great correspondence with psychoanalytic thinking. On the other hand, Freud's own reference to Baruch Spinoza, mediated by Heinrich Heine, led me along the path of pre-psychoanalytic history and thought.

Part I includes two chapters describing seventy years of alignment between Spinoza's *Ethics* and the development of psychoanalysis before Spinoza's silent disappearance, late in the 20th century. Part II expands three published journal articles, describing my first encounters in thinking about Spinoza. Part III presents my reading of *Ethics* I-III in four chapters. Part IV consolidates Spinoza's matrix of psychological considerations, a patterning now familiar to contemporary clinicians, through algorithmic forms such as those presented by Lewin (1933, 1936), Bion (1962), Miller and Sweet (2018), and Levenson (1983). Finally, Part V hypothesizes a solution to the puzzle of Spinoza's late 20th-century psychoanalytic disappearance.

Throughout, I have been mindful of the gaps separating Spinoza's foundation of modern psychology in transformation of medieval philosophy, and late 20th-century training in clinical psychology and psychoanalysis. I have tried to explain clearly, not only what

DOI: 10.4324/9781003246404-1

Spinoza writes, but also how it fits in the history of received ideas eventuating in contemporary psychoanalysis. In journeying, I have encountered a history of psychoanalytic thinking I'd never before heard about or known: a chain of transmission from the turn of the 20th century to the 1960's, integrative of Spinoza's *Ethics* in psychoanalysis. Repeatedly reading *Ethics*, I was led into perplexities in the reception history of ideas: and so, turned to other English-language works from multiple academic fields, themselves locating Baruch Spinoza in relation to history, culture, philosophy, and textual transmission.

Very early, I recognized in *Ethics*, a clinical psychology never formally articulated, but emergent through repetitive readings. It is this *Clinical Spinoza* that I see as congruent with contemporary understanding of our psychoanalytic "vernacular expression", linked in large degree to the thinking of W.R. Bion and D.W. Winnicott (Miller, 2016; Miller & Sweet, 2018); and integrated too, with a focus upon interpersonal relations in clinical practice.

This journey in the transformation of ideas often collapsed time as I traveled from the 21st century, back and forth across two millennia, all the while learning things I'd never considered in clinical training. The reader, traveling with me, will soon understand such rhythms and occasionally, their anxiety-generating perplexities. In passing through multiple transformations of thought and language toward articulating *Clinical Spinoza*, the reader continually encounters unformulated cultural, educational, and philosophical assumptions. These remain more or less present through the development of psychoanalysis as a science more human than otherwise; and are reflective of Spinoza's first and second kinds of knowledge, the distortions of belief and assumptive group consensus as to what constitutes truth.

Throughout, I have relied upon *Spinoza Complete Works*, edited by Michael L. Morgan and translated by Samuel Shirley. While initially introducing a work such as *Ethics* or the *Treatise on the Emendation of the Intellect*, my citation includes "Spinoza, 2002", the date of publication. With repeated reference to a work already introduced, I either use an abbreviation, such as TEI for *Treatise on the Emendation of the Intellect,* or in *Ethics,* the Roman numeral designating Part (I, II, III, IV, or V), followed by subcategory such as Proposition or Definition, together with clarification if appropriate, as when I refer to a Scholium, followed by page number. Contrasting translations of *Ethics*, I clearly state the translation under consideration.

Ian Miller
Dublin
February 2021

Part I

Chapter 1

The Philosopher of Psychoanalysis (I)

Lou Andreas-Salomé glowingly describes Baruch Spinoza as the "philosopher of psychoanalysis" (1964, p. 75).

Reviewing textual history, the clinical reader recognizes strong convergence between Spinoza's *Ethics* and psychoanalytic thought spanning three distinct periods: (1) the early German-language development of psychoanalysis; (2) Spinoza's Anglophone reception; and (3) and the articulation of Spinozan values within humanistic psychoanalysis.

This chapter focuses initially upon Spinoza's reception during the German-language development of psychoanalytic thinking. Next, the focus changes both in geographic location and language. Navigating the English Channel and the Atlantic Ocean, German language reception of Spinoza shifts toward early Anglophone reception.

Chapter 2 reads Spinoza as the precursor to modern psychoanalytic psychology through the vehicle of published journal papers. Philosopher of science Ludwik Fleck, a contributor to Thomas Kuhn's notion of scientific *paradigm shift* (Kuhn, 1970, p. vi), recognizes *journal science* as that period when individual practitioners, working independently and subjectively registering scientific recognitions, announce their findings formally to their larger, scientific thought collectives (Fleck, 1979, p. 118). The journal publications of Amy Tanner in the United States (Tanner, 1907a, 1907b) and M. Hamblin Smith in Great Britain (Smith, 1925, 1926) introduce Spinoza to English-language communities in psychology and psychoanalysis. Smith's (1925) publication, "Spinoza's Anticipation of Recent Psychological Developments" in the *British Journal of Medical Psychology*, the paper

DOI: 10.4324/9781003246404-3

from which his 1926 *International Journal of Psychoanalysis* contribution is derived, provides the journal-based foundation for understanding both Spinoza's anticipations and convergences with then-
emergent psychoanalytic thought. Building on Smith (1925, 1926),
Constance Rathbun's (1934) publication in *The Psychoanalytic Review*
titled, "On Certain Similarities Between Spinoza and Psychoanalysis",
consolidates Spinoza's position within psychoanalysis. Rathbun, in
turn, is referenced by Walter Bernard in his *Psychiatry* publication,
"Freud and Spinoza" (1946). Earlier, Bernard's (1934) monograph on
Spinoza had presented the German reception of Spinozan thought to a
new, Anglophone audience in the United States. Bernard begins,

> There is no doubt that the *Ethics* of Spinoza constitutes an
> extremely important landmark in the history of philosophy.
> From the days that Spinoza was rediscovered by that eager
> group of literary men in Germany with Lessing at their head, the
> influence and the import of Spinoza's philosophy has been
> extending to ever widening spheres; and today there seems to
> be prevalent among philosophers the unqualified opinion that
> Spinoza is one of the very few major thinkers of the world, and a
> first-rate power in the history of thought. All subsequent
> philosophies, with very few exceptions, have taken due cogni-
> zance of, and issue with, the Spinozistic philosophy, and must
> perforce continue to do so. Many philosophers, scientists, and
> literary men have freely confessed a more or less intimate
> devotion to and dependence on Spinoza. Even Hegel was once
> moved to say: *Du hast entweder den Spinozismus oder gar keine
> Philosophie.* (Bernard, 1934, p. 11)

Chapter 2 concludes with the contributions of what were then called
Neo-Freudian psychoanalysts in the United States. As Walter Bernard's
quote suggests, inspired largely by German-speaking refugees from
Nazi Germany, Spinoza became highlighted as representing the enlightened development of humanism in psychoanalytic understanding
(Fromm, 1964a, 1964b; Weiss, 1952). With this development,
America's enthusiastic post World War II embrace of psychoanalysis
underlines the explicit humanism of *Ethics*, Parts IV and V (Fromm,
1964a, 1964b; Weiss, 1952). For the first time, Spinozan clinical

formulation becomes integrated within psychoanalytic discussion (Reid, 1955; Tigner, 1985). Retrospectively, through this opening of the psychoanalytic door to a clinical Spinoza, earlier unattributed Spinozan influences in direct clinical practice become clearer and more greatly distinct to the clinical reader (Tanner, 1907b; Tausk, 1934, 1969; Federn, 1915).

Themes in Psychoanalytic Reception of Spinoza

Chapter 1 is divided into two thematic units. The first, detailing early German language psychoanalytic reception of Spinoza, includes the subsections: (1) themes in psychoanalytic reception of Spinoza; and (2) the German Spinoza, philosopher of psychoanalysis.

The second unit documents early Anglophone reception of Spinoza in psychology and psychoanalysis. It includes three subsections: (1) challenges for Tanner (1907a, 1907b) and Smith (1926); (2) Amy Tanner's "Spinoza and Modern Psychology" (1907a); and (3) M. Hamblin Smith's "Spinoza's Anticipation of Recent Psychological Developments" (1926).

Observing Spinozan reception within psychoanalytic thought across the 20th century, the reader becomes aware of two underlying themes in all writers' presentations. The first is that Spinoza is consistently present *in relation to* the writer's contemporary understanding of psychology and psychoanalysis. Writing at different moments in psychoanalytic development, each writer progressively integrates *Ethics* more tightly into the emerging weave of psychoanalytic conceptions. When Lou Andreas-Salomé and Freud reference Spinoza, it is relative to the opening phases of psychoanalytic development. When M.H. Smith references Spinoza, it is relative to the exciting introduction of psychoanalytic thought in the United Kingdom, just as Smith also references new currents in forensic psychiatry in the United States, represented by William Alanson White. A decade later, Constance Rathbun not only references Spinoza relative to the development of American ego psychology, but also refers to MH Smith's earlier understanding of Spinoza's psychoanalytic links. She is succeeded by integrations of Spinoza within developing interpersonal and humanistic currents of psychoanalysis (Bernard, 1946; Fromm, 1964a; Reid, 1955; Weiss, 1952; Tigner, 1985).

Second, each writer references *their* Spinoza, anchored in *their* psychoanalysis, through consistent use of memory and associative process, psychology's foundational building blocks, observed by Spinoza in *Ethics*, Part II. *Ethics*, in this way, provides both correlative contents and intrinsic psychological processes that align with later writers' subjective understandings of psychoanalytic principles and values. Each text reveals a record of its author's Spinozan discovery relative to his or her time-bound understanding of psychoanalytic psychology.

The German Spinoza, Philosopher of Psychoanalysis

One of the earliest published links between psychoanalysis and Baruch Spinoza is in Freud's critical observation that Leonardo da Vinci's artistic "development approaches Spinoza's mode of thinking" (1910, p. 75). This laconic reference suggests that Freud's affirmation of his own "dependence on Spinoza's doctrine", some twenty years later, may have been more extensive than admitted. Writing in 1931 to Dr Lothar Bickel, Freud confesses,

> I readily admit my dependence on Spinoza's doctrine. There was no reason why I should expressly mention his name, since I conceived my hypotheses from the atmosphere created by him, rather than from the study of his work. Moreover I did not seek a philosophical legitimation. (Bernard, 1977, p. 63)

Freud's suggestion in the context of Leonardo da Vinci is that thinking is foundational to Spinoza's art. Freud's linkage between Leonardo and Spinoza focuses upon the capacity of the artist to intuit clearly from self-experience unbound by biased judgment, in encountering and addressing the world. That Freud's Spinozan reference construes thinking as a *mode* reaches back to the language of Spinoza's detailed explanatory descriptions in *Ethics*. Minimally, Freud would have pondered the definition of *mode* as

> the affections of a substance; that is, that which is in something else and is conceived through something else. (Spinoza, 2002, I. Definition 5, p. 217)

Consistent with Freud's own recognition of psychic determinism from its embodied, physical substrate, *thinking* as Spinoza's functional projection of a pre-existent *something else* becomes represented by Freud, as the functional extension of Psyche, or Mind.

However, Freud's pairing of Spinoza with Leonardo DaVinci is not his first psychoanalytic reference to Baruch Spinoza. Five years earlier, Spinoza enters psychoanalysis through the Freudian backdoor; and Freud's initial reference is anything but straightforward. Rather, the person of Spinoza is referred to as an example of a particular kind of humor, the kind that is constructed economically from what Freud terms "a negative particle" (Freud, 1905, p. 77). Like the construction of the term *unheimlich*, Spinoza is described by Freud as a "fellow un-believer", a witticism attributed by Freud to Heinrich Heine. Later, in Chapters 3 and 12, we return to this initially undignified presentation of Spinoza within psychoanalysis, in consideration of Freud's own ambivalent relatedness to his Jewish cultural identity and its linguistic forms of expression, which he often communicated through reference to Heine.

Two years after Freud's publication of "Leonardo da Vinci and a Memory of His Childhood", writing in December 1912 of her attendance at the Wednesday meetings of the Vienna Psychoanalytic Society, Lou Andreas-Salomé entitles a section of her "Freud School" journal, *Spinoza*. There, she articulates a breathlessly enthusiastic perspective, very similar to that adopted by Gilles Deleuze, seventy years later. Deleuze, writing in the late 1980s would observe that

> Writers, poets, musicians, filmmakers- painters too, even chance readers- may find that they are Spinozists; indeed, such a thing is more likely for them than for professional philosophers. It is a matter of one's practical conception of the "plan". It is not that one may be a Spinozist without knowing it. Rather, there is a strange privilege that Spinoza enjoys, something that seems to have been accomplished by him and no one else. He is a philosopher who commands an extraordinary conceptual apparatus, one that is highly developed, systematic, and scholarly; and yet he is the quintessential object of an immediate, unprepared encounter, such that the nonphilosopher, or even

someone without any formal education, can receive a sudden illumination from him, a "flash". Then it is as if one discovers that one is a Spinozist; one arrives in the middle of Spinoza, one is sucked up, drawn into the system or composition. (Deleuze, 1988, p. 129)

So too, was Andreas-Salomé, who also includes Victor Tausk in her effusions. Tausk, newly discovering himself a Spinozist, had already written an essay on Spinoza five years before Andreas-Salomé's diary entry (Andreas-Salomé, 1964, p. 74). Observing her own enthusiasm as well as Tausk's, Andreas-Salomé writes,

> It is a quality of Spinoza that a few pages by him can teach us whether we are his disciples, whereas big interpretive works have been written about him based on the most erudite misunderstandings. For to think like him does not mean to adopt a system, but just to think. (Andreas-Salomé, 1964, p. 75)

With this, Lou-Andreas Salomé's 1912 lecture diary breaks psychoanalytic conceptual ground in explicitly linking the process of psychoanalytic *thinking* with Spinozan *thinking*; and proceeds through her own comparative equivalence of Spinozan ideas, to discover elements of Spinoza's thinking within the developing system of psychoanalysis.

The first Spinozan linkage cited by Lou Andreas-Salomé is through Tausk's understanding of psychic parallelism in transformation of the physical into the mental. She writes that for Tausk, this idea is "quite representative of his inner allegiance to Spinoza" in that

> to grasp Spinoza it is only necessary to think through to its conclusion the concept that physical and mental manifestations are representations of one another. (Andreas-Salomé, 1964, p. 75)

Translated into other terms, Andreas-Salomé draws a parallel between psychic representation and its physical embodiment within a hierarchical structure of scientific laws traceable from Nature as a whole phenomenon, to its separate aspects, including human psychology.

Freud, in his early monograph on aphasia (Freud, 1953), would argue for the functional difference between body and mind. This difference affirms Hughlings Jackson's neurological understanding of "dependent concomitance" in which one structure relies for its operation on a precursor structure. However related, these domains differ from one another in their functional operation (Grossman, 1992). Another example of dependent concomitance, published at the same time as Freud's thoughts on aphasia, was psychologist John Dewey's interpretation of the "reflex arc" in which he demonstrates that the discrete neurological pairings of electrical stimulus and response cannot account for the transformative chain of neural transmission, empirically demonstrable in the difference between a nerve's original stimulus, and its pathway's final behavioral outcome (Dewey, 1896).[1]

Similarly, Andreas-Salomé addresses the holistic linkage between integrated organic systems. This contrasts with what she refers to sardonically, as then-contemporary psychiatry's "deepest wisdom" in atomistic fascination with "cerebral localization and the like" (1964, p. 75). Elaborating, she writes that the Spinozan contrast between physical and mental representations suggests an

> inward contemplation of the integrity and presentness of two worlds- as we reckon- which nowhere exclude or determine each other, because they *are but one*. (Ibid, p. 75)

Andreas-Salomé's employment of italics underlines the Spinozan principle of monism which she recognizes as

> the philosophical step that goes beyond Freud; he has developed throughout a method of its own for the one of these two worlds which can be grasped psychologically. (Andreas-Salomé, 1964, p. 75)

Turning from monism, Lou Andreas-Salomé recognizes too, that the *overdeterminism* (her italics) fundamental to psychoanalysis also supports a psychoanalytic Spinozism. Passionately, she reasons that

> this insight, that everything is, nay *must*, be psychically overdetermined if only one pursues it far enough, reaches far beyond

the usual logical concept of determination, splits its one-sided concatenation, and ultimately turns it into a principle of universal reciprocity. This reciprocal interaction of everything with everything else needs only to be assumed with all its implications to come, along with Spinoza, from the empirical world of movement to the eternal rest of his philosophy. (Andreas-Salomé, 1964, p. 75)

Andreas-Salomé extends what other theorists (Fromm, 1964a; Rathbun, 1934; Smith, 1925; Tanner, 1907a) acknowledge as the complete determinism of Spinoza's program. She opens the door to what will one day be a parallel extension in the development of psychoanalytic treatment as it deepens from symptomatic relief through recognition of overdetermination in ego-functioning (Waelder, 2007) to primitive psychic functioning, requiring longer durations of therapeutic time than envisioned by Freud, and corresponding to more complex, continuous iterations of action between therapist and patient (Miller & Sweet, 2018; Reiner, 2021). The overdetermined nature of human functioning necessarily generates the opportunity, recognized by Spinoza, to clarify distorted or deformed thinking, recognized today both in parataxic (Sullivan, 1953) and traumatically "mangled" conceptions of mind (Bollas, 2015, p. 539).

Andreas-Salomé also recognizes the centrality of Spinoza's methodological organization in *Ethics*, necessary for the linear development of Spinoza's arguments from Parts I to V: between contemplation of God within the lawful universal rules of infinite nature; to the observables of human psychology; to determined and limited freedom in human conduct.

This top-down approach is reckoned by Spinoza to run in the opposite direction from the approach of earlier philosophers, who begin with the particulars of what people do and conclude with contemplation of the divine. Here, Andreas-Salomé alludes to Spinoza's methodological critique of philosophers'

> failure to observe the proper order of philosophical inquiry. For the divine nature, which they should have considered before all else- it being prior both in cognition and in Nature- they have taken to be last in the order of cognition, and the things

that are called objects of sense they have taken as prior to everything. Hence it has come about that in considering natural phenomena, they have completely disregarded the divine nature. (II. Proposition 10. Scholium, pp. 249–250)

Andreas-Salomé notes that Spinoza's "passionate ecstasy" has never been possessed

by any thinker to such a degree as by this one perhaps who, stammeringly, gave the same meaning to 'nature' and "God", yet without supernaturalizing nature or reducing the name of his God to the level of things. (Andreas-Salomé, 1964, p. 75)

Summarizing her integration of Spinoza within psychoanalysis, Lou Andreas-Salomé writes delightedly that this beloved philosopher of her childhood had become transformed into the *philosopher of psychoanalysis* such that if you

think far enough, correctly enough on any point at all and you hit upon him; you meet him waiting for you, standing ready by the side of the road. (Andreas-Salomé, 1964, pp. 75–76)

As with Lou Andreas-Salomé, Viktor Tausk, and Freud, German language speakers' appreciation of congruence between Spinozan and psychoanalytic systems was broadly recognized through *Bildung*'s cultural acquaintance with classical languages and philosophy (Berman, 1992; Bruford, 1975; La Vopa, 1990; Sterba, 1982; Winter, 1999). Entering medical school, the 19-year-old Karen Horney would confide her intoxication with Spinoza to her diary, writing,

The central point of ethical living is self-preservation. Only through itself, because it owes it to its own persistence, does the mind arrive at happiness; only what its own strength wins for it should it recognize and strive for as the highest good. The mind's only possession is thinking, is reason. Its goal is the truth. Hence happiness is the same as striving after the truth. For the truth is eternal, and the greater our striving, the greater our happiness.

This is easy to understand, for happiness is absence of all influences from outside that threaten self-preservation. (Horney, 1980, p. 93)

Summarizing *Ethics* further, Horney recognizes that

an existence is defective, on the other hand, where outside influences predominate. Where intellect is hampered by passion, suffering remains. Thus the desire to please, voluptuousness, intemperance, greed, sensuality, express surrender to the force of external things. There is suffering too if the mind strives for something transient, changeable, or when its noble striving attaches to perishable things. Only one who lacks true insight can suffer in this way. For true understanding brings about moral behavior this moral behavior must not be the result of fear and hope, for then the mind is in bondage. Hence for Spinoza: understanding is the same as will. (Horney, 1980, p. 93)

The world of early psychoanalytic thinkers was, to echo Freud, animated both by the *atmosphere* and *doctrine* conveyed by Spinoza's *Ethics*. While a comprehensive integration of doctrine and atmosphere was never attempted, textual fragments are sufficient in conveying a general sense of the German-language reception of Spinoza during the early days of psychoanalytic development.

Like Leonardo, Spinoza was construed through the lens of his art, as extending a non-judgmental, balanced apprehension of the human condition, at the center of which was thinking—both as an activity and as a process demonstrated by Spinoza through his writing. Spinoza's philosophical reach was sufficiently broad to meet psychoanalytic explorers at every point along their as-yet unmarked paths. He offered a comprehensive moral philosophy, the central value of which was the willed mobilization of human reason upon the irrational flux of emotion-fused thought. And through interrogation of this continuous action, a therapeutic route to greater ease and happiness was described via rational reflection upon what we do.

The central action of Spinoza's doctrinal *mode* was understood to be a causal relationship between body and mind in a field of psychophysical relations. The permutations of body effect a result, the action of mind. Early psychoanalysts like Tausk and Andreas-Salomé recognized in this, Spinoza's monistic singularity featuring parallel levels of functioning characterized by thought and extension, in which the conjunction of differentiated functional forms eventuated in different types of action. Extended broadly, the determinism apparent under a hierarchy of natural laws allows for broad understanding of *reciprocal interaction of everything* within Nature. That is, under the aegis of God or Nature as the infinite First Cause, our actions and reactions cause effects upon one another in continuous iterations of cause and effect.

From this perspective, individual psychopathology reflects a preponderance of influential effects external to the individual's psychological functioning, first upon body and then upon the body's relation to mind, such that our constellations of ideas and emotions are deformed and distorted.

Finally, the psychic activity recognized by Spinoza in self-preservative striving is understood as the motivational engine of human action, a notion of causality akin to today's vernacular Winnicottian concept of *going on being* (Winnicott, 1960, p. 586), a notion understood by Thomas Ogden as "a phrase that is all verb, devoid of a subject" (Ogden, 2004, p. 1350), similar in this sense to Schafer's earlier "action language" with its emphasis on "verbs and adverbs" (Schafer, 1999, p. 345).

The Anglophone Reception of Spinoza in Psychology & Psychoanalysis: Tanner (1907a, 1907b) and Smith (1925, 1926)

Looking backward, the single largest assumptive difference in the psychoanalytic reckoning with Spinoza between early German language recognitions and later acquaintance in the United Kingdom and in the United States is direct experience: the reader's reading knowledge of Spinoza. Writing in 1977, psychologist Walter Bernard notes that Spinoza "is often praised but not often read" (Bernard, 1977, p. 63). Absent this reading experience, understanding is always reflected through the lens of another's viewpoint. In Spinozan terms, what we come to know is a function of hearsay and external opinion, rather than a function of our own psychological reasoning.

Without the direct experience of reading, what others claim for Spinoza is received like any other piece of information, unmarked by the sudden thrill of what philosopher Gilles Deleuze terms the illuminative "flash", also recognized by Lou Andreas-Salomé in her diary entries.[2] Andreas-Salomé underlines the conjoined experiences of reading and comprehension in recognizing that it is

> a quality of Spinoza that a few pages by him can teach us whether we are his disciples, whereas big interpretive works have been written about him based on the most erudite misunderstandings. For to think like him does not mean to adopt a system, but just to think. (Andreas-Salomé, 1964, p. 75)

"Just to think", under Andreas-Salomé's meaning, includes any and all of elements of Spinoza's thought marshaled in the active work of reasoning: in thinking "far enough, correctly enough" we are met by Spinoza's wisdom, "standing ready by the side of the road" (Andreas-Salomé, 1964, pp. 75–76).

Thinking itself implies not only a general action, but also the specific use of thinking's modes, inclusive of its many contents. Reading "about" what Spinoza says, rather than thinking through what he says via the engaged action of reading, presents us with a generous glossary of terms (not unlike what Spinoza himself presents in his *Definitions of the Emotions*, a summary of psychodynamic positions at the conclusion of *Ethics* Part III (pp. 311–319)), that by themselves are at best, nothing but concepts to be absorbed by rote learning.[3]

Commitment to such passionate reading is reflected in this chapter's central contributions of Amy Tanner and M. Hamblin Smith, two English-language writers integrating Spinozan with modern psychological and psychoanalytic thought, in early 20th-century journals. Their assimilations of Spinoza are bent to the task of inspiring the psychologists and psychoanalysts who are their reading audience. Unlike the private reflections of Andreas-Salomé at the beginnings of the psychoanalytic movement, these English-language journal consolidations of Spinoza are public and programmatic. Constructing the prehistory of their respective theoretical frameworks, both Amy Tanner in psychology and M. Hamblin

Smith in psychoanalysis, present comparative compressions of *Ethics*. Immediately, the reader apprehends a contrast between the extraordinary vivacity in embracing Spinoza reflected by earlier German-language appreciation, and the measured, historical integration of Spinoza into ongoing development in the human sciences, reflected by writers in English.

Hand-in-hand with their readers' assumed absence of having read *Ethics*, Tanner and Smith anticipate reading audiences schooled to different funds of knowledge than the classically educated Viennese of earlier generations. *Bildung* culture, the German-language educational orientation toward self-formation, developed since the 18th century, did not travel well across the 20th-century matrix of geography and time. Indeed, it might be argued not only that contemporary psychoanalysis is heir to Enlightenment thinking through *Bildung*'s cultural lens (Miller, 2018b), but also more specifically, that the transformation of the *Bildung* cultural orientation of self-formation, shorn of its early pioneers' intellectual apparatus (Berman, 1992; Goetschel, 2004; Mosse, 1985; Sorkin, 1987), became professionalized through psychoanalysis, with contemporary clinicians functioning as "practitioners rather than discoverers" (Bergmann, 2017, p. 87).

Reading across the 20th-century assimilations of Spinoza from within multiple writers' excitement and hope for psychoanalytic contribution toward the transformation both of individual and societal relations, the clinical reader observes that as Spinoza is increasingly understood to anticipate psychoanalysis, direct acquaintance with *Ethics*, through reading, declines. Unlike the early days of psychoanalysis in Vienna's *Freud School*, when Lou Andreas-Salomé joyfully linked the controversial, progressive thought of Freud with Spinoza as the *philosopher of psychoanalysis*, subsequent development of psychology and psychoanalysis as independent fields of study in the human sciences, subordinate the now-antique Spinoza to new muscular advances in 20th-century thinking. However, Spinoza's long-closed inquiry would be shown to correspond to exciting new parallels with modern conceptual advance. Spinoza consistently passes the test. As Lou Andreas-Salomé observes, we continue to meet him as psychoanalysis develops forward.

What does change, given readers' lack of direct acquaintance with Spinoza, is recognition of the vibrancy in his writing: not only as powerful argument, but also in his attentions to consideration of the reader. Indeed, as we shall see, Spinoza's care relative to the resistance of his reader, reminds us of the psychoanalyst's own method in the face of clinical resistance, urging slow progression step by step, without the necessity of forced conviction (II. Proposition 11, Scholium). Together with lack of direct acquaintance in reading Spinoza and the ascendency of 20th century striving for psychoanalytic transformations of individuals and societies—first enthusiastically intimated by Smith (1925, 1926)—the psychoanalytic Spinoza collapses into a dry, fragmentary correlation with Freud, reduced almost to a footnote, as in Erich Fromm's observation in the first issue of *Contemporary Psychoanalysis* that

> Spinoza expressed the idea of the unity of the human race in his concept of "the model of human nature" to which certain laws apply, laws which neither completely determine man or leave him completely to be free. Instead of calling him, as is often done, a "determinist", it would be better to call Spinoza an "alternativist"; by this I refer to the concept that man has freedom to choose, but that he can choose only between certain alternatives which are determined from his nature in general, and from the character of each individual, personally. Spinoza became the father of modern scientific psychology, and he is closely related to Freud not only through the concept of the model of human nature, but also by his idea of the unconscious, by the idea that man is guided by forces that he is not aware of. As he put it, man believes himself to be free because he knows his desires, but he is not aware of the causes for his desires. (Fromm, 1964a, pp. 70–71)

By the late 20th century and the passing of what a former psychoanalytic trainee called "the old Berlin analysts" (Galdi, 2019), recognition of Spinozan integration within psychoanalysis almost vanishes into oblivion. It is only with today's re-reading of Spinoza, from the perspective of a much later psychoanalytic moment, that Spinoza's thinking is found in continued alignment with 21st-century psychoanalysis, not only in theory but in clinical practice.

Challenges for Tanner (1907a, 1907b) and Smith (1926)

The presentational hurdles for Tanner and Smith are twofold. First, the theorist must suggest a contemporary definition of psychology or psychoanalysis as the criterion by which Spinoza's thought will be judged. Next, the theorist must present compelling evidence meant to convince the reader of the linkage between 17th-century and 20th-century thought. Each struggles valiantly, but fails because the on-going rush of disciplinary advance in contemporary thought can never be fully anticipated by the past. For example, Tanner (1907a), the earliest of the 20th century Anglophone psychological writers on Spinoza, severely misconstrues the internal functioning of mind, described in *Ethics* Parts I, II, and III. She limits her focus to the motoric aspect of Spinoza's psychology, itself congruent with the experimental orientation of early 20th century American university psychology departments (Ross, 1991; Tanner, 1907a, p. 516). Yet, in presentation of her applied social science research, Tanner provides an entirely Spinozan alternative depiction of human thinking. As if emending her "Spinoza and Psychology" (1907a), Tanner's self-reflective fieldwork, "Glimpses at the Mind of a Waitress" (1907b), enlivens motoric action as thought's transformation. This narrative demonstration of Spinozan psychology includes the elements: (1) perception, feeling, imagination, and the strivings of her will, even-tuating (2) in a process psychology of thought's motoric extension into object-related action; (3) followed by the internalization of that action's subjectively assessed efficacy, which is further (4) reunited in mind toward (5) a new iteration of externalized action (Tanner, 1907b). Significantly for us, Tanner's careful fieldwork narrative represents our earliest 20th century social science approximation to a *clinical Spinoza*.

Amy Tanner's *Spinoza and Modern Psychology* (1907a)

Amy Tanner presents a paradoxical reading of Spinoza, gearing what she terms this first "modern theory of the origin and development of the mind" to the measure of the American experimental psychology laboratory (1907a, p. 514). Tanner positions Spinoza as the intellectual forerunner of William James, with Tanner narrowing the breadth of Spinozan thought to a psychology of consciousness. She observes that

we could hardly have James' theory that all consciousness is
motor, stated more explicitly in the absence of modern proofs of
it. The denial that mind and volition have an abstract existence,
an existence apart from thinking and willing, and the assertion
that the essence of mind and will are identical- these assertions
take Spinoza over into the most modern of modern thought.
(1907a, p. 518)

Tanner maintains a grumpily dissatisfied tone toward Spinoza, who
is taken to task for his lack of appeal to contemporary psychologists; as if specific address to Tanner and colleagues had been
Spinoza's intent. Fairly spluttering, Tanner construes Spinoza's
geometric demonstration to proceed in labored fashion through
"stilted phraseology" calculated to blind "the student to the true
modernity of his ideas" (1907a, p. 514). Tanner's Spinoza seems to
get in his own way; and from this tendentious viewpoint, Tanner
presents a reading lacking depth and aesthetic possibility. Tanner is
baffled by Spinoza's expressive literary style; and interpretively, she
judges the 17th-century philosopher from the perspective of character flaw, assuming that Spinoza's

> inner need for exact proof must indeed have been compelling in
> order to force such ideas into the strait-jacket of geometrical
> presentation. (1907a, p. 518)

Demeaning Spinoza's methodological presentation, Tanner frees
herself from his complex structure of thought; and so, reduces
his thinking to discrete elements. Unfortunately, this reduction
is equivalent to taking-apart a fine clock and throwing its
disassembled parts into the kitchen drawer for further use.
Indeed, thinking through the separate elements of Spinoza's argument requires patience and the capacity to bear complicated
thought. Spinoza's five-part presentation of *Ethics* contains 259
discrete "propositions", supplemented by seemingly innumerable
definitions, appendices, prefaces, axioms, scholia, corollaries, and
lemmas. Like modern builders, Tanner's approach appears to tear
down the older structure, rebuilding it in simpler form with dec-
orative embellishments suggestive of earlier substantive forms.

Ironically, although Tanner confronts Spinoza naively, her pugnacity reflects a certain Spinozan quality of *thinking*, that striving noted both by Andreas Lou-Salome and Freud. Though today's reader might not agree with Amy Tanner's conclusions, that she battles mightily in her arguments is beyond contest. In so doing, she unwittingly replicates a traditional dimension of geometric demonstration, a philosophical model in use since the time of Euclid in the 4th century, BC. This is a positioning of its propositional markers as pivotal points for later philosophical argument and the transformation of ideas. Spinoza himself illustrates this process in his wrestling with the ideas of Galileo and Descartes, just as with Hasdai Crescas and Maimonides, each influential in Spinoza's thought development, had actively grappled with earlier philosophical propositions, such as those conveyed by Arabic transformations of Plato and Aristotle by Avicenna, al-Farabi, and Averroes (Harvey, 1981; Rudavsky, 2018; Strauss, 1952; Wolfson, 1934).

An example from "Spinoza and Modern Psychology" is Tanner's confused challenge to Spinoza's differentiation between adequate and inadequate ideas. She writes,

> here at the very beginning we see an interesting obscurity in Spinoza's thought. He says distinctly that mind and extension are not different substances but the same seen under a different attribute. Is it not then quite as unsuitable to speak of a parallelism between them as of a causal relation? Ought we not rather to say that when God reveals himself as thought then this extension appears? But leaving this aside, if he admits that there is but one substance, how can he deny a causal relationship between all forms of this substance. (1907a, p. 514)

While Tanner does cite a number of Spinoza's contributions, these are more comprehensively assembled by Smith (1925, 1926). Instead, the reader's attention is drawn to Tanner's apparent ambivalence in presenting her subject. Tanner's several references to Spinoza's *inner need* and *unconscious* determination, however leveled aggressively at Spinoza contrary to her praise for his imputed psychology of consciousness, betray Tanner's own fascination with the dynamic psychoanalytic psychology of Freud. Tanner's "Spinoza and Modern

Psychology" is a work divided within itself, limiting Spinoza's breadth within the confines of the academic psychology laboratory as Tanner cautiously hints at his progressive thought; and at the same time, arrogant in Tanner's tendentious and uninformed interpretation of Spinoza's character, while hinting at a broader admiration of what she otherwise excludes.

Recognition of this split is founded literarily. Alluding to unconscious determination, a concept still somewhat alien in American psychology prior to Freud's 1909 visit to Tanner's own institution, Clark University, Tanner hypothesizes that Spinoza's psychological system was "probably the theory which he employed unconsciously in everyday life" (Tanner, 1907a, p. 514). As we shall see in Chapter 4, Spinoza's own endorsement of his method toward an *emendation of the intellect* was nothing if not a conscious, determined effort to acquire clarity of thought. Tanner's subversively pejorative attribution to Spinoza of unconscious determination in relation to everyday life, instead suggests a then-recent title by Freud, *The Psychopathology of Everyday Life* (1901). Curiously, Tanner's own methodological assimilation of Spinozan ideas in her fieldwork, hints at her own very different, if unspoken, attitude toward *Ethics*.

Not only does "Spinoza and Modern Psychology" itself reflect a conceptual splitting between different apprehensions of Spinoza, but together with her "Glimpses at the Mind of a Waitress" (1907b), Tanner's conflictual apprehension of Spinoza is amplified. Spinoza would term such splitting indicative of the *vacillation of mind*. Amy Tanner's simultaneous 1907 presentations suggest a doubling: or the presence of two very different readings. These mirror Deleuze's observation of Spinoza, that

> the *Ethics* is a book written twice simultaneously: once in the continuous stream of definitions, propositions, demonstrations, and corollaries, which develop the great speculative themes with all the rigors of the mind; another time in the broken chain of scholia, a discontinuous volcanic line, a second version underneath the first, expressing all the angers of the heart and setting forth the practical theses of denunciation and liberation. (Deleuze, 1988, pp. 28–29)

Today, knowing something about Tanner's own harsh treatment as a pioneering feminist in a male-dominated university system, consistently denied tenure and ultimately departing the field of academic psychology in order to find a reliable means of economic support (Diehl, 2010; Petit, 2008), the reader might conjecture a personal complication within her conflicting presentations. Tanner's narrow reading, triumphalist in heralding the development of academic psychology, is markedly contrasted with a more personal reading, suggesting unconscious determination and the inner workings of mind, both present in Spinoza and in Tanner's fieldwork, itself departmentally displaced from academic psychology and published in *The American Journal of Sociology*, just as American social science was itself splitting into separate academic siloes (Diehl, 2010; Petit, 2008; Ross, 1991). In "Glimpses at the Mind of a Waitress" (1907b), Tanner demonstrates her own identification with Spinoza's sensitivity to social oppression as well as the care he demonstrates, especially in *Ethics* Part III, in illustrating the complexity of psychological dynamics as integrations of thinking and extension in action. "Glimpses at the Mind of a Waitress" is probably the first published example of a *clinical Spinoza*, however unattributed.

To her credit, Tanner's emphasis on the psychodynamic complexity of *Ethics* Part III is clear and crisp in "Spinoza and Modern Psychology". She notes that Spinoza's motivational premise and the essence of each living thing, is the general principle of endeavoring to persist in their own being, akin to today's Winnicottian notion of *going on being* (Winnicott, 1960). Tanner also recognizes Spinoza's clear discernment of functionally differentiated psychic fields. Willing, striving, or the action of endeavoring to persist in one's own being, is only labeled as *will* when it is contained solely within the internal realm of thought. However, once paired in extended action with the world of things, such *will* becomes transformed into *appetite*. Further, when the relative state of unawareness characterized by *appetite* achieves consciousness, its linguistic marker shifts to the idea of *desire*. Today's clinical reader will immediately recognize a transformational progression across situated psychic fields, from the wholly internal world, to the external world, to conscious awareness of that external world, in these Spinozan vicissitudes of willing,

leading to desire. Clinically, this is marked along a path later discerned by W.R. Bion in the elaboration of a transitory thought from
its position at time (n) to its position at time (n + 1) to its position at a
later time (n + 2). Each Spinozan integration of psychic function
is both integrated within its psychological field of operation, and also
available through reflection along the continuum from unconscious
to conscious awareness (Bion, 1963; Miller, 2017; Miller & Sweet,
2018). Remarkably, in differentiation from other 20th-century writers
on Spinoza, Tanner effectively summarizes this depiction of psychological process from internal thought through external extension,
today empirically demonstrable in clinical psychoanalysis.

Tanner also notes Spinoza's "striking similarity to our modern
conception" in understanding mind as "the residium of countless
efforts at self-preservation", predicated on the organism's receptivity
to pleasure and pain, with our transit to registrations of pleasure
indicative of "passage to a greater perfection" and our transit to
registrations of pain, "the passage to a lesser one" (1907a, p. 515).

While Tanner scoffs at Spinoza's desire to arrive at a mathematically precise theory,[4] she admits that his psychology is presented as an evolutionary theory of human development. Again
though, Tanner substitutes her knowledge of the 20th-century
university laboratory for Spinoza's 17th-century writing desk,
archly observing that

> if instead of geometry, he could have used such forms as now are
> employed both in our physical and psychological laboratories, he
> would have had the exactness for which he so longed without at
> the same time petrifying his theory. But he was too early in time
> for those forms of mathematics. (1907a, p. 515)

Significantly, Tanner makes several observations that are crucial for
contemporary clinical thinking. The first is that Spinoza's interest is
not in the origin of knowledge, but rather in observation of human
functioning. We shall encounter this idea in our close reading of
Ethics. Tanner also notes the intrinsic, object-related quality in
Spinoza's description of human thought. All "modes of thinking", all
of our cognitive-emotional affective constellations, explicitly relate

the individual thinker with "an idea of the thing loved, desired, etc" (Tanner, 1907a).

Additionally, as we have also seen in the early psychoanalytic Viennese understanding of Spinoza, Tanner recognizes that Spinoza begins

> with the body as the idea constituting the mind, as the idea of some particular thing actually existing, i.e., without some material with which to work the mind would have no existence. (Tanner, 1907a, p. 516)

She reprises *Ethics* II, proposition 23, which allows that the mind cannot know itself except through the mind's own perceptual experience of sensation; that is only by tracing the consequences, the cause-and-effect trail of outside stimuli in psychological experience (Tanner, 1907a, p. 517). In this, Tanner forces Spinoza into a psychology of consciousness, obscuring the profundity of the unconscious world he describes.

Tanner observes that

> we can imagine that Spinoza would heartily adopt experimental psychology especially as it would afford some of the mathematical demonstration which he loved so well. (Ibid, 517)

As we shall later see, contemporary clinical thought continues to benefit from abstract mathematical models not unlike those imagined by Spinoza. But these inhere in clinically applied dynamic models, with their generalities applied to the specific uniqueness of clinical emergence, rather than Tanner's sterile portrayal of convergence between Spinoza and the psychological laboratory. Such dynamic models include: the Lewinian field or lifespace (Brown, 1936; Lewin, 1933, 1936); WR Bion's algorithmic expansion of Melanie Klein's shuttle between Paranoid/Schizoid and Depressive positions (Bion, 1963; Miller & Sweet, 2018); and methodological recognition of Freud's

> unwitting application of a linguistic *algorithm,* a systematic series of steps for achieving an outcome. An algorithm, it must be

noted, can work even if the theoretical underpinnings are wrong or irrelevant; ancient algorithms for making bronze, tin, even steel existed long before the onset of scientific metallurgies. (Levenson, 1983, p. 9)

M. Hamblin Smith (1926)

Just as Amy Tanner anchors American experimental psychology in the early modern thinking of Baruch Spinoza, M. Hamblin Smith, a British forensic psychologist, recognizes in Spinoza's *Ethics*, the anticipation of the applied, transformative potential of Freud\s psychoanalysis, both for individuals and societies (Smith, 1925, 1926).

Smith's enthusiasm is palpable in his 1926 *International Journal of Psychoanalysis* presentation, an abstract of a paper earlier published in the *British Journal of Medical Psychology* (1925), "Spinoza's Anticipation of Recent Psychoanalytic Developments". Smith's (1926) presentation is the first in a succession of psychoanalytic journals featuring direct links between Spinoza's *Ethics* and evolving psychoanalytic thought. These journals, reflective of differing institutional training traditions also include: *Psychoanalytic Review* (Rathbun, 1934); *Psychiatry* (Bernard, 1946); *The American Journal of Psychoanalysis* (Reid, 1955; Weiss, 1952; Tigner, 1985); and *Contemporary Psychoanalysis* (Fromm, 1964a).

Smith folds Spinozas *Ethics* into Freud's psychoanalytic project, writing that

> every epoch-making hypothesis has had its anticipators, who have groped after the truth without finding it. Freud's theory was, in part, anticipated by Spinoza, whose system, like that of Freud, is based upon a strict determinism. (Smith, 1926)

Like Tanner, Andreas-Salomé and Tausk, Smith observes with Spinoza that mind and body are "but two aspects of one reality". Like Tanner, Smith finesses the transformational difference between intellect and will, terming them "identical", whereas Spinoza's presentation is more highly nuanced, describing them in *Ethics* Part I, as functionally differentiated and parallel divine attributes, *Thought* and *Extension*, expressed in Cartesian language. Unstated in Smith's condensation is Spinoza's monistic consolidation of these binary elements, differentiating Spinozan thought from Cartesian dualism.

Smith, like Tanner (1907a, p. 514), addresses Spinoza's treatment of God, writing that "the *Deus* of Spinoza is divested of all anthropomorphism". Oddly, Smith does not make the jump toward recognition of God as a synonym for Nature, the very understanding that would cause Albert Einstein, Freud, and Heine, to claim Spinoza's God as their own with Spinoza as Freud's fellow *un-believer* (Freud, 1905, p. 77).

Here, Smith momentarily loses the conceptual thread of *Ethics*: that Spinoza is arguing for a thorough-going natural universe, presided over by an infinite God as the infinity of Nature, knowable only through attributes of Thought and Extension. Nevertheless, Smith regains his footing in addressing Spinoza's orientation toward human psychology, observing that Spinoza

> desires to deal with human emotions in a purely scientific spirit, and as conforming to the ordinary laws of nature. (Smith, 1926, p. 492)

Next, in short order, Smith reconstructs Spinoza along the lines of psychoanalysis observing: (1) that "only by thus understanding emotions can we obtain any power to control them"; (2) that the *Ethics* contain, "the conception of mental conflict and repression and the distinction between conscious and unconscious desire"; and (3) that Spinoza's motivational engine of *conatus*, corresponds to the evolutionary premise that "everything endeavours to persist in its own being" (Smith, 1926, p. 492). Here, Smith ventures an uncharacteristic boldness. He opines that Spinoza's *conatus*, might be "preferable to that of libido", an unwitting echo of Andreas-Salomé's understanding that Spinoza's systematic thought is unique in its immediate psychological apprehension, distinct from physical interpretation (Andreas-Salomé, 1964, p. 75). Almost immediately, however, Smith backpedals, fusing conatus with libido.

Just as Tanner grants herself the ahistorical freedom to accuse Spinoza of rigidity while suggesting his *unconscious* use of his own theory, Smith also extends judgmental interpretation. He folds libido into conatus while commenting upon what he takes to be Spinoza's disability—"indications that he had not overcome his own sex repressions"—which in his earlier 1925 paper, he suggests were instead, subject to the intellectualized process of sublimation.

Aligning Spinoza's written thought with their own conceptual schema, both Tanner and Smith feel free to interpret his personality. Reading this today, the reader wonders about such aggressively judgmental positions; might it be that Spinoza's 250-year-old insights threatened the newly established 20th-century forms of psychology and psychoanalysis in evoking such response?

Smith (1926) reels off some more Spinozan anticipations of psychoanalysis including: the concept of narcissism; and the defensive structure of reaction formation. He concludes by doubling down in his parallels between Spinoza and Freud, writing first that the Spinozan intellectual love of God "bears a striking resemblance to that which is attained by a complete analysis"; and next, that Spinoza's idea of human freedom, mediated by reason, leads to "the fully analysed man".

Pausing for a moment, the reader of Tanner (1907a) and Smith (1926) thinks about the scope of Ethics' anticipations of contemporary vernacular notions in psychoanalytic psychology, at least through its early reception by the English-speaking world. These include: (1) that mind is functionally different but determined by and dependent upon body, reflecting two aspects of a singular reality; (2) the question of thought's relation to action as mediated by the emotions; (3) the differentiation between different apprehensions of emotion, exemplified by will, appetite, and desire—each corresponding to different fields of the mind's focus, its internal world and the external world; (4) the idea that mind is itself the result of the cumulative effects of conatus, the human drive to persevere in its going-on-being; (5) that all thought is intrinsically object-related. Smith also adds a few more observations, independent of Tanner: (6) that the goals of psychoanalytic experience and the application of Spinoza's practical philosophy are similar in using the understanding of our emotional and intellectual processes toward greater and more efficient personal and social agency; and (7) the anticipated presence in Spinoza's thought of such psychoanalytic notions as defensive operations, repression, and narcissism.

Fuller consideration of Smith's contributions is explored in Chapter 2, which begins with attention to the conceptual elements in his 1925 paper, "Spinoza's Anticipation of Recent Developments in Psychoanalysis".

Notes

1 A similar example of dependent concomitance, illustrating structural change, is provided by Alfred North Whitehead, in harmonizing Newtonian corpuscular physics with early 20th-century wave theory. Illustratively, he writes, "For both a corpuscle, and an advancing element of a wave front, are merely a permanent form propagated from atomic creature to atomic creature. A corpuscle is in fact an 'enduring object'. The notion of an 'enduring object' is, however, capable of more or less completeness of realization. Thus, in different stages of its career, a wave of light may be more or less corpuscular. A train of such waves at all stages of its career involves social order; but in the earlier stages this social order takes the more special form of loosely related strands of personal order. The dominant personal order gradually vanishes as the time advances. Its defining characteristics become less and less important, as their various features peter out. The waves then become a nexus with important social order, but with no strands of personal order. Thus the train of waves starts as a corpuscular society, and ends as a society which is not corpuscular" (Whitehead, 1978, p. 36).

2 Vermorel (2009) links Romain Rolland's recognition of *oceanic feeling*, later commented upon by Freud, to a similarly illuminative Spinozan flash.

3 Spinoza's Part III catalog of emotional definitions may also be understood as a turning-point in philosophy. The form of this glossary is similar to earlier presentations of virtue and vice, such as Spinoza would have read in Maimonides' *Eight Chapters* and in Stoical literature. While assuming the classical form of such ethical presentations, Spinoza's summary entails a radical doubling: his focus is upon the dynamic character of human psychology.

4 Tanner writes oblivious to the integrative presence in Spinoza's thought of Galileo and Copernicus, in their striving for the depiction of science in mathematical terms (Rudavsky, 2001). Spinoza's own probable Galilean influence was through the writing of Joseph del Medigo, whose work *Sefer Elim*, published by the press of Menasseh ben Israel, one of the rabbis of Spinoza's Amsterdam *esnoga* (synagogue), reflected del Medigo's own study with Galileo at Padua (Adler, 2014, p. 34; Barzilay, 1974).

Chapter 2

The Philosopher of Psychoanalysis (II)

Glimpsed through time's rearview mirror, the 20-century Anglophone reception of Spinoza within psychoanalytic psychology first flourishes and then founders as a result of untranslatable cultural caesurae, breaks in understanding and recognition. Apparent from the first comparative studies of contemporary psychology and *Ethics* in English-language scientific journals, this tension is illustrated by the gap between Amy Tanner's (1907a) incomprehension at the formal structure of Spinoza's *Ethics*, and M. Hamblin Smith's (1925) re-cognition that Spinoza's *geometric demonstration* is a philosophical form meant to approximate mathematical truth, and a mainstay of philosophical inquiry for over two millennia.

Smith's recognition of Spinoza's presentation as Euclidian de-monstration derives from his pre-professional education (Smith, 1925, p. 257); just as earlier, the diaries of Lou-Andreas Salome and Karen Horney reflect acquaintance with Spinoza from adolescent philosophical encounters. By contrast, Tanner operates from an impatient frustration with Spinoza's lack of accessibility to her con-temporaries' scope of knowledge. Despite her announcement of Spinozan parallels with modern psychology twenty years before Smith's, Tanner's American obliviousness to Spinoza's method and her resulting impatience, is a sign of the educational and cultural divide that will continue to confound Spinoza's wide acceptance by twentieth-century clinicians.

Readers will note too, that unlike Tanner, Smith relies upon non-psychological Spinoza scholarship, as do both Constance Rathbun

DOI: 10.4324/9781003246404-4

(1934) and Walter Bernard (1933, 1946), the latter two writers, through acquaintance with works written in German.

Two dynamic currents mark the trajectory of Spinoza's 20th-century psychoanalytic reception. The first is broadly Oedipal, indicative of intergenerational incomprehension. Writing from New York late in the 20th century, Martin Bergmann illustrates this dynamic in idealized observation that

> the psychoanalytic pioneers were inspired by a sense of identification with Freud and co-engaged in one of the great discoveries of the century. (Bergmann, 2017, p. 87)

By contrast, Bergmann characterizes succeeding generations as

> practitioners rather than discoverers, members of a profession whose services were available to the rich and not-too-severely disturbed of the general population. (Bergmann, 2017, p. 87)

Bergmann's reductive binary leaves out both Freud's continuous professionalization of psychoanalysis as well as the mortal necessary of its locational shift from Vienna and Berlin to London and New York, omissions no more unfair than Tanner's lack of acquaintance with Spinoza's expressive forms. The difference is that Tanner cannot understand what came before and that Bergmann does not fathom clearly and distinctly what develops later. Each distortion of perspective takes refuge in the correctness of its respective generational orientations.

Paul Federn (1940) addresses such problems of intergenerational communication both within psychoanalysis and more broadly, within the scientific reception of psychoanalytic ideas. He writes that

> every creative worker solves problems which took hold of him already when he was young, long before his companions became aware of them. Only when he has reached full maturity does he solve the problem. He is ahead of his time and ahead even of the next and perhaps later generations. He becomes the leader of millions yet to be born after his own death. The millions who are alive are not really lead by their great contemporaries, but by the

genius of bygone generations. Even his colleagues and experts in his own field are unwilling to accept the new discoveries, do not understand what is really new. Besides, by preoccupation with the new, they would lose contact with their contemporaries. This produces a tension which is hard to stand. Most people compromise and follow the herd whom they are expected to guide. Teaching prevents learning! This is a general though not the only form of resistance to analysis. (Federn, 1940, p. 66)

Martin Bergmann, like the German-language Spinozists and the English Spinozist M. Hamblin Smith, shares a socio-cultural root-edness in Latin and Greek classics. It is from this classical vantage point that Spinoza is recognized in comparison with contemporary thought, although he also fits the bill as Federn's "genius of bygone generations". Writing of the early psychoanalytic generations marked by Bergmann as "discoverers", Sarah Winter observes that

> because school is the crucial institutional space in which formal knowledge is reproduced in the form of culture, one's thinking bears the mark of the respective school one attended. Through the nineteenth and well into the twentieth centuries, the crucial institutional location for the passing on of knowledge about classical Greek culture in Europe was the secondary school- in the German speaking countries, the gymnasium- with its classical curriculum. (Winter, 1998, p. 140).

Richard Sterba, commenting on his own secondary school experience, explains that

> the gymnasium gave me not only the knowledge of the subjects but, more important, a familiarity with the broad cultural aspects that the ancient languages transmit. Greek I loved for its poetic beauty, but Latin fascinated me by its clarity of expression and the exactitude of its statements in the shortest and most precise possible form. The study of Latin in itself provided training in logical thinking: the mere sentence structure is the result of concentration on the precision of expression in briefest form. (Sterba, 1982, p. 16)

Continuing, Sterba views the deficiencies in contemporary American education, a viewpoint paralleling Bergmann's observation of early discoverers and later practitioners. Writing pejoratively of difference between his own gymnasium and the educational curriculum of his transplanted mid-century Detroit home, Sterba comments,

> In my opinion, the Western world is greatly impoverished by the abolition of Latin from the curricula of higher education. Besides, Latin is the basis of all Romantic modern languages, like Romanian, Italian, Spanish, French, and some of English. It is much easier to learn any of these languages when one knows Latin. In law and medicine, Latin terms are an indispensable part of the professional language; I find it deplorable that lawyers and doctors use these terms without being familiar with their original meaning. (Sterba, 1982, p. 16)

The educational background of early psychoanalytic thinkers was germinated not only within the German language gymnasium, but also within the cultural orientation of *Bildung,* an educational philosophy of self-formation, not only as process but also in the development of character. Sterba comments that Freud himself had attained an unusual degree of *Bildung,* cultivated from within "the educational model of the liberal bourgeouisie in Austria- the background of most Viennese analysts" (Sterba, 1982, p. 81). Reminiscing about the Vienna Psychoanalytic Society, the very *Freud School* of Lou Andreas-Salomé's Spinoza recognitions, Sterba writes,

> In general, the society meetings were peaceful and dignified. They were, after all, an assembly of *"gebildete"* people. The noun form of *gebildete, Bildung* is generally translated into English as "education". However, one would not call somebody who has merely graduated from the university a *gebildeter Mensch.* To be considered *gebildet,* one had to be able to speak at least two living languages (predominantly English and French) besides German, the language of the meetings; less important were Italian and Spanish. The knowledge of ancient Greek, the obligatory studies at the gymnasium, was taken for granted. A *gebildeter Mensch* had to be familiar with the most important works of Western

literature and the most important events of the history of Western culture. He had to be familiar with its outstanding artists and their chefs d'oeuvre. Interest in and information about current events should not be missing. One expects a *Gebildeter* to be well mannered and to use the vocabulary of the *gebildete* circle. A great deal of the behavior, interests, and mentality of the *Gebildete* is absorbed from childhood on if he is brought up in a *gebiltete* milieu; it is difficult to acquire it later. Of course, the *gebiltete Mensch* as I have described him here was an ideal; however, most of the society members attained some degree of this *Bildung*. A few of them like Bernfeld, Hartmann, Kris, and Waelder, even attained an unusual degree. Sigmund Freud was above all of us; his *Bildung* was of the highest level, as one can easily recognize in his publications and letters. (Sterba, 1982, pp. 80–81)

The second complicating current in the 20th-century psychoanalytic reception of *Ethics*, was the rapidly developing pace of psychoanalysis and psychology as broadened disciplines, requiring that workers link their own clinical understanding with consolidating trends in their respective fields, differentiated one from another. In academic psychology, this is illustrated by an empirical ethos affirming a narrow positivism as against a holistic view of the person within competing models of social science (Koch, 1999; Sarason, 1981). Under such conditions, the commitment of early psychoanalysts to the vanished, broadly intellectual world of *Bildung* strains against a narrower disciplinary demand for psychoanalytic independence and consolidation. Intellectually, this shift is represented by Freud's continuous differentiation of his "movement", *die sich*, from philosophy[1]; but, as Alfred Tauber notes of Freud,

> while he was not a philosopher, Freud knew philosophy and drew from that tradition as he built his theory, consciously or not. (Tauber, 2010, p. 25)

Spinoza's location as *philosopher of psychoanalysis* strains against this developmental imperative. By 2021, the PEP archive, the digital psychoanalytic library, would contain over 1.2 million pages of theory, research, and commentary (http://www.pep-web.org/) in a discipline itself already characterized half-a-century earlier by John Reid, as having three distinct strands,

> it is a technical procedure for investigating unconscious mental processes and for treating psychoneuroses; it is a systematic body of fact and theory concerning the relations of conscious and unconscious mental processes; and it is, finally, a philosophy of life, in the sense that it is a way of looking at, of thinking about, and of appraising some our basic habits, attitudes, and beliefs. (Reid, 1955, p. 115)

Together with changes in education, in culture, and in the on-rushing pulse of disciplinary development, the 17th-century Spinoza at best, resounded in anticipation of the psychoanalytic present. The record of journal science reflects two significant 20th-century movements in Spinozan reception. The first is the early, strong recognition of Spinozan thought within the currents of developing psychoanalysis during the interwar period. The next is a diminution of Spinozan integration. In this latter development, following World War II, Spinoza's *Ethics* in much reduced form, becomes notable only as the humanistic marker of a *Bildung* lost in the evolutionary process viewed narrowly by Bergmann as the professionalism of psychoanalytic practice.

This chapter details these two movements. It concludes with consideration of implicit demonstrations of Spinoza's *Ethics* within the development of clinical psychological and psychoanalytic practice.

Spinoza's Foreshadowing of Psychoanalysis: M. Hamblin Smith (1925), Constance Rathbun (1934), and Walter Bernard (1946)

Reading M. Hamblin Smith (1925), Constance Rathbun (1934) and Walter Bernard (1946) after reading *Ethics*, one appreciates the effort each author has extended toward consolidation of Spinoza's thinking. An acuity of recognition and commitment to intellectual honesty, as well as shared enthusiasm toward Spinoza's happy reintegration within a psychoanalysis he unwittingly inspired, is reflected by each. That these generalized presentations are uneven, imbued with the respective author's subjective link to Spinoza, is to be expected. Reading Spinoza is hard work, demanding the reader's subjective consolidations. Encompassing Spinoza in a relatively brief communication meant to alert the development of psychoanalysis to his importance is harder still.

The ambitious scope of these projects, joined by the reliance of later authors on the contributions of their predecessors, also contributes to a cumulative weakness. Overall, the reader is left with a Spinoza reduced to a glossary of psychological definitions, aligned as a concordance with psychoanalysis. Approaching Spinoza through these introductions, this difficulty arises because while agreeing on multiple points, each author understands Spinoza slightly differently; and because each presents a series of interpretive generalizations, the comparative format provokes confusion. Necessarily, the reader is set down in the *middle* not only of Spinoza (Deleuze, 1988, p. 129), but also in that middle's conjunction with three writers' interpretive commentaries.

Additionally, each of these authors also writes for a different moment in psychoanalytic development; and so, definition of psychoanalysis. Publishing in the *British Journal of Medical Psychology* (1925) and *The International Journal of Psychoanalysis* (1926), Smith addresses a psychoanalysis construed as classically Freudian. Nine years later and across the Atlantic Ocean, Rathbun, publishing in *Psychoanalytic Review*, addresses ego psychology; and thirteen years after that, Bernard publishes in *Psychiatry*, the interpersonal journal of the Washington School of Psychiatry.[2]

The commentaries of Smith, Rathbun and Bernard begin in joint agreement, recognizing the congruence of Freud's psychoanalytic perspective with Spinoza's philosophy. As Bernard states, in both

> the attitude is that the same logic, the same procedure, the same method of inquiry that prevail in the physical sciences must be applied to the mental realm as well- an approach that is typically Freudian and typically Spinozistic. (Bernard, 1946, p. 101)

Where Smith affirms that Spinoza's thinking "can be accepted, without much alteration, by students of psycho-analytic theory today" (Smith, 1925, p. 257), Rathbun recognizes that there is a closer alliance of Spinoza's psychology and psycho-analysis than there is with any other modern school of psychology. (Rathbun, 1934, p. 99)

And Bernard concurs, writing that

the congruence in essential elements is indeed so striking, the mood and direction of both thinkers, especially with regard to the theory of emotions are so similar and so close that one must of necessity be angered that no real attempt has hereto been made on the part of the psychoanalyst to compare and to correlate their theoretical views and those of Spinoza. (Bernard, 1946, p. 99)

Of these three presentations, only M. Hamblin Smith's attempts to follow Spinoza's five-part structure of *Ethics*. This sequencing spans the organization of *Ethics* from the foundational premises of Part I to the basic operations of human psychology in Part II to the clinical dynamics of human psychology in Part III. Parts IV and V, which are Smith's major humanistic interest, concerning the ethical choices available to each of us under the conditions and laws of psycho-physical determination.

The first part of *Ethics* is the most profoundly foreign to con-temporary clinical readers. Smith, like Tanner, Rathbun and Bernard, attempts to lift Spinoza's psychological system from its ancient frame of philosophical demonstration.[3] Readers traverse conceptual territory far distant from our familiar clinical categories. None of these authors explains that Spinoza's philosophy, despite its difficulties, is positioned as *practical* philosophy, meant for application toward personal and societal betterment, within the medieval binary splitting philosophy into theory and practice. Yet, each strives to elevate such elements in *Ethics* that might be directly linked to psychoanalytic practicality. Too often, the effect is forced, while descriptively general enough to con-vince us of Spinoza's role in anticipating psychoanalysis.

Each commentator agrees that like Freud, Spinoza maintains

that a strict determinism rules all psychic events and that even the transient, the trivial, and the seemingly superficial point

to definite causes which often may go deep into the structure
of the mind and the personality of the individual. (Bernard,
1946, p. 101)

Our immediate confusions, distortions and reservations, according to
Rathbun, are caused by the way in which we categorize these two
related, determinist theories. Compressing each to what today we
call "key words", we erroneously group psychoanalysis together
with such bullet points as *libido* and the *unconscious* while we locate
Ethics under such terms as *absolutism* and *rationality* (Rathbun, 1934,
p. 1). In so doing, we distort clear thinking; and fail to recognize the
corresponding unconscious and motivational forces within Spinoza's
thinking. Necessarily, and intrinsic both to psychoanalysis and to
Spinoza, we must act to broaden our thinking.

All three writers agree that Spinoza founds his *Ethics* from a richly
contextual holistic perspective. Spinozan *Ethics*, for Smith,

> is the study of man's relations to the universe as a whole,
> not merely the study of his relations to his fellow-men. (Smith,
> 1925, p. 257)

Rathbun comments that this approach aligns with the psychoanalytic

> in the sense of being synthetic psychologies attempting to present
> the mental processes of the individual as a relatively unified whole
> and not merely as an aggregate of elements. (Rathbun, 1933, p. 2)

This holistic reading distinguishes Smith, Rathbun, and Bernard
from Amy Tanner (1907a), who more narrowly construes her theory
from the observable effects of psychological action. Tanner's
Spinoza is contained within the holistic Spinoza of Smith, Rathbun
and Bernard.

Plunging into *Ethics* Part I. in order to make sense of Spinoza's
systemic thinking, Rathbun and Bernard recognize that Spinoza's
monistic holism is an advance upon Cartesian dualism (Bernard,
1972, p. 209; Rathbun, 1934, p. 4). For Spinoza, mind is dependent
upon, if functionally different than, body. Rathbun writes that
Spinoza's

analytic approach to the nature of emotion remains far more valuable in the light of present day psychology than the then accepted Cartesian account of passions and affections with "emphasis on the activity of man as a whole, behaving as a relatively integrated being, self-directed rather than at the mercy of every whim, desire, and compulsion, is of permanent value". (Rathbun, 1934, p. 4)

Spinoza's integrative approach to body and mind transforms dualism. Where Descartes separates, Spinoza integrates. Spinoza begins with the idea that God (or Nature) is the first and primary, infinite substance; and that the different attributes or modes[4] of *thought* and *extension* emerge from this primordial point of origin. Rathbun explains that

substance is one quantitatively, even if containing within itself qualitative differentiations. Since the universe from the point of view of being can be dichotomized into substance and modes, all that there is of finite reality must be contained in substance. Man, then, as a finite entity is not composed of two different kinds of reality, thought and extension, but is one real being possessing these two essential aspects, each of which expresses the whole of him from a different point of view. Such a unity is no bare abstraction; that Spinoza thought it to be a complexly differentiated one is shown by his discussion of emotions and passions, yet it is a unity continuously striving to maintain and to preserve its own equilibrium and balance. (Rathbun, 1934, p. 4)

Throughout *Ethics*, Spinoza maintains this parallelism within his reasoning. Smith emphasizes the seemingly paradoxical idea of conjoined similarities coexistent with qualitative difference. Introducing *Ethics* Part II, he writes that

Spinoza does not look for any explanation of the correspondence of two such dissimilar things as mind and body; he simply says that they are the same thing, and that they differ only in being two aspects of the same thing. (Smith, 1925, p. 261)

Smith recognizes that there is

> no mystery about the parallelism or the mutual interaction of
> mind and body. The mystery is resolved into an elementary fact.
> To ask why mind should correspond with matter is like asking
> why the convexity of a curve should answer to the concavity.
> Mind and body are distinguishable but not separable. (Smith,
> 1925, p. 261)

The clinician-reader must pause here, considering the relation of
these concepts to elements active in contemporary clinical psychoanalysis. First, is our appreciation of the *caesura*, a Bionian idea, with
its necessity of often-incomprehensible gaps existing between things.
Caesurae, in this sense, populate Spinozan thought as they do the
clinically psychoanalytic. Without too much of a stretch, for example, we can understand the intergenerational difference implied in
the Oedipal situation as a concretized, mythologized instance of a
caesura, the gap between one generation and the next. From the
Spinozan perspective, the ongoing imperative of striving for the
Aristotelian goal of a "greater perfection" in psychological understanding and balance (as opposed to the regressive "lesser perfection") marks the bridgeable gap between one therapeutic moment
and another.

W.R. Bion also wrestles with the Spinozan idea of the conjoint
union, reflected in observable clinical forms, under his idea of *constant conjunction* in clinical experience (Bion, 1992, p. 14). One such
conjunction speaks directly to Spinoza's relation of *thought*-to-*extension* that lawfully and theoretically precedes the parallel relation of
body and mind. Such relationship is also central to Edgar Levenson's
recognition, drawn from General Systems Theory, of clinical *transformation* (Levenson, 1978) which exactly replicates the Spinozan
parallelism implying sameness and difference, quantitative and qualitative dimensions. Observed ninety years ago by Constance
Rathbun, such parallelism expresses discernible instances of Nature's
substantive essence (Smith, 1925, p. 260).

Before continuing on with Smith, Rathbun, and Bernard, the
reader would be well advised to consider what we have generated in
this pause by association with our current vernacular understanding

of psychoanalysis (Miller, 2015). Respectively, our focal Spinozan authors were published in 1925, 1933, and 1946—leaving the better part of a century to future, psychoanalytic practice and development. M. Hamblin Smith comments on the Spinozan distinction between complete, or *Adequate* causation and incomplete, partial, or *Inadequate* causation (Smith, 1925, p. 264). What might seem almost completely explanatory in one historical moment is demonstrated as incomplete at a later time. This process, originally observed clinically by Melanie Klein and expanded into a handily applied algorithm by WR Bion, tracks moments of earlier psychological positioning in evolution across time toward moments of more mature functioning, themselves equally transient (Miller & Sweet, 2018).[5]

In the same way, clinical psychoanalytic explanation discovered in one historical moment forms the ground for progressive discovery at a later moment. Considering such empirically demonstrable process, the clinical reader associates backward in time to Lou Andreas-Salomé's observation that Spinoza meets us at every stage of our clinical psychoanalytic journey; and then wonders, how Spinoza might further inform the psychoanalysis that our earlier psychoanalysis itself recognized in his anticipation of modern psychology. The answer must come from our own close reading of Spinoza's *Ethics*.

Returning to the essentials of Spinozan thought as glimpsed by 20th-century psychoanalysts, the reader is exposed to three theorists' different deconstructions of a singular, five part philosophical demonstration. The result is a wealth of observations drawn from an impoverished conceptual scheme, stripped from Spinoza's geometric model. Often, our authors effuse generality. For example, Constance Rathbun comments that

> although there is a certain difference of emphasis of concepts among psychoanalysts, it is nevertheless the purpose of all to view the man in the totality of his relationships, as the nexus of a complex interplay of libidinal factors, rather than to resolve his psychic life into a set of fixed elements. Certainly the technique of analysis proceeds on the assumption that none of the aspects of behavior, none of the apparently insignificant tangents of thought are to be considered as unimportant and meaningless;

to acquire an understanding of the nature of the individual as a whole, all must be included. Since every act, every aspect of psychic life is determined wholly by preceding states, there is no such thing as a completely inexplicable act. Hence any psychology of the total personality must take into consideration, as far as possible, all phases of activity as internally related to one another. Spinoza seems to be saying the same thing in asserting that what is real is the essence of the individual, his activity in all its forms and stages of development as a concrete individual. To view man as a differentiated dynamic unity it is requisite to see him not simply as a rational social being but also as one possessing impulses, desires, feelings, without which rationality would become the emptiest of abstractions. (Rathbun, 1934, pp. 4–5)

Rathbun here recapitulates the recognition of Lou Andreas Salome, that Spinoza postulates a compelling psychological system of interrelations, effectively linking any discrete aspect of psychic activity with anything and everything else, both in the individual's internal world and in the external environment.

And then, a raft of concepts is unfolded. These include the here and now immediacy of experience in nature as well as the anthropocentrism of man. Smith observes Spinoza's challenge to the common belief that human weakness is attributable to a deficit of resolve; and that such beliefs are often coupled with ridicule or abuse. For Spinoza, as for the later Freud

the emotions are exactly like any other natural phenomena, and follow natural laws, which laws it is our task to study. (Smith, 1925, p. 264)

Quoting from Spinoza, Part III, Definition 3, Smith explains that emotions themselves are

modifications of the body by which the power of action in the body is increased or diminished, aided or restrained, and at the same time (for body and mind are one), the ideas of these modifications. (Smith, 1925, p. 264)

Remembering the parallelism that characterizes Spinozan thought, the reader observes both the active part of the emotion, its capability in *extension*, and the ideational part of the emotion, its *thought*. Similarly, association, and memory are mental functions dependent upon the body. Smith observes that the psychoanalytic practice of *free association* necessarily combines both the function of memory and association (Smith, 1925, p. 261).

In rapid order, each author provides a grocery list of psychoanalytic concepts, observed through a Spinozan lens. Most notable, especially at the time they were written, given the development of psychoanalysis, are the concepts of the Unconscious and the motivational nature of the Freudian libido. The Unconscious described by Freudian repression is only one aspect of the Spinozan unconscious. Smith reminds us that "it is not within the free power of mind to remember or forget anything" writing that repression, while unnamed by Spinoza, is explainable when the "memory of painful experience is removed from the conscious mind" but not forgotten, remains accessible (Smith, 1925, p. 264). A broader unconscious is summed up by Rathbun, who writes

> while Spinoza never mentions the unconscious as such, there is the possibility that in Spinozistic terminology the unconscious is a collection of the most confused and inadequate of ideas, especially those which correspond to unperceived bodily movement. Thus the problem for psychoanalysis of how the unconscious becomes conscious is for Spinoza the problem of how confused ideas are transformed into clear and distinct ideas. (Rathbun, 1934, p. 3)

Spinozan attention to distorted, inadequate, and confused ideas corresponds to the concept of the parataxic, originally imported into American clinical practice by George Herbert Mead (from Wilhelm Wundt) and transformed during World War I by T. V. Moore, later to be integrated into Sullivanian interpersonal understanding (Mead, 1904; Moore, 1921; Sullivan, 1953). Christopher Bollas' concept of "mangled" ideas (Bollas, 2015), similarly corresponds to this Spinozan model.

Notably for psychoanalysis, Spinoza's concept of human motivation is a variation upon Will, to which he gives the name (also used by Hobbes and Descartes) of *conatus*, endeavoring or striving. Rathbun comments that there is

> a striking resemblance between Spinoza's doctrine of the conatus or impulse toward self-preservation which constitutes the essence of every man and what was originally called the libido by analysts containing both the sex and the ego impulses. (Rathbun, 1934, p. 2)

Rathbun observes further that

> what is not found in Spinoza's concept of the conatus is what Freud terms the death instinct. There are, however, for Spinoza those passions which decrease and lessen the activities of the body and which in a sense imply a regressive turning inward of the conatus and thus might be said to foreshadow the theory of the death instinct. (Ibid, p. 2)

Writing in 1934, Rathbun updates Freudian libido through Freud's dualistic extension of drives, paralleling Empedocles' early instinctual theory. However, in Rathbun's desire to prove Spinoza's foreshadowing of psychoanalysis, she stumbles. Her drive-related, dualistic extension of Spinoza sacrifices Spinoza's monism. Smith, by contrast, only reluctantly equates conatus with Freudian sexuality, stating that

> in my judgment, there is much to be said in favor of the psychoanalytic use of conatus, in place of the somewhat unfortunate term libido. (Smith, 1925, p. 256)

Conatus alone maintains first, that "everything endeavours to persist in its own being"; and secondly, that such "endeavour is the actual essence of the thing" (Smith, p. 265). Almost as an afterthought, Smith realizes that perhaps he has tweaked psychoanalytic orthodoxy a bit too much and recants, harmonizing that when we remember, as we always must remember, the extended meaning which Freud attaches to the term 'sex', we shall find that the essentially sexual character of the emotions can be quite well fitted in with Spinoza's definitions. (Smith, 1925, p. 266)

Despite his back-pedaling, Smith alone seems to grasp a critical, if otherwise un-noted aspect of Spinozan thought which we shall encounter in our later reading of *Ethics*, the difference between *First Cause* and *Efficient* or *Proximate Cause*. In implicit recognition of this distinction, Smith hints at Spinoza's greater conceptual consistency, than in Freud's later development of psychoanalysis.

While Smith, Rathbun and Bernard uncover far more parallels, we shall follow their tracks in our own later reading of *Ethics*. However, relating back to the regularity of Spinoza's scientific method and clinical psychoanalytic method, it seems fitting to conclude this section with Smith's observation that

it is Freud's great offence, as it was Spinoza's, that he insists that man should regard himself as part of nature, and not as something outside and above nature. Spinoza's teaching is exactly that. Human motives must be analysed in just the same way as the relations of lines, circles, and planes. (Smith, 1925, p. 266)

Rathbun would both differentiate and collapse Spinoza's ideas into psychoanalytic conceptual advance, writing

psychoanalysis uses in its investigation of "the dynamics of mental life" methods unknown to Spinoza; free association, dream analysis, the interpretation by the analyst of material offered by the patient in the course of analysis, and positive and negative transference. The object of these methods is identical; to strengthen the ego, to modify the super-ego, to bring as much of the unconscious material into consciousness as is possible, and so to enable the individual to achieve a satisfactory adjustment to reality through insight into his own character. (Rathbun, 1934, p. 12)

Finally, commenting on desire, which Tanner recognized early was the conscious transformation of Spinozan willing, extended into behavioral appetite, Bernard writes

> from the very principle of self-preservation and considering the fact that our body, our life, is at no moment stationary and self-sufficient but always rather in a state of insufficiency, lability, and imbalance- consider the continuous necessity for breathing- it follows that we must always be in a *state of desire*, no matter how minimal its degree, either in order to continue the state of pleasure and well-being or in order to avoid and ward off that of pain and destruction. (Bernard, 1946, p. 104)

Bernard brings the psychoanalytic linkage to Spinoza full-circle, as the imperative mobilization of conatus through will to appetite and then, to desire, also implies a continuing imperfection, always reaching to what the ancients, with Spinoza, called "a greater perfection", which in our day, is the patient's experience of valued, positive change, through the work of clinical psychoanalysis.

Valuing Humanism: Postwar Spinoza as the Psychoanalytic Remnant of *Bildung*

Constance Rathbun, publishing in 1934, brilliantly summarizes the mid-century rush of psychoanalytic development, confident in its own terms, yet anticipated by Spinoza's differently worded conceptions.

Through such translation, the parallel form of *Ethics* became easily absorbed by psychoanalytic development. After all, according to M. Hamblin Smith, the objectives of both *Ethics* and psychoanalysis are similar in orienting the individual to "how a complete adaptation to reality can best be obtained" (Smith, 1925, p. 257). Smith's own dominant interest, writing as a forensic psychologist, is in Spinozan morality. He writes that

> Spinoza also points out how determinism confers advantages upon social as well as upon individual life, inasmuch as it teaches us not to despise, hate or ridicule any one, to be angry with and

envy no one (II49). Further, it teaches us that each one should be satisfied with what he has, and should be ready to help his neighbour, from the guidance of reason. Can more than this be claimed for psychoanalysis? (Smith, 1925, p. 262)

This claim of similar value positions is drawn from *Ethics*; and, as we shall later read, it links *Ethics* Part II with Parts IV and V. Yet, despite Smith's secondary-school recognition of Euclid, he seems not to have made the same differentiation as the later Deleuze in that Spinoza himself argues at two separate levels. The first, linear and unbroken, is the primary vehicle of geometric demonstration; while his second, occasional and broken throughout Spinoza's arguments, is a collection of opinion-pieces, each called a *scholium*. Here, Spinoza follows Maimonidean philosophical tradition, which facilitates both explicit, exoteric communication, as well as implicit, esoteric communication which only the philosophically attuned can hear.[6] In this, Spinoza's own method of theoretical conveyance itself demonstrates Freud's parallel, clinical recognition of conscious versus preconscious or unconscious communication.

Smith's claim of goal similarity between *Ethics* and psychoanalysis results in distortion between Spinoza's own aspirational passions and his geometrically demonstrable method of proof. Still, Smith's emphasis falls within the three-fold nature of psychoanalysis: its clinical facts and findings, its theoretical underpinning, and its argument for a specific value orientation in living (Reid, 1955).

It is toward this third strand of psychoanalytic understanding that Spinozan reference is channeled, beginning in the early 1950s. Writing in the *American Journal of Psychoanalysis*, Frederick A. Weiss presents the central humanistic argument for continued Spinozan influence in psychoanalysis. What remains implicit in Weiss' paper is its cultural rootedness in *Bildung*, however separated by distance and *Shoah* from that vanished German language culture. Similar to the late 20th-century writing of Bergmann cited above (Bergmann, 2017, p. 87), reading Weiss demands the broad acquaintance with historical, philosophical and literary understandings of Western culture ascribed by Richard Sterba to the *gebildeter mensch* (Sterba, 1982, p. 81). Weiss refers not only to Freud, Paul Schilder, and Karen Horney, but also to Karl Jaspers, John Dewey,

Jeremy Bentham, Epicurus, William Butler Yeats, Henri Bergson, Mo-Tse, Lao-Tzu, Plato, David Reisman, Hobbes, Goethe, the Earl of Shaftesbury, Albert Schweitzer, Kurt Lewin, Kant, and, of course, Spinoza. The effect is not only encyclopedic, integrating historical wisdom from ancient times to the present, but also serves as a critical supercommentary[7] upon the initial psychoanalytic position of Freud, just as Freud's expanded essays in the *Standard Edition*, serve as his later commentaries upon his own earlier, foundational postulates.

Comparing the aesthetic of such social science presentation, the contemporary reader, unschooled as a *gebildeter mentsch*, recognizes great affinity with the integrative, inclusive argumentative form of *Ethics*. That is, the breadth and scope of Weiss' argument, contrasts positively with Spinoza's philosophical-literary presentation, which itself features such luminaries as Descartes, Maimonides, Hobbes, Hasdai Crescas, Cicero, Seneca, Cervantes, Ovid, and the writer of Ecclesiastes, foundational in medieval Jewish philosophy and attributed to King Solomon (Robinson, 2007).

Weiss' "Psychoanalysis and Moral Values" is a fascinating document, resulting from psychoanalytic growth, integration, and redirection. Its confidence is anchored in the conviction that cultural acceptance of psychoanalysis had, by the early 1950s, already affected contemporary morality; and that with this achievement, post-Freudian psychoanalysis required critical reassessment.

Weiss enlists reference to Paul Schilder in arguing that Freud's theory is insufficiently founded upon isolated theoretical knowledge, stripped of context (Weiss, 1952, p. 39). Because of such limitation, psychoanalysis itself cannot assess its own cultural impact. Following Karen Horney, Weiss observes that morals themselves represent a compromise (Weiss, 1952, p. 39). Horney's argument triggers the reader's memory. Her formulation, conveyed by Weiss, implies a conjoint action extending from neurotic origin and inclusive of the functional idea and action of maintaining neurosis. Horney posits without attribution, the basic Spinozan relationship of modes and attributes, originating in *Ethics*, Part I. By association, the reader immediately recalls Horney's early recognition of Spinoza (Horney, 1980).[8]

Positioning himself in the American here-and-now of psychoanalysis following the Second World War, Weiss recognizes the holistic necessity of locating psychoanalysis in its context of time, place, and relative internal or external definition, linking such contextualization with the field theory of Kurt Lewin (Weiss, 1952, p. 45). Weiss argues from German-Swiss psychiatrist/philosopher Karl Jaspers' stern warnings of man's self-destructive perils. But it is in the action of translation between philosophy and psychoanalytic application that Weiss, shines. He *translates* Jaspers

> into analytical language: the danger facing man is self-idealization which, by producing either neurotic pride or self-complacent satisfaction with the status quo, blocks the struggle for self-realization and thereby makes him 'immoral' in light of the morality of evolution. (Weiss, 1952, p. 48)

Weiss' conclusion leads to a psychoanalysis integrative both of Karen Horney's formulations and of the ancient philosophical desideratum of endeavoring toward "greater perfection", originally Aristotelian, recognizably Spinozan, and attributed now by Weiss to John Dewey—whose position of continuous purposive change Weiss opposes to Kantian rigidity and adherence to duty (Weiss, 1952, p. 45).

Weiss' psychoanalytic argument is that Freud's tragic dualisms: (1) between instinctual drives themselves and (2) between drives and civilization, must be addressed holistically; and argues too, that the 19th-century biology that formed Freud's Darwinian underpinning must be integrated with later considerations of psychology, anthropology, and sociology. Weiss argues that Freud himself represented Victorian man. He writes

> that the Freudian man appears deeply split is due not only to the theoretical fact that in basing his picture of man only on isolated instincts, Freud excluded and therefore neglected essential parts of whole man; it is due also to the clinical and cultural fact that the type of man who served him as case material for his interpretation of what he believed to be universal human nature was a rather odd creature. There has hardly existed in history a man more split and more alienated from himself than *homo victorianus*—alientation from body, sex, and all his genuine feelings. (Weiss, 1952, p. 44)

The therapeutic goal of healing such splits is tinctured with the *Freudian pessimism* that

> pervaded his writings, especially his last ones. He did not expect that the split could ever be healed. The only solution he could conceive of was resignation. He asked man to accept his tragic fate; understanding that it might make it somewhat more tolerable. But the essential task of *therapy* is to heal the split. (Ibid, p. 44)

The clinical reader here recognizes the setting-up of another binary, powered by the same optimism that M. Hamblin Smith recognized in Spinoza's aspirational hopes: in the therapeutic power of rationality presiding over emotion. Indeed, Weiss is so ardent in this position that he misreads or misrepresents Spinoza, inverting the very order of *Ethics*, as if by *Freudian Slip*: that Spinoza's "first chapter of his *Ethics*, (is) entitled 'On Human Bondage'" (p. 41). In fact, "On Human Bondage" is the title of Part IV of *Ethics*, the beginning of Spinoza's aspirational depiction of ethical conduct. In hurrying toward Spinoza's application of his developed psychology, Weiss evades the dynamic psychological foundations of Spinozan thought.

Weiss' slip, however, represents the effective fate of Spinoza within psychoanalysis. Whether absorbed as a precursor idea or integrated within newly expanded theory, as demonstrated by Horney in her formulation of morality, the dynamic psychological underpinnings of Spinoza go unattributed; at the same time, the hopeful trajectory of a now-annihilated *Bildung* culture is reconstructed as American humanistic psychoanalysis.

A decade after Weiss, Erich Fromm recapitulates Weiss' understanding of Spinoza in the first issue of *Contemporary Psychoanalysis*, writing that

> Spinoza expressed the idea of the unity of the human race in his concept of "the model of human nature" to which certain laws apply, laws which neither completely determine man nor leave him completely free. Instead of calling him, as is often done, a determinist, it would be better to call Spinoza an "alternativist"; by this I refer to the concept that man has freedom to chose, but

that he can chose only between certain alternatives which are determined from his nature in general, and from the character of each individual, personally. Spinoza became the founder of modern scientific psychology, and he is closely related to Freud not only by the concept of the model of human nature, but also by his concept of the unconscious, by the idea that man is guided by forces he is not aware of. As he put it, man believes himself to be free because he knows his desire, but he is not aware of the causes for his desires. (Fromm, 1964a, pp. 70–71)

Together, with Horney's morality itself as the structuralizing compromise between causation and maintenance of neurosis, Fromm places the Spinoizan imperative of inquiry into human desire and desire's alternatives,[9] front and center in humanistic psychoanalysis.

Fromm's more extensive integration of Spinoza is found in *The Heart of Man* (1964b). Connected to his idea of *biophilia*, Fromm, like the earlier M. Hamblin Smith, advocates for the superiority of the Spinozan conatus to the Freudian dualism of life/death instincts, writing of such intrinsic striving that, "it is an inherent quality of all living substance to live, to preserve its existence" (Fromm, 1964b, p. 41).

Enlisting Spinoza as a lover of life, Fromm recognizes such unfolding as representative of humanity's productive orientation. Arguing that Freud's generation of the death instinct emerged from the demoralization of World War I, and citing *Ethics* Part IV, Proposition 41, Fromm writes,

> Spinoza's *Ethic* is a striking example of biophilic morality. 'Pleasure', he says, 'in itself is not bad but good; contrariwise, pain in itself is bad'. (Fromm, 1964b, pp. 43–44)

Expanding from Weiss' depiction of pride as arrogant self-idealization and self-complacent satisfaction[10] (Weiss, 1952), Fromm contrasts group narcissism with individual humanism. He reflects that the group narcissisms of the Second World War "have brought the world to the abyss of total destruction" (Fromm, 1964b, p. 80). Contextualizing historically and signaling the demise of *Bildung* culture, Fromm reflects on this "severe blow" to an individual humanism that

> in the eighteenth and nineteenth centuries- from Spinoza, Leibniz, Rousseau, Herder, Kant, to Goethe and Marx- the thought developed that mankind is one, that each individual carries within himself all of humanity.[11] (Fromm, 1964b, pp. 80–81)

Like the earlier Spinozan commentator M. Hamblin Smith, Fromm underlines the necessity of doubt within Spinoza's thinking. Doubt, for Spinoza, operates as a counter-balance, reducing the fixed rigidity of a prized idea through the leveling effect of unpleasure. As we shall observe in Chapter 11, with its clinical application reflected in Viktor Tausk's case presentation of Ibsen the Druggist (Tausk, 1934), the clinical application of doubt in psychoanalytic psychotherapy is as a mechanism affirming rationality in the face of the irrational. Unfortunately, Smith distorts the Spinozan centrality of scientific questioning, of doubting, by forcing a comparison with Freudian repression, writing

> Spinoza notes that doubt is an essential element in both hope and fear, thus anticipating the views of modern psychology. He says that we endeavour to affirm concerning ourselves everything that we imagine to affect ourselves with pleasure. And what we find repugnant or conducive to pain we endeavor to remove. Here we have repression again. (Smith, 1925, p. 268)

Smith would have been more accurate in typifying the mind's intrinsic refusal to allow a diminution of its power, to the psychoanalytic notion of repression (Part III, Propositions 12 & 13). Fromm, however, gets it right. He integrates scientific skepticism with Spinozan defiance in the face of popular, unfounded opinion, reflected from the beginnings of Spinoza's ethical writing in the *Treatise on the Emendation of the Intellect*. But the self-satisfied arrogance of popular opinion, located for Spinoza both in Church and Synagogue,[12] is refracted through Fromm's post-war lens as *group narcissism*. He writes, the growing intensity of group narcissism- only shifting from religious to national, racial, and party narcissism- is, indeed, a surprising phenomenon. First of all because of the development of the humanistic forces since the Renaissance, which we discussed earlier. Furthermore, because of the evolution of scientific thought which undermines narcissism. The scientific method requires objectivity and realism, it requires seeing the world as it is, and not distorted by one's own desires and fears. It requires being humble toward the facts of reality, and renouncing all hopes of omnipotence and omniscience. The need for critical thought, experimentation, proof. The attitude of doubting- these are characteristic of scientific endeavor, and they are precisely the methods of thought which tend to counteract the narcissistic orientation. Undoubtedly the method of scientific thinking has had its effect on the development of contemporary neo-humanism, and it is not accidental that most of the outstanding natural scientists of our day are humanists. But the vast majority of men in the West, although they have 'learned' the scientific method in school or at the university, never really have been touched by the method of scientific, critical thinking. Even most of the professionals in the field of the natural sciences have remained *technicians*, and have not acquired *a scientific attitude*. For the majority of the population, the scientific method they were taught has had even less significance. Although it may be said that higher education has tended to soften and to modify personal and group narcissism to some extent, it has not prevented most of the 'educated' people from joining enthusiastically the national, racial, and political movements which are the expression of contemporary group narcissism. (Fromm, 1964b, p. 120)

The reader also detects in Fromm's observation of higher education's failures, a not-so-veiled lament for the "scientific, critical thinking" that *Bildung* inspired. Fromm's relegation of the educated to the role of technicians exactly parallels Martin Bergmann's later condemnation of post-*Bildung* psychoanalytic practitioners, as mere "professionals" (Bergmann, 2017, p. 87), itself congruent with Richard Sterba's condemnation of contemporary American education (Sterba, 1982, p. 16).

Fromm returns to the adequacy of ideas, earlier commented upon by Smith (1925). Fromm recognizes that

> according to Spinoza, freedom is based on 'adequate ideas' which are based on the awareness and acceptance of reality and which determine actions securing the fullest development of the individual as psychic and mental unfolding. Human action, according to Spinoza, is causally determined by passions or by reason. When ruled by passions, man is in bondage; when by reason, he is free. (1964b, p. 126)

Fromm's humanistic conclusion, drawn from Spinoza, returns to the concept of essence, originally located by Spinoza in the substantive idea of Nature in *Ethics* Part I, and extended through the lawful natural order to the modes and attributes of human functioning. Fromm underscores Spinoza's Aristotelian essentialism in our shared, deterministic humanity, from within which limited freedoms of action are possible. Fromm affirms our inquiry and humanistic refinement of human nature writing that

> logically, for Spinoza, 'a horse would be as completely destroyed by being changed into a man, as by being changed into an insect' (*Ethic*, IV, preface). Good consists of transforming our existence into an ever increasing approximation to our essence; evil into an increasing estrangement between existence and essence. (Fromm, 1964b, p. 144)

The humanistic integration of Spinoza concludes with two technical papers. The earlier paper, by J. Reid (1955), focuses on the centrality of values in psychoanalysis. The second paper, written by Joyce A. Tigner (1985), and following the observations of arrogance and self-esteem suggested by Weiss (1952), is an integration of clearly applied Spinozan thought within clinical psychoanalysis. Emulating Spinoza's own manner of explanation, demonstrated from Propositions 18 to 59 in *Ethics* Part III, Tigner's publication remains the singular explicit, historical example of *clinical Spinoza*. Unfortunately, after her brilliant foray, the rest is silence. Spinoza disappears from explicit reference in psychoanalytic thinking.[13]

Notes

1 Freudian metapsychology endures as metaphysics disavowed as philosophy, defending psychoanalysis itself against inquiry into its own preconceptions. Late 20th-century psychoanalysts have argued for psychoanalytic evolution beyond metapsychology, including a shift away from anthropomorphic descriptive language (Grossman & Simon, 1969; Schafer, 1976), toward a renewed discipline founded on the empirical facts of clinical practice.

2 It is indicative of the interactive, germinating nature of psychoanalytic development that Smith's (1925) paper references William Alanson White (Smith, 1925, p. 259), the mentor of Harry Stack Sullivan, founder of the Washington School of Psychiatry (Perry, 1982, pp. 187–188) Citing Rathbun (1934) who herself cites Smith, Bernard's scholastic placement of Spinozan integration in *Psychiatry* solidifies Smith's anticipatory Spinoza relative to what would become the American "school" of interpersonal-relational psychoanalysis (Stern, 2017).

3 Readers of Spinoza may note that *Ethics'* demonstrative presentation does not characterize all of his writing. For example, his incomplete essay, *Treatise on the Emendation of the Intellect* (Spinoza, 2002, pp. 1–30) does not follow this form. Later, his *Short Treatise on God, Man, and His Well-Being* (Spinoza, 2002, pp. 31–107) playfully contrasts different forms of writing, including fanciful dialogues reminding the reader of Leone Ebreo's *Dialogues of Love* (Ebreo, 2016), a popular work known by Spinoza and written by a Renaissance "cultural intermediary" between Jewish and gentile worlds (Ruderman, 2004, pp. 1–23; Veltri, 2004, pp. 55–66). It is only beginning with Spinoza's critique of Descartes, that he deploys the geometrical method of demonstration, mirroring and challenging that of Descartes. Introducing Spinoza's *Principles of Cartesian Philosophy and Metaphysical Thoughts* (Spinoza, 2002, pp. 108–212), Spinoza's colleague Lodewijk Meyer writes, "It is the unanimous opinion of all who seek wisdom beyond the common lot that the best and surest way to discover and to teach truth is the method used by mathematicians in their study and exposition of the sciences, namely, that whereby conclusions are demonstrated from definitions, postulates, and axioms" (Meyer, L. in Spinoza, 2002, p. 116). Together with Spinoza's Cartesian challenge, it may be that Spinoza's awareness of Maimonides' standard of philosophical demonstration also underwrote his style of presentation. Writing in *The Guide of the Perplexed*, I:68, referenced by Spinoza in the *Ethics* II scholium for Proposition 7, Maimonides writes that the nature of God's unity as "intellectual cognition as well as the intellectually cognizing subject and the intellectually cognized object".....is a matter of *demonstration*" (the italics are mine, ISM; Maimonides, 1963, p. 163).

4 What our psychoanalytic commentators may not recognize is that the very idea of godly attributes had been the focus of medieval theological contemplation long before Spinoza; and that Spinoza's own considerations may be traced to his integration, cited in his correspondence with Lodewijk Meyer (Spinoza, 2002,

Letter 12, p. 791), of the 15th-century post-Maimonidean philosophical thought of Hasdai Crescas (Fraenkel, 2009a; Harvey, 1998; Wolfson, 1916).

5   Such transitions are also illustrated in earlier and later ideas, as one generation's imagination becomes realized only generations later. One such example is in Maimonides' fantasy of what would one day be an airplane (Gorfinkle, 1912, p. 41). Another is reflected by Spinoza's argument about water, accurate for his time but erroneous in light of Henry Cavendish's later discovery of water's divisibility into Oxygen and Hydrogen (I. Proposition 15 Scholium, p. 227).

6   Deleuze comments that this equivocal form of communication "that consisted in concealing the boldest or least orthodox arguments in appendices or notes", is paralleled by Spinoza's "systematic method of scholia" (Deleuze, 1988, footnote 21, p. 29). Josef Stern observes that such traditions of concealment were understood by the medieval Islamic world, "most notably by Al-Farabi" in reference to "secret doctrines" held by Plato and Aristotle (Stern, 2013, p. 56). Receptive of medieval Islamic philosophical tradition, Maimonides' interpretive use of layered parables, disclosing philosophical levels of Scriptural meaning, is illustrated by Stern, in the parable of the silver filigreed apple (Stern, 2013, p. 27), which I recognize below, as illustrative of Spinoza's methodological transformations.

7   Reading the receptive history of Spinozan ideas, the reader encounters the medieval form of supercommentary, as later philosophers wrote their own commentaries upon an earlier philosopher's reading of Aristotle. Similarly, beginning in early medieval time, biblical textual commentaries would themselves forward differing interpretive, often competitive, positions relative to the same text, in the form of supercommentaries. Focusing upon the 12th-century scholar, Abraham ibn Ezra, Uriel Simon writes

> a supercommentary, as a commentary superimposed on a commentary, does not refer directly to the primary text being glossed and explained. Whereas a commentator on Scripture deals with a single text, the supercommentator has in front of him two texts of quite unequal status: one is sacred and obligatory, whereas the other is merely revered and indispensable. The truth of Scripture is absolute, inasmuch as it is the product of revelation; but the validity of the commentary depends on its powers of persuasion, inasmuch as it is the result of human logical processes. (Simon, 1993, p. 86)

From this perspective, this present reading is itself a supercommentary, both upon other Spinozan commentaries on *Ethics* and upon the history and forms of Spinoza's psychoanalytic reception.

8   While Karen Horney's psychoanalytic publications contain no explicit reference to Spinoza, the oral transmission of Spinozan reference by "old Berlin analysts" is still remembered by late 20th-century graduates of Horney's American Institute (Galdi, 2019). It is noted that Frederick Weiss, like Karen Horney, like Paul Schilder, like Walter Bernard, like Richard Sterba, like Martin Bergmann,

like Kurt Lewin, like Erich Fromm, had all been educated in Central Europe, and reared under its dominant middle-class German-language culture of *Bildung*.

9　Fromm's focus on desires links the reader back to psychology's earlier Spinozan commentators. Amy Tanner (1907a) provides the clearest, most differentiated Spinozan consideration of desire relative to conatus, in recognizing the different forms of desire along the unconscious<> conscious continuum, from our internal psychological worlds to our extended appetite for external objects and again, conjoining in reintegration with ongoing internal process.

10　Focused on the Ethics IV and V, Weiss misses the opportunity to link this cardinal theoretical observation to Spinoza's clinical recognition in Part III that such arrogance reflects the essence of madness, of dreaming with one's eyes open (III Proposition 2, Scholium; III Proposition 26, Scholium).

11　We have noted above that Walter Bernard (1934) similarly recognizes Spinozan influence in 18th–19th century German thought as do other commentators including Goetschel (2004) and Wolstein (1953).

12　The reader is reminded of Spinoza's epigram to his *Short Treatise on God, Man, and Well-Being,*

> ... now translated into the Dutch language for use of the Loves of Truth and Virtue; so that they who spout so much about it, and put their dirt and filth into the hands of simpletons as though it were ambergris, may just have their mouths stopped, and cease to profane what they do not understand: God, themselves, and how to help people to have regard for each other's well-being, and how to heal those whose mind is sick. (Spinoza, 2002, p. 33)

13　An example of tacit Spinozan influence within psychoanalytic thought is in Benjamin Wolstein's differentiation of the ego-interpersonal sphere of psychic functioning from what he terms the self's "psychic center" (Wolstein, 1987). As sharply differentiated as Amy Tanner's depiction of Spinozan operations separating externally verifiable and internally private fields of psychological functioning, Wolstein both: (1) shifts Freud's libidinally derived interpretation of ego to the individual's internalization of interpersonal relations, as does Spinoza in his distinction between internal conatus and externalized appetite and desire; and (2) establishes a "psychic center", functionally distinct from its bodily dependency, and congruent with Spinoza's conatus as the locus of private self-definition.

Part II

Chapter 3

Freud's Negative Particle

The previous section concluded with my observation that after the creative clinical work of J.A. Tigner in 1985, the synthetic integration of Spinoza within the psychoanalytic field became silent. As I have researched *Clinical Spinoza*, I have wondered about this phenomenon; and return to it in Part V, after close reading of *Ethics* and a summarizing of *clinical Spinoza*.

For now, it is sufficient to note that this silence mirrored my own obliviousness to Spinoza both as a philosopher and relative to psychoanalytic psychology. Among psychology's Spinozans, Amy Tanner's (1907a) impatient incomprehension came closest to my own lack of preparedness for encountering *Ethics*. Unable to recognize Spinoza historically in the onrushing flow of received, psychological thought, I only discovered him at the margin of another, related deep-dive into oblivion, as I set out to unpack a famous joke described in 1905, by Freud (Miller & Sweet, 2018, Ch 8; Miller, 2019). What oriented me to Spinoza was an odd Freudian observation: on the one hand, objectifying Spinoza under the example of a humorous "negative particle"; and, on the other hand, smuggling in a certain cautious identification with Spinoza as a "fellow un-believer", expressed by Freud's ironic spokesperson, Harry Heine (Freud, 1905, p. 77). What was unambiguous was that Freud himself, through such *unheimlich* misdirection, directed me to Baruch Spinoza.

The next three chapters mark my step-wise observation of Baruch Spinoza within the conceptual fabric of psychoanalysis. Thinking about this process, I can have no better thought partner than Samuel Ibn-Tibbon, Maimonides' 13th-century Hebrew translator.

DOI: 10.4324/9781003246404-6

Considering his own commentary on the book of Ecclesiastes, Ibn-Tibbon wrote that while he hoped his thinking might stir thought either in his own or later generations, the utility of the work at least served him as a marker of his own thinking, a place-holder of where his thoughts had taken him, that

> even if many of the people of my time speak against me, it is impossible that not one or two will receive some benefit- during my own generation or that which follows. Even if something like this does not come to pass, it can still serve me as an aid to memory. (Robinson, 2007, p. 176)

Over these next chapters, I present revised versions of journal papers that served me as memory aids, in assembling my own understanding of Freud, Heine, and Spinoza: first, in relation to the problem of personal identity under societal intolerance; and next, as integrative factors in the development of psychoanalysis. Besides identity, the reader will recognize the recurrent topic of doubling, of multiple levels of understanding. As we have already seen, such equivocal communication had already been present in medieval writing; and through Freud, Heine, and Spinoza, also seems to have become supercharged through personally undergone experiences of exclusion and oppression. As is clear from these papers, I wondered about both of these currents, one literary-philosophical and the other, drawn from directly lived experience, in contributing to the central psychoanalytic premise of unconscious and conscious experience and communication.

The first paper in this process of rediscovery is a revised version of "Doublings Between Bewilderment and Enlightenment: Reading Freud With Heine on the Troubled Identity of Hirsch-Hyacinth", published in 2019 in *The American Journal of Psychoanalysis*.

Freud, Heine, and the Tragedy of Hirsch-Hyacinth

This section follows Freud's reading of a joke excerpted from the *Reisebilder* or *Travel Pictures* of H. Heine (Heine, 2008, p. 124) in illustrating the action of doubling between unconscious and conscious registrations as fundamental within psychoanalytic psychology.

Whether through the one-person psychological act of reflection observed in dreams or joke construction (Freud, 1900, 1905) or through the two-person psychological acts present both within the apprehension of jokes and within the clinical discernment of symptomatic meanings (Freud, 1901, 1905, 1927), Freud's examples of psychological doubling present transformations akin to literary translation. His initial recognition of the Hirsch-Hyacinth vignette compresses Heine's wit to what appears in "Standard Edition" English to be a neologism[1]; but the illuminative meanings of Hirsch-Hyacinth remain deceptively complicated, audaciously defiant of Freud's linguistic explanation.

This presentation is divided into two parts. The first, "(No)Joke", illuminates Freud's personal identification with Heine as signaled by the Hirsch-Hyacinth example. The second, "Arabic Curse and Jewish Malady", drawn from the same literary text as the Hirsch-Hyacinth joke, conveys a doubling within Heine's writing similar to Freud's illuminative interpretations of Hirsch-Hyacinth: as if two scansions are equally present in a single expression, addressed to two different levels of apprehension.[2] In addressing Hirsch-Hyacinth while following Heine's doubled literary form of presentation, Freud's descriptive demonstration mirrors the multiple levels of experience and meaning continuously emergent in the daily work of psychotherapy (Miller & Sweet, 2018).

Freud overtly turns away from his culturally "beloved mother-tongue" (Freud, 1915, p. 177) in the service of consolidating the objective, scientific practice of psychoanalytic method (Gilman, 1990). Rhetorically, if from the cultural currents of *Bildung*, Freud consigns to oblivion the civilizational elements inherent in multiple Jewish languages. Operating from the dynamic Erich Fromm will later term "group narcissism" (1964b, p. 120), Freud reduces Jewishness to his own commonly shared large group assumptive fantasy. Robbing the Hebrew bible itself of language, Freud locates Jewish culture within an unlanguaged essentialism, which is "the more powerful the less they could be expressed in words"[3] (Freud, 1926, p. 274). Effectively, Freud's strategic move parallels Austro-Hungarian political definition of Jews as a people with neither territorial nor linguistic status. Jay Geller observes,

following Article 19 of the 1867 Imperial Constitution, the Jews, unlike other nationalities such as the Ruthenians and the Czechs, were recognized as a people (Volksstamm) but not as a nation (Nationalität); hence, they had neither language nor territory rights. Every recognized nationality had the right to teach its children in the 'language customary to the land'—Croat, Czech, German, Magyar etc. Austria-Hungary recognized 11 national groups and their languages, but the state did not confer such status on either the Jews or their languages, Hebrew and Yiddish. (Geller, 2004, p. 1211)

This disability, uniquely extended to Jewish citizens of the Austro-Hungarian Empire, antedates Freud's similar cultural reduction of Jewishness; but is background to the emancipated Austrian Jewishness in which Freud had grown up, from the age of 11. In this light, Freud's ambivalent depictions of Jewishness resemble the defensive posture later psychoanalysis recognizes as "identification with the aggressor", in the sphere of gentile-Jewish relations (Ferenczi, 1933; Freud, 1936; Howell, 2014). Yet, as Freud demonstrates, such identification is incomplete. Freud's strategic definition of a Jewishness depleted of its cultural voice is contradicted by his counter-narrative through which vibrantly living forms of Jewish expression, such as those comprising the bulk of his 1905 *Jokes and Their Relation to the Unconscious,* as well as his own literary mirroring of Heine's overtly ambivalent Jewish preoccupations, continue from Hirsch-Hyacinth to *Moses and Monotheism* (Gilman, 1990; Yerushalmi, 1991). Within this persistently repetitive doubling in literary equivocation, Freud undercuts his formal identification with the conventional Austro-Hungarian portrayal of Jewishness as an *unheimlich,* ghostly carapace of antiquated civilization in exactly the same way the unconscious illumination of a joke's doubled meaning undercuts its initial premise. While contemporary categorical definition of such cultural emotional striving was unavailable to Freud, its historical, psychological, and associative mnemic currents become culturally discernable by the late 20th century in the particular expressive forms that Yerushalmi recognizes as, "the faith of fallen Jews" (Yerushalmi, 1982, p. 101).

Significantly, the Hirsch-Hyacinth joke functions to illustrate Freud's discernment of psychoanalytic auto-emancipation through interpretive method reliant on subjective particularity but oriented toward illuminating the universal human condition; and at the same time, models Freud's cautiously audacious use of doubling to address the ongoing psychological situation of cultural prejudice, particularized in his participant-observer role as Austro-Hungarian Jew. Freud conveys his doubled psychological reference to a Jewishness he defines as inexpressible in words yet at the same time, actively demonstrates through its particularisms of language and expressive forms, as well as through his personified identification with Heine, the creator of Hirsch-Hyacinth.

I. (No) Joke

We begin with a joke told by Freud. In actuality, Freud doesn't tell the joke but rather gestures to the joke in summary. In this way, the disclosure in enlightenment that is the yield of the joke, both for teller and listener, lies obscure and distant from its initially conscious surface. Freud as raconteur is aware not only of the conscious and unrecognized levels of the joke's meaning; but is also mindful of its intended effect upon the listener. He pays attention to the joke itself in its polyphonic meanings as well as to his participatory actions in its conveyance to an audience (Freud, 1927). Freud's skillful presentation parallels the manner in which a joke works through revelation of its doubled meanings. In abstracting from the complex specificity of the joke's contents, Freud describes its mechanics in precise prose.[4] He discerns the triggers that evoke recognition and laughter as an interpersonal psychological creation, through the infusion of the joke's surface by a doubling of underlying meanings.

But in reading Freud more than a century after the writing of this densely constructed text, contemporary readers face a challenge that is also central within clinical practice. We engage an experiential field defined between amnesia and oblivion, with amnesia representative of the generative pole from which memory might be evoked (Freud, 1910a). Oblivion represents its opposite pole, evocative of nothing at all, as the requisite experience upon which recognition depends is missing or obscured by gestural repetitions operating beneath linguistic vocalization (Bion, 2005; Miller, 2015; Miller & Sweet, 2018). As in the practice of psychotherapy, where "living through" or "learning from experience" must be wrested from meaningless re-petition (Bion, 1962; Ferenczi & Rank, 1924; Waelder, 1951), so too, the integration of what has become dissociated from within literary, historical memory, is crucial in recovering meaning from textual oblivion in psychoanalytic history.

Contemporary psychoanalysis, mindful of annihilative human destruction, societal dislocation, large group social dynamics, xeno-phobia, the binocularity between individual subjectivity and external group experience, and the necessity of integrating history's external facts within internal subjectivity (Boulanger, 2015; Davoine & Gaudilliere, 2004; Ferenczi, 1932, 1933; Fromm, 1973; Grotstein, 2007; Kogan, 2017; Mucci, 2014; Volkan, 2017) extends a psycho-analytic method founded by Freud into a 21st century future of which Freud had no experience.

Unlike Freud's registration of societal racism in its characteriza-tion of Jewishness as genetic infirmity, believed through Lamarckian distortion to have been transmitted by the intergenerational cove-nantal practice of male circumcision, in fascinated focus upon the Jewish phallus as congenitally feminized within the Habsburgian social imaginary (Boyarin, 1997; Geller, 2004; Gilman, 1990, 1992), today's psychoanalysis celebrates civilizational aspects of Jewishness in relation to their wealth of psychoanalytic contribution (Aron & Henik, 2010). To the end of Freud's life, he would express a Spinozan vacillation of mind, an oscillation between regard and disdain for Jewishness, similar to Heine's. Writing of the Heine-Freud pair, Yosef Hayim Yerushalmi observes,

> in a footnote to a passage in *Moses and Monotheism* on the alleged Egyptian origin of Jewish circumcision, Freud writes, "And incidentally, who suggested to the Jewish poet Heine in the nineteenth century A.D. that he should complain of his religion as "the plague dragged along from the Nile Valley, the unhealthy beliefs of ancient Europe? (Freud, 1939, n. 2; Yerushalmi, 1991, p. 31)

Heine's disruptive and provocative voice, sometimes darkly con-demning, sometimes praising, and frequently mocking both Jewish and Gentile cultures, articulates the mid-20th century epitome of "marginal man", partaking variably and ambivalently in multiple cultural identifications (Stonequist, 1937, pp. 153–154). His voice is relatively unknown today, especially within Anglophone psychoanalysis (Miller & Sweet, 2018); but not for Freud, who recognizably enlists Heine

> as his own rhetorical double-the object of his study as well as the voice into which he can slip. What is uncanny in Freud's text is the regularity with which Heine's voice appears in this manner. Freud's poetics of quotation reveal themselves to be a politics of quotation. His appropriation of Heine's voice in the 'scientific' context of psychoanalytic theory reveals itself to be a dialogue with the voice of the Jew within a discourse initially labeled as scientific, but also understood by Freud within his thought-collective as Jewish as well. Heine remains for Freud the sign of the double bind of being both the authoritative voice of the observer and the ever suspect voice of the patient, a voice which remains one of the signs and symptoms of the disease from which Heine and Freud suffered, their Jewishness. (Gilman, 1990, p. 94)

Recognizing this of Freud and Heine, we turn to Freud's joke sample, his literary case presentation of Herr Hirsch-Hyacinth. Freud begins this particular academic demonstration of the joke with concentration upon a single aspect of humor, "the factor of bewilderment and illumination" (Freud, 1905, p. 12). He then leads the reader through an allusion to Kant upon the general nature of the comedic before proceeding to G. Heymans' 1896 commentary upon bewilderment and illumination, itself elaborating a dimension of the comic made by T. Lipps (Freud, 1905, p. 12; Gilman, 1990, p. 89). Boldly, Freud now reveals his active participation in this imagined debate, his own mental representation of an academic symposium about the dynamics of psychology, extending across a century of Enlightenment. Freud reintroduces a joke used as an example by Heymans by writing that Heine

> makes one of his characters, Hirsch-Hyacinth, the poor lottery agent, boast that the great Baron Rothschild had treated him quite as his equal- quite 'familionairely'. Here the word that is

the vehicle of the joke appears at first simply to be a wrongly constructed word, something unintelligible, incomprehensible, puzzling. It accordingly bewilders. The comic effect is produced by the solution of this bewilderment, by understanding the word. Lipps (1898, 95, *citation as in Freud's text*) adds to this that this first stage of enlightenment- that the bewildering word means this or that- is followed by a second stage, in which we realize that this meaningless word has bewildered us and has then shown us its true meaning. It is only this second illumination, this discovery that a word which is meaningless by normal linguistic usage has been responsible for the whole thing- this resolution of the problem into nothing- it is only this second illumination that produces the comic effect. (Freud, 1905, p. 13)

Freud next gestures to a more pointedly if particular form of doubling in the Hirsch-Hyacinth sample through revelation that this example of wit is no joke at all, but a statement of an uncomfortably borne societal alienation within which both Heine and Freud are embedded respectively, to their bewilderment. Addressing this issue obliquely if boldly, within the context of his imagined symposium with Kant, Lipps, and Heymans, Freud writes

What Heine has put into Hirsch-Hyacinth's mouth is a correct and acute observation, an observation of unmistakable bitterness, which is understandable in a poor man faced by such great wealth; but we should not venture to describe it as in the nature of a joke. If anyone is unable in considering the translation to get away from his recollection of the shape given to the thought by the poet, and thus feels that nevertheless the thought in itself is also in the nature of a joke, we can point to a sure criterion of the joking character having been lost in the translation. (Freud, 1905, p. 17)

Freud recognizes that this joke discloses a significant fact, Heine's poetic observation of the bitter suffering of Jewish poverty, emitted through the vehicle of Hirsch-Hyacinth's mouth. But now cautious, Freud goes no further. Indeed, his silence is deafening as he leaves the reader only marginally advanced along the path from bewilderment to illumination. Perhaps the particular suffering to which he alludes might genuinely concern one Jew's envious desire for another Jew's wealth? This interpretation would be congruent with traditional anti-Semitic derogation (Nirenberg, 2013), so probably sufficient to make the Heine example laughable for some. But knowing Freud as we do, such limitation while sufficient, lacks necessity.

Alternatively, Freud seems engaged in the psychological action of doubling, of demonstrating a ghostlike and uncannily *unheimlich* resonance which remains inexplicit, so formally undisclosed. Like the dynamism of the joke itself, it is as if an alter-ego undoes the ostensible placidity of social presentation (Freud, 1919; Frosh, 2013; Kilborne, 2014; Rank, 1914). If so, Freud signals one rendition of his interpretative story at one level while signaling a counter-rendition of the story at another level: exactly the disruptive marker of the psychoanalytic double. Here, Freud,[5] mindful of Heine's original contextual location of Hirsch-Hyacinth in the "The Baths of Lucca", stylistically mirrors Heine's subversive presentation of doubling discussed below in section II, "Arabic Curse and Jewish Malady" (Freud, 1905, p. 77; Heine, 1826, p. 183), as if with an insider's wink that those in the know will recognize what is meant.

Modern readers are aware that historically

> Austrian Jewry was caught in a double bind. The Viennese society into which many sought admission demanded complete assimilation, even to the point of obliterating any traces of Judentum[6]; yet, often accompanying the demand was the assumption that Jews were constitutionally incapable of eliminating their difference. (Geller, 2004, p. 1210)

The man who Freud considered his contemporary literary doppelganger, Arthur Schnitzler, observed that such Jewishness remained conspicuously and painfully present in everyday Viennese life where there was neither respite nor exit from this social condition. This societal force induced a hyper-conscious state of self-awareness upon the individual, the sense of one's own threateningly sinister alter-ego imposed socially, psychoanalytically framed by Rank as a double (Rank, 1914).

The situation described by Schnitzler and lived by Freud and

Heine, has been described as an "existential aporia", placing Jews in a "no man's land" of cultural homelessness: resident in Germany or Austria but with a socially induced self-consciousness through racial objectivization as society's "Other" in a dichotomized and xenophobic social world, split into mutually negating depictions of "us" and "them" (Kogan, 2017; Schlesier, 1990; Volkan, 2017).

Immediately recognizable to the fin-de-siecle German readers of the Hirsch-Hyacinth joke is the character's hyphenated name. Hirsch is the original Jewish name and Hyacinth, the post-baptismal name of the character, just as its author, another H-H, was originally known as Harry Heine and after baptism, Heinrich Heine. The social-psychological context for Freud's Hirsch-Hyacinth is within Heine's sarcastic depiction of German-Jewish bourgeois pleasure in the Tuscan spa resort of Lucca. Here, Heine archly observes, is where imperfectly acculturated Jews have opportunistically fantasized an escape route to the inescapable Gentile-Jewish dilemma through baptism as the "entry ticket to European culture" (Schleiser, 1990, p. 39). This attempted, if impossible, escape reduces confessional faith to the throughput of "religious conversion companies" (Heine, 1826, p. 182) as newly Christian, Heine's characters now revel in hopeful awareness that the freedoms and pleasures of societal acceptance will be theirs, ambivalently self-conscious that the "Jews have cornered the Christian market" (Heine, 1826, pp. 182, 190).

Freud's own "Signorelli" dream specimen, presented both in *The Interpretation of Dreams* and in *The Psychopathology of Everyday Life*, reflects contextual similarity to Heine's depiction of assimilated German-Jewish interaction in "The Baths of Lucca". Freud arrives at the universal nature of dream dynamics via the elemental particularities of the dreamer's specific associations. Here, the associative framework is particularized by Freud's narrative context of two Austro-Hungarian Jews from different regions of the Empire, expertly discussing the nuances of church art as they sit in a Mittleuropean train carriage (Freud, 1901, pp. 6–7). Creating his narrative setting, Freud blends two discernable forms of Jewish linguistic expression. The first is his utilization of the train motif that is a mainstay of 19th-century Jewish humor; and that is explicitly depicted in his 1905 text (Freud, 1905, p. 80; Wisse, 2013). Combined with this familiar set piece is a motif resonant of Heine, whose hyphenated Jews of Lucca, educated in secular European culture, observe

> you can bind my eyes and take me to an art gallery in Florence and every painting you put me in front of I can tell you the painter who painted it or at least the school he belonged to. (Heine, 1826, p. 106)

Uncannily present in its absence from Freud's dream associations is the recognition that Signorelli's first name is "Luca", similar in pronunciation to the setting of Heine's story (Freud, 1900; Miller & Sweet, 2018).[7]

Sardonically, Heine reduces what in earlier times had been the idealized domain of transcendent religious faith, to its down-to-earth value as practical utility in daily life, a unique marker of an adaptive Jewish social form also recognizable in the 350-year-old culture of Iberian Conversos, the descendants of forcibly baptized "New Christians", under the lethal force of the Spanish Inquisition, still operative during Heine's lifetime (Gilman, 1972; Yovel, 1989b, 2009). Self-consciously aware of a similar social imperative, facing societal contempt and disability rather than the *auto-de-fe*, Heine's newly Christian Jewish characters affect a similar pragmatic stance.

The fin de siècle German reader of Freud's Hirsch-Hyacinth joke immediately recognizes the impossibly obstructed societal dead-end of Jewish striving, whether for character Hirsch-Hyacinth or author, Harry-Heinrich Heine.

Heine's vocalization of Hirsch-Hyacinth's contempt shifts the narrated locus of Jewish suffering, highlighting its interior dimension of self-hatred. Hirsch-Hyacinth's rebellion turns against Jewishness itself whereas Freud's interpretive sensitivity toward "the shape given to the thought by the poet", addresses Heine's more expansive critique of insoluble cultural prejudice in regard to the problem of being Jewish in enlightened Europe (Heine, 2006, 2008),

> You can keep your old Jewish faith Doctor, I wouldn't wish it on my worst enemy. Gives you nothing but scorn and shame. I tell you, its no religion at all, just a lot of hard luck. I try to avoid anything that could remind me of it, and since Hirsch is a

Jewish word and means Hyacinth in German, I even gave old Hirsch his walking papers and now sign my name: 'Hyacinth, Collection Agent, Operator Extraordinaire and Taxator'. Fortunately, my signet ring already has an H on it and I don't have to get a new one engraved. I assure you, your name matters a whole lot in this world, your name is everything. When I sign, 'Hyacinth, Collection Agent, Operator Extraordinaire and Taxator,' it sounds altogether different than if I'd just signed Hirsch, and nobody can treat me like a common ragamuffin. (Heine, 2008, p. 127)

Whether as Hirsch-Hyacinth or as Harry-Heinrich Heine, the unsuccessful assimilation of Jews to cultural acceptability through the baptismal ticket of admission is doomed to fail. The German or Austrian Jew as socially imagined was stuck within an irremediable racial category from which there was no exit. This is Freud's tacit social critique in the Hirsch-Hyacinth interpretation, a subsidiary illumination requiring further inquiry along the path of primary illumination, Freud's discernment of psychoanalytic method.

Freud's self-formation as a scientist would pivot upon the same exclusionary social dynamic. Jewish definition within the German cultural imaginary was externally imposed rather than resultant intrinsically from Jewish civilizational contents.[8] Indeed, identification with this environmentally aggressive racial definition, was also reflected in Jewish self-representation. Heine himself is recognized as the epitome of this marginal situation, oscillating between idealized and denigrated states of identification, at times celebrating Jewish identity, at times in self-hatred, and at times, aligned in non-Jewish identification with the secular environment (Gilman, 1990, 1992; Stonequist, 1937) in a manner resembling today's contemporary psychoanalytic observations upon self-identity relative to external environments (Boulanger, 2015; Howell, 2014; Mucci, 2014; Volkan, 2017).

Freud's affirmation of scientific role allows him the social status of observer wherein his societal definition as Jew permits him the access to the experience of society's Other, believed in his time and place to be equivalent to society's congenitally diseased patient (Gilman, 1990). Freud obliquely addresses this doubled assumption of biological incapability relative both to Jewishness and to emotional suffering in his 1909 Clark University lectures. There, he upsets the characterization of the hysteric as genetically impaired, through two contrasting images. The first is the biologized pictograph of hysteric as overwhelmed shopper, incapable of supporting multiple parcels. Freud's counter-image is of Bertha Pappenheim's fluid facility in expressing herself verbally, together with Josef Breuer, across multiple European languages (Freud, 1910).[9] Jews and their languages remain markers for Freud, in demonstrating universal capability against the 19th-century anti-Semitic claim of Jewish cognitive and emotional incapacity (Makari, 2008; Geller, 2004; Gilman 1990, 1992).

However, Freud strategically heightens his observational position by favoring the then-common Jewish identification with the gentile social imaginary through characterization of Jewishness as "*unheimlich*" or ghostlike (Geller, 2004). As Rank later documents through psychoanalytic interest in the "double" (Rank, 1914), this ghostlike quality is imputed to be an internal, pathological characteristic rather than either an external projection upon a socially demeaned group (Volkan, 2017) or the result of complex individual identifications within a traumatizing social environment. Thirty-five years before Freud's own work on the *unheimlich*, or uncanny, Jewish nationalist Leon Pinsker had argued that the parasitic and ghostly Jewish condition that he termed *unheimlich*, would require the remedial action of *auto-emancipation* through realization of national territory and language (Freud, 1919; Geller, 2004; Pinsker, 1882).

Freud's interpretive method provides a very different route to the self's auto-emancipation, accessible universally both to Jew and Gentile, along the *Bildung* path of self-formation (Mosse, 1985; Sorkin 1983, 1987). For Freud, this requires a strategically reductive turning from Jewish civilizational contents in the service of elevating psychoanalytic method. Such orientation extends beyond our contemporarily popular, if limited, faith-based understanding of Freud as "Godless Jew" (Gay, 1988). Indeed, it is Heine, as cited by Freud in *Jokes and Their Relation to the Unconscious* who links such Godlessness to Spinoza as Heine's and Freud's "fellow un-believer" (Freud, 1905, p. 77); and Heine, too, who construes the modern individual's self-authorizing autodidactic thinking as reflective of "Godless self-gods" (Schlesier, 1990, p. 26).

Heine also articulates a philosophical turn that is enacted by Freud as assumptive behavior: the modernist idea of individual self-formation. Freud's developing method derives from observation of the world through the individualistic lenses of identity determined by Heine, to have been "ground" by Spinoza.[10] The individual's acquired personal definition individual is the basis of *Bildung* ideology of self-formation (Sorkin, 1983; Sterba, 1982), in contrast to the late medieval social definition of the individual within the context of confessional or legal large group social definition (Nadler, 1999).

But powerful cultural definition of the Other continues in social reality, despite modernity's post-Spinozan shift. Freud accommodates this contradiction by generating one of his own: he reduces Jewish particularity and identity to a cipher, while he continues throughout his lifetime, to reference Heine as his literary alter-ego; and so, keeps Heine's "incurable malady" of Jewishness in continuous awareness as a subjectively meaningful form of psycho-social awareness.

Throughout his career, Freud would retain a fine appreciation for Heine's presentation of the ironic, jarring social contradictions of the German Jew. With escape impossible from the self-consciousness of Jewish racial definition, imposed both internally and externally, Freud identifies with Heine in addressing his own multiple, conflicting forms of social identification (Stonequist, 1937). As Gilman observes

> Heine, about whom one laughs, with whom one laughs, is seen as the epitome of both subject and object, both the means of analysis and the object of study. (1990, p. 92)

But where Heine is painfully overt in surfacing the cultural divide in marginality between dominant cultural judgment and the demeaned racialized Jew of the gentile cultural imaginary with which both Freud and Heine also identify, Freud attempts his own disappearance of Jewishness into an *unheimlich* silence. Famously, in Freud's (1926) 70th birthday address to the B'nai Brith, he defines Jewishness as sharing

> many obscure emotional forces (*viele dunkle Gefühlsmächte*), which were the more powerful the less they could be expressed

in words, as well as a clear consciousness of inner identity, the safe privacy of a common mental construction (*die Heimleichkeit der gleichen seelischen Identität*)". (SE 20:274; see Gilman, 1992, p. 157)

Freud's pathway to the scientific discernment of psychoanalysis remains caught in a doubled bind. The first concerns his oscillating personal identifications with Jewish and non-Jewish cultural elements. Contrasting with this personal identification within an obscure and unlanguaged ("the more powerful the less they could be expressed in words") Jewish mental construction both private and shared, Freud is also remembered for the doubled sentiment that he could not live anywhere else on earth after the World War I collapse of the Austro-Hungarian Empire (Kilborne, 2014). Indeed, in his elegiac "Thoughts for a Time of War and Death", written at the beginning of that global conflict, he would mourn the passing of universalized freedoms, among the multiple ethnicities representative of Austro-Hungarian citizenry

Relying on this unity among the civilized peoples, countless men and women have exchanged their native home for a foreign one, and made their existence dependent on the intercommunications between friendly nations. Moreover anyone who was not by stress of circumstance confined to one spot could create for himself out of all the advantages and attractions of these civilized countries a new and wider fatherland, in which he could move about without hindrance or suspicion. In this way he enjoyed the blue sea and the grey; the beauty of snow-covered mountains and of green meadow lands; the magic of northern forests and the splendour of southern vegetation; the mood evoked by landscapes that recall great historical events, and the silence of untouched nature. This new fatherland was a museum for him, too, filled with all the treasures which the artists of civilized humanity had in the successive centuries created and left behind. As he wandered from one gallery to another in this museum, he could recognize with impartial appreciation what varied types of perfection a mixture of blood, the course of history, and the special quality of their mother-earth had produced among his compatriots in this wider sense. Here he would find cool, inflexible energy developed to the highest point; there, the graceful art of beautifying existence; elsewhere, the feeling for orderliness and law, or others among the qualities which have made mankind the lords of the earth. (Freud, 1915, pp. 176–177)

This, Freud's mournful recollection of a destroyed civilization, is a dream memory of *Bildung*, a socially mobile, pluralistic society, providing intellectual and aesthetic challenge and pleasure. Quite passionately, Freud articulates the freedoms of emancipation, only dreamed of by Heine (2006), as the foundation of his own generational experience, two generations later. He articulates a transit between the particularity of Jewish experience to the generality of secular citizenry after Emancipation, with membership in the larger world of universalized enlightened thought. He writes,

from among the great thinkers, writers and artists of all nations he had chosen those to whom he considered he owed the best of what he had been able to achieve in enjoyment and understanding masters of his own tongue. None of these great men had seemed to him foreign because they spoke another language— neither the incomparable explorer of human passions, nor the intoxicated worshipper of beauty, nor the powerful and menacing prophet, nor the subtle satirist; and he never reproached himself on that account for being a renegade towards his own nation and his beloved mother-tongue. (Freud, 1915, p. 177)

Here are Freud's individualized choices of writers and thinkers with who he wished to identity and from who he derived the productive contents upon which his own creative thought emerged, as shown above in his intellectual engagement with Kant, Lipps, Heymans, Heine, and Spinoza. Freud, the ardent and representative son of *Bildung* (Sterba, 1982), the German languaged ideology of educative self-formation, discloses a difficulty that otherwise becomes effaced in his development of psychoanalytic method: the continuing fact of particularistic experiences and civilizational contents (such as language and expression) from and through which, individuals strive to express the universality of the human condition. And with it, his enduring awareness that he never reproached himself on that account for being a renegade towards his own nation and his beloved mother-tongue. (Freud, 1915)

In contrast to Freud's cautious audacity, Heine is strident and direct in expression of Jewish suffering: as forthright as his creation, Hirsch-Hyacinth, the butt of Freud's (un)joke. Throughout his prose writing, Heine describes a doubled state of socially induced psychological identity, both German and Jewish. Heine, as Freud's Jewish muse, rejecting of religious faith and observant of the political rights of man, but himself the imperfect paraway to reveal what is Jewish participant observer of this Jewish dilemma, remained with Freud throughout his career from Hirsch-Hyacinth to *Moses and Monotheism*. Freud overtly reduces Judentum to the dessicated and unlanguaged, ghostly uncanny, where its contents are disappeared into subjective and collectively shared obscurity, like Freud's own declared turn from his own "beloved mother tongue"; and then proceeds to illuminate his psychoanalytic journey from German-Jewish particularity to Kantian universality. Freud's more outrageous alter-ego, through whose voice Freud sometimes speaks, remains Heine, the incurably provocative Jew, consigned to oblivion in Anglophone psychoanalysis (Miller & Sweet, 2018).

II. Arabic Curse and Jewish Malady

Freud is correct in promising the reader, like the audience of the joke, a journey from bewilderment to enlightenment through multiple illuminations (1905, p. 13). The primary illumination of *Jokes and Their Relation to the Unconscious*, like the *Psychopathology of Everyday Life* and *The Interpretation of Dreams*, is in discernment of what clinicians will come to recognize as psychoanalytic method; and especially in the applicability within clinical psychoanalysis of recognizing the disruption of consciousness by the uncanny emergence of a previously unrecognized, unconscious illumination. This broadly describes the repetitive clinical journey from bewilderment to enlightenment (Miller & Sweet, 2018).

Yet Freud, who fashions himself a 60-year-old "renegade towards his own nation and his beloved mother-tongue" (1915), seems anything but. Rather, this written presentation of his thinking, like that of Heine's, is thickly doubled, like the form of the Hirsch-Hyacinth joke he describes in 1905. Freud writes voluminously and declares much, so it is easy to focus on what he writes as immutably central within our attentions. Escaping our notice, the forms by which he conveys his thoughts in writing become peripheral or *un-heimlich* to us. For example, the self-styled 60-year-old renegade from 1915 repeats his argument fifteen years later in a manner that would greatly please Heine (Freud, 1913, p. xv). For Freud does here exactly what he did in his earlier telling of the "Signorelli" parapraxis: he causes the oblivious reader to focus on the central fact of content while ignoring the peripheral fact of context. In "Signorelli", Freud reprises Heine's depiction of acculturated Jews at Lucca, down to the last jot and tittle. He addresses two audiences: those he seeks to teach through demonstration of psychoanalytic method and also those who recognize what he is doing by means of the particularity with which he does it: the fine art of the Jewish storyteller. And Freud should know: he wrote the book on how Jewish stories work.

Later, the 74-year-old Freud's attestation in the preface to the Hebrew language version of *Totem and Taboo* repeats the same pattern. He affirms his programmatic reduction of Jewishness to a vague essentialism, without language or content; and at the same time winks at his own fine contradiction through the particular fact of the written context, signaled by the specific occasion for this address. The location for this extension of *Bildung* through psychoanalytic auto-emancipation is founded in the particularity of its placement as preface to the Hebrew language translation of *Totem and Taboo*. Hebrew, of course, is one of the several Jewish languages Freud tactically disappeared as he elided his own Jewish identity into the identity of the objectively "scientific" cultural observer, all the while allowing Heine's mischievous expressions, complaints, and diatribes, to speak Jewishly, for him. And in 1930, Freud repeats his repetitive claim of absent Jewish civilizational forms in the context of another auto-emancipation, the nationalist revival of the Hebrew language in modern form after 2000 years of survival in textual and liturgical use. Freud's expressive audacity and hilarious irony faces down his life-long experience of anti-Semitic racism (1) by affirming the method of psychoanalysis and (2) by affirming the particularity of specific, linguistic Jewish civilizational contents with a comedic irony that rivals Heine's.

Perhaps the ultimate psychoanalytic Jewish joke is constructed not by a Jew, but by a gentile, affirming the genuine universalism in psychoanalytic method through the fact of Jewish particularity, foundational in psychoanalytic thought. Each of us comes from somewhere; and that somewhere shapes the particularities of our experience. Yet, psychoanalysis discerns what is common or universal in the deep patterning of our shared human journeys.

The particular variables that characterize both Heine's and Freud's lifetime struggles with the emergence of self in relation to the externally imposed cultural barrier of anti-Semitic definition, become writ large in the translation from German to English of Freud's (1923) work, *Das Ich und Das Es*. Here, what is German within German-Jewish relations drops away to reveal what is Jewish (at least from the perspective of gentile definition) and continuously known both to Heine and Freud. Perhaps mirroring Hirsch-Hyacinth's earlier neologism, the significance of this fact emerges in "Standard Edition" English through the faux-Latinate neologism adapted by its British translation committee; and so remains circumcised within the textual body of Anglophone psychoanalysis.

Writing to his wife, translator James Strachey explains how the contemporary London street derogation for Jews, "Yidd", is consciously affirmed as the translation of the German word "Es", the earlier, culturally indistinct agency that Groddeck had termed the "It" (Freud, 1923; Groddeck, 1923; Strachey and Strachey, 1985, p. 83). The Strachey-Jones "(Y)idd" operates unceasingly and persistently until its socialized transformation by the acculturated Ego, a linguistically marked route familiar both in Heine's and Freud's acquaintance with the existential aporia that had denied both awareness and expression of the self's multiple forms of subjective identity under externally imposed cultural exclusions. However, Strachey's audacious translation misses the doubled, if internally Jewish aspect of language, perhaps unknown from the external, gentile perspective. This is that the word, "Id", as transliterated from Yiddish, simply connotes the Jew as human: the Freudian idea of the Kantian universal.

But the gesture of doubling itself remains in what might be here, Strachey's greatest (unconscious) appreciation of the psychoanalytic tension between what is conscious and unconscious. For the large group awareness of us/them is an enduring cultural fact whether in the relation of German-to-Jew or in Viennese psychoanalysis-to London psychoanalysis. What remains is for this fundamental splitting to be addressed in its recognition. And here, the following passage from the same Heine text from which Hirsch-Hyacinth is drawn, would not have escaped Freud's attention. The scene Heine sets is in exit from the Cathedral at Lucca, similar to Freud's memory in the "Signorelli" parapraxis, of the Cathedral at Orvieto. Two characters emerge, having visited the church's interior.

Heine writes,

> when leaving the cathedral, she dunked her index finger three times into the holy water, sprinkled me each time and muttered, "Damn, Zefardeyim, Kinnim", which, she maintained, was the Arabic charm wherein sorceresses transformed a man into a donkey". (Heine, 2008, p. 183)

Here is the essence of Heine's "Jewish malady" (Draper, 1982, p. 399). For this curse is not an Arabic charm at all. Stylistically, Heine has borrowed from Cervantes, who substitutes Arabic for Hebrew in *Don Quixote*, transforming the Jewish Marrano in Toledo's Alcana Market into the Moslem Morisco, both forcibly converted to Catholicism and linguistically mocked through the particularity of Spanish word usage representing foods ritually proscribed under Jewish and Moslem practice, but now demanded to be eaten as a sign of Catholic religious conviction (Cervantes, 1615, p. 67)

But unlike Heine, who references Cervantes in the same text (Heine, 2008, p. 198), the reader needn't have read *Don Quixote* to understand the joke. Indeed, the Cervantes reference only provides literary heft to what is already baldly provocative and weighty. For the three Arabic words uttered are Hebrew; and immediately recognizable to anyone with experience of the Jewish celebration of Freedom, the Passover Seder. They specify the biblical plagues imposed by God upon Egypt, in forcing the conditions for Jewish liberation. Yet under Heine's usage at Lucca, the doubling of the joke from Hebrew to Arabic is doubled again. The specifically Jewish image of historical freedom is doubled into universal freedoms, in accordance with the revolutionary French, "Rights of Man". Even the sprinkling of water is doubled: whether of the baptismal font or of the commemoration of the plagues, at Seder, by the gesture of the little finger in spilling tiny droplets of wine. Still, Heine cannot resist another kick at his great bugbear as Godless Jewish Christian: that religion itself turns people into asses.

Yet, Heine's compressed Jewish meanings, here expressed in a universalized Moslem-Jewish curse against external Catholic religious coercion, endures unrecognized by any except those who recognize it[11]; and this exactly mirrors Freud's compressed second illumination drawn from within the textual context of the Hirsch-Hyacinth joke. Whether in Heine's Arabic Curse that expresses the Jewish malady or in Freud's passionate exegesis of Jewish suffering in the Hirsch-Hyacinth example, even the most acculturated, secular Jew would recognize this broad wink: and this is the doubling of unrecognized meanings, provocatively emergent and discernable in the vocalized, conscious surface of text, either written or verbalized, as in the mechanics of wit.

Freud's reading of Heine traces the multiple hyphenations of language and culture from linguistic, literary expression, particularized in Jewish forms, to psychoanalytic recognition of universality in what people do. Freud's (1905) demonstration of universal psychoanalytic method underlies the functional utility in clinical discernment of the interpretive significant fact (Miller & Sweet, 2018).

Willi Goetschel's essay (2004, pp. 266–276) on Heine's poem *Rabbi Yehuda HaLevi* highlights what, for the psychoanalyst, is an aspect of the untranslatable, evanescent and shimmering quality of psychoanalytic experience. This is the containment of an oscillation in process between instances of history, perceptual viewpoints, at the cusp of meaning and affect.

The significant literary form focused upon by Goetschel is a singular word that illuminates through its presence, a transformative aesthetic meaning beyond Heine's German (or English, if read in translation). This word is the Hebrew *shalshelet*, which assumes two meaningful or doubled forms in this poem. Goetschel recognizes its meaning as a diacritical symbol within the written cantillation of Torah reading, assigning a quavering musical expression to a particular word or syllable. Together with this vocal quaver, the literal meaning of *shalshelet* as "chain", indicating its endurance and strength, forms the leitmotif of Heine's poem. This is expressed in Heine's poem through the imagery of a pearl necklace across ages of historical time.

Heine employs a single Hebrew word in its complex pluralities of meaning, embedding it in the German text to establish a new, thickened and transformed meaning which becomes discernable through his quavering homage to the medieval poet Yehuda HaLevi; but there is more.

Yehuda HaLevi is also the subject of Moses Mendelssohn's poetic linkage with Jewish tradition (Goetschel, 2004): and so, Heine extends consciousness of the poet's integrative synthesis of Arabic-language forms into Hebrew poetry as both Mendelssohn and Heine extend Jewish sensibilities into German linguistic expression.

Heine's conscious poetic integration of Hebrew together with German poetry stands in marked contrast with Freud's strategic consignment of Jewish languages to the domain of the *unheimlich*. And Heine, being Heine, goes further: in another poem from the same period as *Rabbi Yehuda HaLevi*, he praises the simple Jewish Sabbath stew, called *schalet* in Germany, itself an unmistakable onomatopoeic compression of his use of *shalshelet*, which also extends the shimmering, atemporal depiction of Jewish civilization into the sensuous realm of smell and taste (Draper, 1982, p. 653).

Like Heine's hidden reference to the Jewish celebration and hope for emancipatory freedom in his allusion to the Passover Seder through his misattribution of Arabic nonsense syllables—ironized by his conscious knowledge of Yehuda HaLevi's literary integration of Arabic forms in Hebrew expression—the untranslatable Jewishness of such elements in his work are immediately recognizable to his readers. By contrast, Freud's demonstrated, strategic wit relative to "unlanguaged" Jewish identity, both denies the linguistic bonds of Jewish expression and at the same time, affirms them through his doubled and continued reference to Heine.

What remains, especially within our 21st-century awareness of continued traumatization and divisiveness, of racism and splitting between "us and them" (Volkan, 2017), is another, continuously bewildering significance, beyond immediate illumination, as in the quavering sound of the *shalshelet*. This is the fact that the effects of traumatization eventuate in human suffering. Freud and Heine demonstrate that creative sublimation may be possible in the humorously adaptive addressing of suffering; but that the universal fact of human destruction and traumatization continues to challenge not only the field of psychoanalysis, in recognition of its various psychological forms across the continuum of human adaptability, but also the question of species survival itself (Fromm, 1973).

Psychoanalytic texts themselves bear the scars of institutional intolerance and doubling; and our institutional oblivions to the particularities of psychological experience in different times and places cause us to foreclose consideration of the complex particulars eventuating in clinical presentation, just as Freud (1919) and Rank (1914) imputed the *unheimlich* to be an exclusively internal registration rather than an internal response to the societal traumatization within Gentile-Jewish relations. Freud's complex Jewish identification with Heine returns our understanding of psychoanalytic history from the foreclosed ignorance of oblivion to reckoning through the restorations of memory as we consider the complexities of our current psychoanalytic moment.

Notes

1 As Sander Gilman observes (1990, p. 90), the spoken quality of this neologism is immediately recognizable by the German speaker as a dialect joke, a distortion caused by the mispronunciation of German from an imperfectly accented "jargon", the Yiddish employed by Hirsch-Hyacinth. Here, the sensuous nature of discordant sound together with its contemporary (if derogatory) social signification compounds the cognitive registration of discordant word meaning.

2 The reader will remember Deleuze's observation that Spinoza too, operates by such doubling, through the literary device of a "broken" chain of scholia serving as essays commenting upon the "unbroken" succession of propositions and axioms (Deleuze, 1988, footnote 21, p. 29).

3 As Abigail Gillman (2018) documents through close study of commentaries and illustrations within Hebrew bibles intended for a German-speaking audience, Freud's own historical location occurs within a process of deteriorating Jewish Hebrew language competency between the 17th and 20th centuries. From this

perspective, Freud's renowned pride and shame at viewing the Parthenon, disclosed in 1936 on the occasion of Romain Rolland's 70th birthday, is not only an index of a son's progression from his father's life status, but also a final repudiation of Jakob Freud's competency in midrashic Hebrew composition (Ostow, 1989) relative to the triumphalism of Freud's gymnasium competence in Greek and Latin (Winter, 1997–1998). Vermorel (2009) also comments on the presence within this communication, of Freud's conception of Spinoza as Heine's "fellow (un)believer", with its extension to Rolland as a Christian unbeliever.

4 In adolescence, Freud would comment to a friend that because of racially ima- gined, congenital disability, Jews were capable of writing prose but incapable of the creativity required by poetry. In momentary youthful literary enthusiasm, he seems to suppress his own awareness of Heine's popular range in both forms. Later, Freud would frequently reference both Heine's poetry and prose (Gilman, 1990, 1992, p. 159).

5 Freud explicitly cites "The Baths of Lucca" within Heine's *Reisebilder*, "travel pictures" or postcards, later in his *Jokes and Their Relation to the Unconscious* (1905, p. 77).

6 Geller (2004, p. 2010) defines Judentum in the following context, "The tacit familiarity for Central Europeans of Judentum, that condensation of ethnos, ethos and ethic (i.e. of Jewry, Judaism and Jewishness), lay in more than its function as the necessary and proximate other or older would-be superseded sibling by which Christentum, a comparable condensation of the communities, beliefs and practices of Christians, continued to define itself. With the advent of Emancipation, Jewry lost more and more of its manifest difference without losing its structural otherness necessary for first Christian and then German self-definition".

7 Another stylistic similarity between Freud and Heine is in the Jewish childhood fantasy of identification with the Semitic Hannibal in opposition to the Romans. Heine antedates Freud's telling of this fantasy by about sixty years (Heine, 2006, p. 16), with Heine's description occurring in relation to his meeting with Ludwig Borne—whose work was also known by Freud (De La Durantaye on Borne, 1964). Heine's depiction focuses upon the ubiquitous fantasies of ghetto children in Frankfurt, educated not in traditional Hebrew texts but like Freud, in the secular study of history as counter-cultural, providing subversive childhood role models for addressing gentile power (Heine, 2006, p. 16).

8 The Heine/Freud characterization of schoolboy identification with Hannibal results from exposure to secular historical study, itself a function of increasing Jewish acculturation in gentile society. This contrasts sharply with Spinoza's 17th-century education within the faith community of Amsterdam's "New Jews", where he represented the first generation of his family after more than a century of living as Iberian "New Christians", to be educated entirely in tradi- tional Hebrew texts (Nadler, 1999).

9 Bertha Pappenheim's final work, before her death in 1936, was both historical and linguistic. Mindful of the degraded position of women in the medieval Jewish world, she nevertheless began a translation project of the traditional "women's bible", the *Tsene-Rene*, no longer available to German-speakers who had lost Yiddish literacy. Abigail Gillman comments,

> The tension within Pappenheim's translation project is that she values the Yiddish classics both positively, as repositories of Jewish women's spiritual experience, and negatively, as they codify the wound, the exclusion, a depreciation of women that "cast its fateful shadow onto the present day". She did not seek to reintroduce these books to modern German Jewish reader for their intellectual content, nor did she aim to awaken interest in Yiddish. She aspired rather to channel the aura of belief and devotion, the religious sensibility that imbued the pages of the *Tsene-Rene* and, even more important, that infused the souls and minds of the readers of that book over the centuries, for a new generation". (Gillman, 2018, p. 248)

10 Heine's description is an argument in the history of ideas. He writes

> Nothing is more absurd than ownership claimed for ideas. Hegel did, to be sure, use many of Schelling's ideas for his philosophy, but Mr Schelling would never have known what to do with these ideas anyway. He always just philosophized, but was never able to produce a philosophy. And besides, one could certainly maintain that Mr Schelling borrowed more from Spinoza than Hegel borrowed from Schelling. If Spinoza is one day liberated from his rigid, antiquated Cartesian, mathematical form and made accessible to a large public, we shall perhaps see that he, more than any other, might complain about the theft of ideas. All our present-day philosophers, without knowing it, look through the glasses that (optician) Baruch Spinoza ground (Heine, 1826, quoted from Boon, J (1996) "Levi-Strauss, Wagner, Romanticism" in *Romantic Motives. Essays in Anthropological Sensibility* (GW Stocking, ed); *History of Anthropology*, v6, p. 137).

11 As we shall later see, this idea of acquired knowledge, in recognizing what is equivocally represented, is also indicative of Maimonidean method, as it was of his Arabic-language predecessor, Al-Farabi (Stern, 2013; Strauss, 1952). From this perspective, albeit without demonstrating the historical line of transmission between Maimonides and Freud via the intermediation of Spinoza, David Bakan's posthumous publication points in the right general direction, but without compelling forward linkage in the receptive transmission of ideas (Bakan, Merkur, & Weiss, 2009). The clinical reader recognizes in the incremental transformation of the patient's understanding, the same shape of newly available acquired knowledge, to extend rational reflection toward the conjoined operations of perception, feeling, imagination, and desire.

Chapter 4

Contextualizing Spinoza

Freud's reduction of Heine's quip about Spinoza to a "negative particle" is as quietly eloquent an analysis as his more extended exegesis of Hirsch-Hyacinth's existential challenges. It speaks both to the shared desires of Heine and Freud to develop as secular Europeans thinkers, independent of their Jewishness; and also, to the vacillations observed long before by Spinoza, between registrations of pleasure and pain through conscious expression of love and hate, however in relation to shared Jewish identities.

At first glance, a *negative particle* seems almost insignificant. Yet, for Freud, it was powerful enough for Spinoza to rival the creativity of Leonardo da Vinci in creative breadth (Freud, 1910, p. 75), while remaining otherwise absent within the development of Freud's psychoanalytic conceptions. As I read, I would learn that from the earliest moments of psychoanalytic development, Freud's own Viennese colleagues recognized the parallelism between Spinoza's thinking in *Ethics* and their developing clinical practices (Andreas-Salomé, 1964). In much the same way that certain aspects of Heine's thoughts are remembered, filtered through Freud, as in the *familionarity* of Hirsch-Hyacinth with the Rothschilds as against the stridency of Heine's literary voice twinned with Freud's *unlanguaged* silence, much about Spinoza was also jettisoned, split off and lost to psychoanalytic memory.

What came next for me was the natural outgrowth of graduate school discipline: a self-generated reading curriculum. This branched into several different domains. The earlier chapters on Spinoza as the *philosopher of psychoanalysis* represent the most focal tranche.

DOI: 10.4324/9781003246404-7

But I also sought to understand Spinoza in relation to his history, socio-cultural background, and philosophically received ideas. Initially, texts written by three scholars provided me with a foundation: Steven Nadler's *Spinoza. A Life* (1999) and *Spinoza's Heresy. Immortality and the Jewish Mind* (2001); Jonathan Israel's *Radical Enlightenment. Philosophy and the Making of Modernity 1650–1750* (2001) as well as his *Diasporas within a Diaspora: Jews, Crypto-Jews, and the World Maritime Empires 1540–1740* (2002); and Harry Austryn Wolfson's (1934) classic, *The Philosophy of Spinoza. Unfolding the Latent Processes of His Reasoning.*

As this book's bibliography reflects, I benefited greatly from the academic surge in Spinoza interest during the past thirty years. Contemporary scholars in Judaics, philosophy, and the history of ideas challenged me; and I dove into fields of perplexity far from my familiarities in clinical psychology and psychoanalysis. New ideas zig-zagged back and forth, mediated by continuous reading of Spinoza's texts. One example of such wandering followed the influence of Islamic thought upon medieval Jewish thought, as in Bahya ibn Pakuda's 11th century *Duties of the Heart* (Lobel, 2007; Mansoor, 1973) forward to Maimonides' 12th century *Eight Chapters* (Gorfinkle, 1912), both of which would reflect precursors to the therapeutic use of doubt, fundamental to Spinoza's *Ethics*. Done with one consolidated idea, I found my curiosity setting off on another journey. Often, my interests were piqued by footnotes.

Originally, the present chapter was presented at the 2018 meeting, in Florence, of the *International Federation of Psychoanalytic Societies*. The conference topic, "New Faces of Fear", fit the scope of my then-current readings, which oscillated between the Spanish Inquisition and the history of Spinoza's immediate forbearers, Portuguese Jewry from the 15th to the 17th centuries (Israel, 2002; Kaplan, 1989; Swetschinski, 2000; Wachtel, 2013; Yerushalmi, 1971).

Rereading the paper, I recognize in it, an element of observation located in the psychotherapeutic field. Signaling the clinical process described by Melanie Klein, a shuttling between psychic states she termed the Paranoid-Schizoid and the Depressive positions, its origins were in the methodological clinical algorithm discerned by W.R. Bion (Bion, 1962; Miller & Sweet, 2018). Reckoning from Bion, I observed the patient's transient if cohesive and coherent arrival at different consolidations, subjectively good enough to remember as clinical milestones. Calling these points *d* to distinguish them from the more robust Kleinian notation of *D*, I was further able to discern such inflection points both in literature and in daily processes of unpacking life's general confusions: I called such emergence, **d**, emboldening the symbol's font to differentiate it from the clinically-specific *d* (Miller & Sweet, 2018). I found in this paper my own expression in **d** relative to my Spinoza interests, a marker in an extended process toward some unknowable future understanding.

Diving again and again into a Spinozan ocean of ideas and references, following footnotes across multiple texts in discovery of facts themselves fascinating, if off the point of a *clinical* Spinoza, I was reminded, time and again, of historian Adam Sutcliffe's caveat in attempting understanding of Sephardic traders, former New Christians who had become New Jews in 17th-century Amsterdam. Essentially, Sutcliffe's is an inter-disciplinary reprise of William James' *psychologist's fallacy*, a warning not to mistake one's own viewpoint for that of one's subject of interest (James, 1981). Sutcliffe writes that these individuals

> should not, then, be regarded as pioneering yet essentially familiar "founding fathers", but rather as fascinatingly alien inhabitants of a world- and a culture- very different than our own. (Sutliffe, 2009, p. 30)

Much of the perplexity in rediscovering a Spinoza significant for contemporary clinical psychoanalytic practice lies in this fundamental distortion. Not only ideas, but also cultural, philosophical, and literary transformations, both known and unknown to us, have preceded the social, cultural, communal, and interpersonal forces shaping our psychologies. Not only 17th-century Amsterdam, but also the assumptive world of 18th- and 19th-century *Bildung* influence psychoanalysis today, conditioning both what has become taken for granted as authoritative, and also left to oblivion, much like oblivion's physical marker, the statue of Heinrich Heine on the Grand Concourse in the South Bronx (Miller & Sweet, 2018, Ch 8).

Just as analysts continually plunge into unconscious depths with our patients, there is no reason to avoid inquiry into the obscurity of cultural assumptions and worldviews, seeking linkage to useful, present formulations (Miller, 2016). What follows is my first, public presentation toward consolidating Psychology's Spinoza.

Situating Spinoza

Despite Freud's renowned disavowal of links between philosophy and psychoanalytic thought (Holowchak, 2013; Rathbun, 1934), the Anglophone reception of psychoanalysis resonated with interest in the parallels between psychoanalytic conceptions and the psychological considerations of the 17th-century Dutch thinker, Baruch Spinoza (Brill, 1931; Rathbun, 1934; Smith, 1926; Tanner, 1907a). Spinoza conceives of human striving as *conatus*, an organic conception of mind as the containing, processing center of conflicting, deformed ideas, arising from the body, but absent Freud's later energic formulation of libido. Like Freud, Spinoza hypothesizes a pleasure principle, as well as the workings of desire. The Spinozan conception of desire conforms more to operational definition than does Freudian wish. For Spinoza, desire is the self-preservative extension of internal states, directed outward as action. Its operation is well-depicted in Daniel Defoe's *Robinson Crusoe*, written only a generation after Spinoza's death, in a repetitive narrative pattern demonstrating how bits of learning, garnered through conscious observation and accommodation in enduring life experience, are later remembered and pressed into new service (Defoe, 1719). In this way, the autodidactic attitude of learning through experience expands self-knowledge, forming a precursor idea to the 18th-century German development of *Bildung*, or the Enlightenment culture of self-formation, reflected in Goethe, Schilling, Humboldt, Lessing, Mendelssohn, Heine, and Freud (Bruford, 1975; Goetschel, 2004).

As within psychoanalysis, Spinoza construes not only the actions of loving and loss, but also an internal representation of the loved object (Tanner, 1907a, p. 515); and conceives not only of associational processes, but also the fundamental necessity of clarifying deformed or parataxic ideas, registered via sensation and perception. Spinoza's concept of self-consciousness is in the individual's recognition that external objects are affected by the body's actions as directed by the mind, linking thought and action along the same lines as Bion's psychoanalytic theory of thinking, some three hundred years later (Bion, 1962).

Additionally, in observing human construction of religious belief, Spinoza pioneers the concept of an idea's projection onto an external object which is then understood to behave independently of the individual projecting the idea—an early illustration of the dynamics of projective identification (Spinoza, 2007, p. 26). Erich Fromm writes of Spinoza that he

> became the founder of modern scientific psychology, and he is closely related to Freud not only through the concept of the model of human nature, but also by his concept of the unconscious, by the idea that man is guided by forces he is not aware of. As he put it, man believes himself to be free because he knows his desires, but he is not aware of the causes of his desires. (Fromm, 1964a, p. 70)

More recent scholarship observes Spinoza's

> redefinition of autonomy and independence as self-determination and self-realization and his argument that the psychodynamic play of the affects represents a crucial form of self-liberation. (Goetschel, 2004, p. 4)

The present chapter addresses the psychosocial context from which Spinoza's radically individualistic psychology arose, paired in seeming paradox with his Latin watchword, "*Caute*", or caution. Focused upon social experience, its elements range across disciplines beyond the formal boundaries of clinical psychoanalysis to philosophy, history, anthropology, biography, and Hebrew letters. It tracks the intergenerational cultural effects of fearful external threat upon individuals, beginning centuries before Spinoza's birth, in recognizing Spinoza's development of an attitude, later conveyed clinically by analyst to analysand, of reasoned thinking in the face of the unknown, anchored in the here and now immanence of affective and ideational experience. Within psychoanalysis as within Spinozan psychology, the mind attends to some thought so as to examine it and to deduce from it in proper order what can legitimately be deduced, if it is false, the mind will detect its falsity; but if it is true, the mind will proceed fruitfully without interruption to deduce truths from it. This, I say, is what our purpose requires. (Spinoza, 2002, p. 28)

The analyst's verbalization of such intuitive reasoning is often received by the patient as a disturbance of momentary equilibrium, with its reception met on a continuum between denial and recognition. Mindful of interventions' effects, the Spinozan caveat of "Caute" must inform the clinician's participation in interpersonal engagement because such intervention is not simply intellectual, but experiential, and may involve what Ferenczi and Rank term a "wounding of the narcissism of the patient" (Ferenczi & Rank, 1923, p. 9). Through the dyadic process of action and reaction

whereas formerly, one tried to obtain the therapeutic result as a reaction to the enlightenment of the patient, we now try to place the knowledge obtained by psychoanalysis directly in the service of our therapy, by directly provoking the corresponding personal experience on the basis of our insight, and explaining to the patient only this experience, which is naturally directly evident to him also. (Ferenczi & Rank, 1923, p. 91)

The theoretical orientations both of psychoanalysis and of psychology discern individual and social experience from the viewpoint of psychic causation. Divergent, particularized, explanatory languages both within and between disciplines create the impression of what Spinoza terms, "distorted ideas". However, many general ideas are actually shared across divergent theoretical orientations. For example, the internalizing subjective processes of introjection discerned by Ferenczi (1909) are paralleled by the internal world of recognitions observed by psychologist Edward C. Tolman as "means-ends-readiness" (Tolman, 1932, p. 30) which in turn, are recognizably similar to George Herbert Mead's descriptions of symbolic social experience (Mead, 1922, p. 162). Mead, a self-described "social behaviorist" writes of the "significant symbol",[1] linking internalization of the environing world within the individual's subjective psychological structures of languaged and non-languaged experience as

> the gesture, the sign, the word which is addressed to the self when it is addressed to another individual, and is addressed to another, in form to all other individuals, when it is addressed to the self. (Mead, 1922, p. 162)

This binocular psychodynamic view provides us with a vertex observing the individual within the social and the social within the individual, recognizing that "the more points of view we have, the firmer our sense of conviction about our observations" (Mason, 2000, p. 984).

Observations of fear require this binocular perspective. Fear operates from the outside, in the socio-political world, penetrating the internal or psychological world, where it is registered individually. Sandor Ferenczi wisely reminds Sigmund Freud that while fear itself paralyzes, the individual's state of fearfulness may facilitate thinking and productive action (Brabant, Falzeder, & Giampieri-Deutsch, 1993, p. 4). WR Bion advises that the analyst, like the patient, must feel fear of the unknown, but demonstrate to the patient, a willingness to surmount it through the toleration of containment (Bion, 1990, p. 5).

Addressing Spinoza in his contribution to the later emergence of psychoanalytic psychology, I proceed through four interlocking sections which I term, (1) Social Doubling; (2) Pragmatic Immanence; (3) The Forces of Inquisition and Synagogue; and (4) and The Social Audacity of Individual Emergence. In considering this journey of actions and ideas across time, it is necessary to begin with the caveat that we cannot understand from today's historically changed vantage-point, the originating norms of the 17th century which was

> a period in which Christian nations went to war with each other over religious differences, people were thrown into prison (and sometimes burned at the stake) for heresy, and books were placed on the Catholic Church's Index of Prohibited Books if they were deemed inconsistent with the dogmas of faith. (Nadler, 2011, p. 78)

It will be helpful in reading, therefore, to remember the broader cultural contexts of the developments that are traced.

Social Doubling

Separating himself Oedipally from the social stigma he felt regarding his family's Jewishness, Freud abandoned his given name of Sigismund Schlomo, changing it to Sigmund. Dennis Klein observes that

> by replacing the name given to him with a Germanic-sounding name, Freud severed this important link with his Jewish background to identify more closely with the progressive German-liberal culture. (Klein, 1981, p. 46)

Freud's conscious act of doubling would not be so noticeable if his own borrowing from literary muse, Heinrich (Harry) Heine for commentary in *Jokes and Their Relation to the Unconscious*, had not been through a character with similarly doubled names of Hirsch and Hyacinth. Heine's character, drawn from his 1836 *Travel Pictures* (*Reisebilder*), is remembered by psychoanalysts for his *familionarity* with the wealthy Rothschilds. What is concealed in plain sight was readily apparent to Freud and his 19th-century fin de siècle German reading audience: the fact that Hirsch's attempt at secular acceptance, like author Heine's, through baptismal name change, did nothing to change who he was to the world: a Jew. The Yiddish inflection in his spoken German betrayed him (Gilman, 1990, p. 90).

Freud went to great lengths to obliterate the linguistic tie between Jews and their subjective identities. Historian Jay Geller explains that the highly significant granting of Austro-Hungarian citizenship to Jews, in 1867 when Freud was 11, itself concealed the crown's official imposition of an ongoing disability, the denial to Jews of Yiddish and Hebrew from legal recognition as state languages. Aligned with this law, Freud opts for a definition of Jewish identity that is unlanguaged (Erikson, 1956). He construes an essentialist Jewish civilization claimed by him to be "the more powerful the less .... expressed in words" (Freud, 1926, p. 274). Freud definitively consigns Jewish language and language forms to the *"unheimlich"* or uncanny, while continuing to allow its audacious Otherness, attacking prejudicial perspectives and narrowed argument, to be voiced by his literary alter-ego, Heinrich Heine (Gilman, 1990, 1992).

The ironic upshot of this not-so-hidden Jewishness underneath what is consciously named, is psychoanalytically memorialized within the Anglophone *Standard Edition* where a linguistic prank converts the ethnically-neutral terms in Freud's *Das Ich und Das Es*, to the underlying and enduring unconscious fact of the *Id*, a variation of the derogatory *Yid* known to translation committee members, Strachey and Jones, from its anti-Semitic London use (Freud, 1923; Strachey & Strachey, 1985).

Freud's identification with Heine relative to doublings, both of name and identity, illustrates a bifurcation between what is consciously addressed socially if privately unspoken. Tacitly known in suppressed awareness, this is the cultural presence in 19th-century European secular society, of the unseemly, *unheimlich* Yid. Such social experience of doubled identities, continuously pervasive yet often rising to conscious awareness, underlies early formative concepts in psychoanalysis such as Freud's multi-leveled construction of jokes (1905) as well as its later Anglophone reception, tinctured with Strachey's bold wink at the German *Es* as the British (Y)id.

Less pejoratively affirmed is the correspondence between Freud's self-conception as "godless Jew", and Spinoza, through Heine's interpretive characterization (Freud, 1905, p. 77; Gay, 1988). Spinoza, like Freud, Heine, and the comic exemplar Hirsch-Hyacinth, participated in multiple doublings of identity. Spinoza was known by three names: Bento, Baruch, and Benedictus. Each name signaled a bounded sphere of social operations characterizing particularized worlds of thought and action. Each name faced a social world of foreclosed identity, constraining thought and limiting social activity. Testing these boundaries courted potentially annihilative consequences. Anthropologist Nathan Wachtel wrests a depiction of this world from the written court records of Inquisitional tribunals (Wachtel, 2013). He writes that 17th-century *New Christian* descendants of Iberian Jews, coerced through lethal threat into baptism beginning in the 15th century, lived in constant motion: while the New Christians were fleeing the Inquisition and affirming their Jewish faith in Amsterdam and Venice, Jews who had been New Christians returned to Spain, Portugal, or the Iberian colonies, and took up the Christian mask again in the interest of managing their business affairs. Moreover, even in Amsterdam, Sephardic Jews persevered in a kind of double life, reflected in their dual names: in addition to their Hebrew names, used within the Jewish community, they continued to employ their Portuguese or Spanish names for all commercial transactions. (Wachtel, 2013, p. 13)

As in Heine's and Freud's later times, when doubled names were an attempt to secure acceptance in gentile, secular society, for Spinoza as an Amsterdam *New Jew*, the first generation after two hundred years in enforced separation from normative Jewish practices, education, and socially permissible intergenerational cultural transmissions, a fluidity of named identities reflected prudent, self-protective behavior. The wrong name in the wrong place, or through the denunciation by colleagues or Inquisitional spies, would mean asset confiscation, imprisonment, public humiliation through the spectacle of the auto-de-fe, and death through the holocaust of burning at the stake (Kaplan, 1989; Wachtel, 2013; Yerushalmi, 1971).[2] Today, such names can be observed, chiseled in stone at the Beth Haim cemetery, along the Amstel River at Ouderkerk, near Amsterdam—where members of 17th-century Amsterdam's newly Jewish community were buried.

Pragmatic Immanence

Historian of philosophy Yermiahu Yovel introduces us to the cultural marker of the *converso*, coercively baptized Jews also called *marrano*s, or in Hebrew, *anusim*, also reflected in the careful research of Hispanic scholar Steven Gilman (Gilman, 1972; Yovel, 1989a, 2009). He calls this attitude "immanence" and contrasts it, as a reduction of classical, transcendent ideals in philosophy and theology, to the observed forms of what people do, in dynamic recognition of how life and society operates. Spinoza's own reflective observations, compressing divergent human actions into categories useful for empirical inquiry, illustrate this perspective. Reflecting upon his own psychological journey he observes that

> for the things which for the most part offer themselves in life, and which, to judge from their actions, men regard as the highest good, can be reduced to these three headings: riches, honour, and sensual pleasure. With these three the mind is so distracted that it is quite incapable of thinking of any other good. (Spinoza, 2002, p. 4)

The attitude of immanence reflects a clear-eyed pragmatism, stripped of nostalgia in reducing the poetics of life to the mechanisms by which the individual not only survives but also thrives under daily conditions of threat and fear. This attitude is boldly exemplified in the late 15th-century picaresque *converso* text, still taught in Spanish schools for its classical Castilian, *La Celestina* (Gilman, 1972; Gonzalez-Torres, 2017; Yovel, 1989a).

Heine would also echo this orientation in his own time. In his assessment of baptism as an entry-ticket to Western civilization, he would reduce religious belief to a business; and a business fueled by Jewish desire to escape the social stigma of anti-Jewish hatred. Still Heine tried; and loudly protested when, as with his tragic character, Hirsch-Hyacinth, his path to secular acceptance as newly Christian was blocked. Self-consciously, Heine, an 18th-century German, identified with Iberian *New Christians* (Heine, 2008).

Since the 14th century, paralleling the *converso* fracturing of theology into immanence, Iberian Catholicism had also forsaken ideological transcendence, effectively splitting its membership by racial exclusion through contrast between the *Old Christian,* marked as having genetically pure blood, and the impurity of the *New Christian,* indicative of the *unheimlich* Yid. The medieval problem of Jewish Otherness, foreseen as soluble through religious conversion would continue because

> until masses of its Jews had been brought to the baptismal font, Spain, along with the rest of medieval Europe, had viewed the Jewish problem in one dimension: as a problem of religious

conversion. It was precisely when conversion had been achieved on an unprecedented scale that there had ensued a realization of the basic inadequacy of the conversionist solution. For in the eyes of the rest of the population nothing beneficial had been accomplished thereby. Names had been altered, religious allegiances had shifted, but, even discounting the question of religious sincerity, today's Christian was still recognizable as yesterday's Jew. (Yerushalmi, 1971, p. 13)

Both Spanish and Portuguese *conversos* shared not only suffering and the suppression of their Jewish origins, but also a similar, socio-historical drift away from traditional Jewish practices, enforced by fear of lethal threat both by state and by Church. Against externally hateful definition and together with the continuing erosion of normative knowledge about Jewish civilization, the *converso* would construct a subjective definition of Jewishness, often based upon an inversion of anti-Jewish Catholic claims (Wachtel, 2013). Internal self-definition in the Iberian Peninsula was idiosyncratic rather than socially consensual. It operated from within a continuum of *New Christian* belief from fervent Catholicism to crypto-Judaism, compressed by survivalist reduction of worldly events to how things are in terms of probabilistic cause-and-effect. By the time such *New Christians* had migrated to Spinoza's Amsterdam, they were also defined within the loose brotherhood termed in Portuguese, *homens da nacao*, "Men of the Nation". Historian Miriam Bodian observes that

> collectively, the Portuguese conversos were known as *la nacion portuguesa* or *la genta portuguesa*. These terms were adopted in European countries outside the Peninsula as well. The Portuguese Jesuit Antonia Vieira lamented the misunderstanding this produced, noting that in popular parlance, among most of the European nations, 'Portuguese' is confused with 'Jew'. (Bodian, 1999, p. 13)

But there was no misunderstanding in Amsterdam's Jewish mercantile community. Identification with the *Nacion* both at home and on the Peninsula stood as terminological witness to the fact that in the Portuguese mind the New Christians were, above all, the men of business and commerce. (Yerushalmi, 1971, p. 16)

Hampering Jewish attempts to reeducate these *New Christians* in the 17th century,

> the problem was not that they knew nothing of Judaism, but that what they knew was often a pastiche of fragments inherited from parents, gleaned haphazardly from books, disorganized, with significant gaps, sometimes distorted. (Yerushalmi, 1980, p. 165)

Spinoza's Portuguese name, Bento, corresponds to his membership in this social group of secularized, formerly Jewish, now formerly Christian, *New Jews*, resident in religiously tolerant Amsterdam and economically useful in developing mercantile opportunities during this period of early capitalism (Nadler, 1999; Studnicki-Gizbert, 2009; Wachtel, 2013; Yerushalmi, 1971).

Inquisitional and Synagogue External Forces

Bento, as member of the Portuguese *Nacion* faces Baruch as member of the Amsterdam *Talmud Torah* synagogue community. Roughly at the time of Spinoza's birth, the community of *New Jews* in Amsterdam was fragmented by an internal controversy concerning the normative performance of Jewish ritual commandments. The theological issue focused on the system of rewards and punishments eventuating in personal attainment of Eternal Life. Its controversial resolution, endorsed by Spinoza's later teacher, Rabbi Saul Morteira, was to differentiate between *New Jews* capable of observing religious commandments and *anusim* of the Iberian Peninsula, whose Inquisitionally enforced non-Jewish practices precluded ritual observance. At stake was the promise of Eternal Life, to which *conversos* were now excluded (Altmann, 1972; Nadler, 1999, 2001).[3]

Having developed a healthy skepticism toward all forms of idealized faith during adaptation to hundreds of years of Inquisitional threat, *New Jews* were faced with attuning their social behaviors to what for them were often unfair and forcibly imposed, normative Jewish standards in Amsterdam. For former Iberians,

> the problem of adjusting to their new lives within the Jewish community was truly enormous. The Marrano who arrived as an adult had not only to undergo circumcision, but also to acquire rapidly a large fund of Jewish skills and knowledge without which even minimal participation in the life of the community would be impossible, The habits, ideas, and attitudes which other Jews had inherited naturally, and in which they had been educated during their former years, had now to be compressed and assimilated by mature men in a very short time. (Yerushalmi, 1971, p. 47)

Here, Baruch Spinoza differed both from his community's devout advocates and its immigrant heretics. Spanning the languages of both worlds, with daily life activities conducted in Portuguese and Spanish, his formative education in Jewish thought was both in Spanish translation and classical Hebrew texts (Nadler, 2011; Wolfson, 1934). Within the Amsterdam synagogue, Spinoza was raised and educated by the community's rabbis as a beloved son in a resurrected form of Jewishness. His biblical knowledge, with reference to such classical Hebrew commentators as Rashi, Maimonides, David Kimchi, and Abraham Ibn Ezra, would be boldly deployed after the synagogue *herem* or community ban of 1656, as proof for the arguments in his *Theological-Political Tractate*.

The Social Audacity of Individual Emergence

The germination of this paper extends from a vignette related by Steven Nadler in his 1999 biography, *Spinoza: A Life*.[4] It concerns the moment when Spinoza is presented with the fact of this 1656 *herem*. Relying on earlier written sources, Nadler writes that Rabbi Saul Morteira, the chief rabbi of the Amsterdam *Talmud Torah*

> "Urged him in a most formidable tone to decide for repentance or for punishment, and vowed that he would excommunicate him if he did not immediately show signs of contrition". Spinoza's response was calculated to push the rabbi over the edge:

"[I] know the gravity of the threat, and in return for the trouble that [you] have taken to teach [me] the Hebrew language, allow [me] to teach [you] how to excommunicate". The rabbi left the synagogue in a fit of rage, "vowing not to come there again except with a thunderbolt in his hand". (Nadler, 1999, p. 153)

This is a dramatic depiction of Spinoza's challenge not only to synagogue authority, but also to its lived reality as a refuge for *converso* immigrants from the Peninsula, dependent upon the largesse of the Dutch State. Although physically and temporally separated from centuries of ongoing Inquisitional persecution, the Jewish community now imposed its own rigorous demands and constraints upon its members, who only recently had conformed to demands of the Iberian Peninsula, where any hint of Jewish practice might court not simply prison, but death. In this transitional era between medieval and modern times, an individual's personal identity could be secured only through participation in a faith community. The synagogue strove to maintain its internal organizational boundaries through widespread use of the community *herem*, banning the accused from social interaction with Amsterdam's *New Jews*, and so heightening the dangers to these individuals of social, economic, and political isolation. The *herem* was designed to compel the banned individual into conformity with community norms.

Baruch Spinoza courted dismissal from the community, risking personal isolation in an era long before the autonomous identity of the self, Freud's *Ich*, had been societally recognized. Jonathan Israel observes that under the additional strain of debt from the legacy of his father's failed family business, this event signaled that

Spinoza had now definitively made up his mind to cross the Rubicon- discarding respectability, social standing, and commerce and devoting himself wholeheartedly to philosophy. By publicly repudiating the fundamentals of rabbinic tradition and authority in so formal and provocative a manner, the young thinker virtually demanded to be expelled, indeed made it impossible for the synagogue authorities not to expel him. (Israel, 2002, p. 171)

In courting such threat and consequence, Spinoza's demonstration of the capacity to think, through reduction of threat to its utilitarian meanings together with their practical implications—reflects the very mobilization of the *converso* attitude of immanence (Yovel, 1989a, 2009).

I couldn't avoid a clinical reading: its significant fact struck me solidly. Here was Spinoza's watchword, *Caute,* or caution, intertwined with the tremendous audacity of immanent thinking, spoken clearly and rationally, to the authoritative Other. However pictured as provocative by the biographical observer, within this interpersonal pairing, it is a measured meeting of the Other's position that claims, "what you call X, I call Y, and here is how I think about it"; and a willingness to live with the contingent results. Of course, at another level, at the relation of the student to the teacher, it also represents an Oedipal challenge, an individual's act of differentiation from the norms and constraints of the preceding generation.

Spinoza's caution in this example is recognition of opportunity afforded by context. Just as the 17th-century United Provinces provided a momentary gap of public acceptance against Western European Jewish expulsion, with Jews expelled from England in the 13th century, from France in the 14th, and from Iberia in the 15th, so a momentary post-Reformation military truce combined with potential economic benefit to the Dutch state, allowed *conversos* their difficult transition to public Jewish identification, education, and practice (Nadler, 1999).

Burdened by crippling debt received as his patrimony on his father's death, Spinoza located relief in the secular family law of his city of birth. And acting through the civil courts, also recognized that the audacious effect of his legal success would mean a turning from his own determination of personal status from within the authority of the synagogue (Nadler, 1999). Predictably, synagogue authorities would become outraged at his individually opportunistic action in undermining communal authority both in its own eyes and possibly those of the state relative to the community's capacity to police its membership, as reflected in the biographical quid pro quo between Spinoza and Rabbi Morteira.

"Caution" here, is in harnessing what one is already capable of doing through prior learned experience (De Spinoza, 1996); and cautious audacity is the willed extension of this Spinozan definition of desire together with calibration of its contingent effects. For Spinoza as for the later psychoanalysis, this would become a therapeutic attitude effective as an Archimedean lever that might later move interpersonal, intersubjective worlds within the clinical dyad.

The pairing of Spinoza's audacity and caution would require his shift to yet another name, Benedictus, a translation of the Hebrew Baruch, or "blessing", in the global, literary language through which Spinoza would convey his philosophical thinking, Latin. Spinoza's interpersonal capability to form enduring social friendships, extended internationally—as with Henry Oldenberg, the Secretary of London's Royal Society—did not preclude the enduring pejorative characterization by which he was later known as "the Jew of Voorsburg" (Nadler, 1999). Indeed, this external derogatory marker, insistent upon determining personal status by group affiliation as the Jewish Other, was paradoxically paralleled by the never rescinded *herem*, both formally disallowing Spinoza social affiliation with his community of origin during his lifetime and in its intolerant endurance into the present, challenging the centuries-long institutional tenure of Inquisitional persecution which today continues in another iteration as "The Congregation for the Doctrine of the Faith".

Conclusion

Weaving together contemporary and classical scholarship reaching back seven hundred years, we discern the continuum, recognized by Ferenczi and Bion, between traumatizing, paralytic fear, fearfulness, and adaptive caution born of and facilitating contingent thought—reflective of the psychoanalyst's operational position in relation to the patient's claim of immutability in her suffering.

Spinoza's intellectual contribution to psychological thinking marks our conceptual psychoanalytic inheritance. His encouragement to us is not only through the revolutionary nature of his written legacy, but also directly through his conduct: of prescribing individual courage in the face of fearfulness, requiring both caution and audacity, in stating to another, "What you call X, I call Y"; and remaining true to living through the consequences. Toward such ends, psychoanalysis strives to address those situations in which

> people are often reduced to such desperate straits that they cannot arrive at any solid judgment and as the good things of fortune for which they have a boundless desire are quite uncertain, they fluctuate wretchedly between hope and fear. (Spinoza, 2007, p. 3)

Notes

1 Mead's concept of the "significant symbol" is a chronological precursor to Bion's "significant fact" which itself Bion attributes to Poincare (Bion, 1992, p. 5), a contemporary of Mead.

2 On the other hand, doubled identities also provided an experiential basis for the communicative pleasure of polysemic multiplicity. The Spanish-born Hebrew poet and biblical commentator, Abraham ibn Ezra, fluent both in Arabic and Hebrew and cited by Spinoza in his *Theological-Political Tractate,* observes a doubled level of understanding within linguistic meanings in his biblical commentary on Genesis (Ibn Ezra, 1988, p. 28). Spinoza's contemporary, Joseph de la Vega, the first author to write on the workings of stock markets, employs the Spanish word *flor* to indicate both a flower and a card-sharp (De La Vega, 1688, ft 6, p. 5); and Spinoza's posthumous detractor, Daniel de Levi Barrios, recounting the synagogue face-off between Rabbi Saul Morteira and Spinoza, describes the latter as a "thorn" (*espinos*) in a "meadow" (*prados*)—alluding to the link between Spinoza and his fellow in "heresy", Juan de Prado (Israel, 2001, p. 171).

3 Spinoza's concept of Nature attends to what humans do, their lived experience and how they act. In recognizing God as unknowable, Spinoza turns away from theological attention to the relational domain between Man and God. One consequence is in freedom for all—whether *New Jews* or *conversos*—from observance of the Commandments, which practice had been incentivized by the promise of Eternal Life. Indeed, the fantasy of Eternal Life was also negated. Relative to the synagogue controversy which had been the background of Spinoza's childhood, his *Ethics* effectively places *conversos* and religiously observant *New Jews* on the same footing within the immanence of their mortality, not only reversing Rabbi Morteira's ruling decision, but also eliminating the entire question that had roiled the Amsterdam community. As we shall see further below, this continuation of Spinoza's audacity also signals an unspoken

Oedipal victory in his turn from social determination by group membership to affirmation of psychological individuality.

4 I would learn later that this same vignette is also published in the psychoanalytic literature. It is referred to by Feuer in his creative and historically informational, if overly confident, paper, interpreting a Spinoza dream fragment (Feuer, 1957, p. 234), where it is attributed to A. Wolf's 1927 work, *The Oldest Biography of Spinoza*. Feuer's analysis itself becomes the later jumping-off point for later interpretation of this Spinozan dream in the context of post-colonialism (Goetschel, 2016).

Chapter 5

A First Reading

The present chapter is my first attempt at a close reading of Spinoza. Published in the *American Journal of Psychoanalysis* in 2020, the reader can discern my early linkage to *Clinical Spinoza* through reference to a multi-tiered clinical example provided by Spinoza in *Ethics*, Part III.

Introduction

Freud knew his Spinoza. Or "about" Spinoza, a rough reception equivalent to what today's non-specialist might know of Freud. Walter Bernard translates a letter, sent in 1931 by Freud to Lothar Bickel, a colleague in Toronto that reads

> I readily admit my dependence on Spinoza's doctrine. There was no reason why I should expressly mention his name, since I conceived my hypotheses from the atmosphere created by him, rather than from the study of his work. Moreover, I did not seek a philosophical legitimation. (Bernard, 1977, p. 63)

The link to philosophy was present for Freud within the incomplete nature of consciousness relative to mind. The continuously generative psychoanalytic unconscious represents the mental realm between the discernable workings of the body and our conscious actions. Pragmatically, Freud (1938) wrote that what is significant within psychoanalysis is how the unconscious is addressed and mobilized.

DOI: 10.4324/9781003246404-8

Speculative discussion is "reserved to philosophical thought but the justification for which lies in its results" (p. 144).

The present chapter extends psychoanalytic discernment of a bright line from Spinoza's natural philosophy across the evolution of natural and social sciences toward Freud's development of psycho-analysis (Bernard, 1946, 1977; Fromm, 1964a, 1964b; Rathbun, 1934; Smith, 1925, 1926; Tanner, 1907a; Yovel, 1989b). This extension beyond Freud's "dependence on Spinoza's doctrine" links a new reading of Spinoza with contemporary writing on psychoanalytic method (Grossman, 1992; Miller, 2015; Miller & Sweet, 2018).

Focused on Spinoza's first, incomplete methodological statement, the *Treatise on the Emendation of the Intellect,* I track both the developing form and textual literary context from which Spinozan inquiry proceeds, as well as specific anticipations of clinical psycho-analytic phenomena. The chapter unfolds in five sections: Observing the world; Oedipal complexity; Spinoza's model of mind; The pri-macy of love; Analyzing perception and method; and Conclusion.

Observing the World

Spinoza begins his unfinished thirty-page essay, *Treatise on the Emendation of the Intellect* in personal revelation, quickly followed by a startling observation. The reader is swept into what Freud, two hundred fifty years later, will recognize as the shift between "be-wilderment and enlightenment" (Freud, 1905, p. 13). The surprised recognition that Spinoza reveals is familiar to philosophy and lit-erature. It is the strong swerve that for Aristotle, typifies tragedy in two movements: from *anagnorisis* or recognition, to *metabasis,* or directional change. Exemplifying this experiential movement, for Aristotle as for Freud, is Sophocles' dramatic example of *Oedipus Rex.*

Spinoza, in this first paragraph, describes the journey from his own anxiously felt meaninglessness, to firm, testable, recognitions. He writes

> after experience had taught me the hollowness and futility of everything that is ordinarily encountered in daily life, all the things which were the source and object of my anxiety held

nothing of good or evil in themselves insofar as the mind was influenced by them. (Spinoza, 2002, p. 3)

Taking him at his word, Spinoza, like a contemporary psychotherapist, begins with the experience of anxiety. Containing this agitation, he attempts to locate his anxiety's origins; and discovers these not in external reality, but in the mind.

Beginning with inquiry into his own distress, Spinoza discerns not only the foundations of modern psychology, but also the foundations of modern psychological inquiry. Paired with anxiety is "the hollowness and futility" as description of Spinoza's felt mental state, in general observation of human daily strivings, close in time to his expulsion from the Jewish community. Further, he notes the common habit of blaming personal suffering upon accidental experience in the physical world, external to mental functioning. Such recognition is an early anticipation of Melanie Klein's "Paranoid Position" (Klein, 1946). And, as with Kleinian observation of the "Depressive Position", Spinoza arrives at an antiphonal, moderating notion. His "Depressive" correlate is in a temporary recognition that becomes the linchpin of modern psychology. Quite radically, Spinoza overturns the general belief that the press of daily experience operates as the direct "source and object" of his or any other human's suffering. Instead, he locates suffering in the interpretive actions of "perception", the mind's interpretive creation of meaning.[1]

We know from Spinoza's life history that this twenty-something writer had endured much hardship; and not only from early childhood loss. More recently, enormous economic strain had capsized the family business and with it, the status of Spinoza's family in the community (Israel, 2001; Nadler, 1999). Beyond this, the enormous debt that was Spinoza's patrimony upon his father's death would have demanded a lifetime's toil to repay. Spinoza achieved relief of this burden only through ingenious appeal to Amsterdam's civil courts in gaining the legal status of orphan. This move legally absolved him of debt, but also cast him in direct opposition to the authority of the Jewish community, whose members' social and economic activities fell under its executive authority. This audacious act, together with his public claim to a philosophical skepticism shared with other members of the community, were instrumental in precipitating community punishment as the strongly coercive motivation for his return to community authority. This was achieved through the enactment of the *herem* or ban of separation, precluding economic or social engagement between the shamed individual and community members. Proceeding from reflection upon such personal experience, Spinoza outlines his own program of *metabasis*, the foundation of modern psychology, which is also intrinsically, the foundation of modern psychotherapy.[2]

Mindful of his resolve to turn his attention to the study of mind, as with our patients in consideration of today's therapeutic journeys, Spinoza next recognizes his initial ambivalence, to which he now turns toward resolution. His considerations question the guarantee that a decision's consequences will be pleasurable, with pleasure itself as the criterion of efficacy. Here, Spinoza discloses his own insecurities in thought. Given his intention to change "the manner and normal routine of my life" (Spinoza, 2002, p. 4), he proceeds to second-guess his decision; but before taking action, thinks through his predicament. He observes that "at first sight it seemed ill-advised to risk the loss of what was certain in the hope of something at that time uncertain" (Spinoza, 2002, p. 3). His uncertainty emerges from the confluence of two binary mental continua. The first stretches from certainty to uncertainty. He discovers uncertainty not only in the pursuit of philosophy, but also in the pursuits of sensuous desire and greed; and recognizes that to choose one pursuit is not to guarantee the success of its outcome. Only the unchosen outcome is certainly known and final; and what might have been had one pursued it, can be construed only in unhappy fantasy, in imagination rather than in productive thinking.

Thought links affective states with ideas, which Spinoza construes as "nothing but a certain awareness" (Spinoza, 2002, p. 22), joined in a continuous stream of successive moments, subject to perceptual interpretation. The therapeutic task addressed by Spinoza is in clarifying

> the circumstances with which the fictitious, the false, and the doubtful perception are concerned, and how we may be delivered from each of them. (Spinoza, 2002, p. 14)

Along the binary of certainty-uncertainty, one idea generates another, creating doubt. Doubt arises in the conflict between ideas, the first followed by the next "which is not so clear and distinct that we can infer from it any certainty as to the thing that was doubted" (Spinoza, 2002, p. 22). The working-through of doubtful uncertainty is the business of rational intellection, rather than of simple imagination with its generation of believable and fanciful fictions.

Spinoza addresses imagination's distortions of clear thinking through multiple examples including the mobility underlying the transfer of the individual's memories onto the present situation (Spinoza, 2002, p. 16), together with a splitting-off of memorial aspects incongruent with the present. The clinician immediately recognizes such action as a precursor both to the psychoanalytic idea of transference and to dissociation.

Spinoza also considers the inexact nature of memory traces, themselves discontinuously frozen into single moments of deformed certainty through which

> memory fails us, revealing its own limitations, having itself become anchored in singular "determinate duration of the sensation" rather than the continuous, present duration of the sensation to which it transfers. (Spinoza, 2002, p. 23)

Transference and distortion of memory are also joined by Spinoza to observation of delusional fixity or foreclosure of thought, through which the individual so negates the possibility of uncertainty that she is self-convinced her idea "is so in reality", rejecting the possibility of alternative ideas that cast doubt on her position (Spinoza, 2002, p. 17). Each of these dynamically observed forms—whether of transference, memory distortion, or delusional foreclosure, operates from the perspective of Spinoza's conjecture of the psychological binary certainty-uncertainty.

The second psychological continuum operative within mind separates the binary between pleasure and unpleasure that entails the emotional cost of one's enterprise. For Spinoza, as for the later Freud, the seeking of pleasure and the avoidance of unpleasure (or pain) is the subjective fulcrum of an act's wisdom. This psychological criterion of personal wellbeing hearkens back to Lucretius' Epicurean poem, *De rerum natura* (On the nature of things), which rediscovered in the Renaissance, was known to Spinoza's contemporaries Bacon and Descartes, cited by the later Freud, and alluded to in Spinoza's *Ethics* (Ford, 2007, p. 238; Freud, 1900, p. 8; Gillespie, 2007, pp. 251–252; Greenblatt, 2011).

Together with the two psychological continua of certainty/uncertainty and pleasure/unpleasure, Spinoza again foreshadows his more complete discernment of how we think, in the *Ethics*, by construing the functional realms through which "conatus", his term for our fundamental human striving, willing, desiring, or what today, following Winnicott, we term, *going on being*, operates (Winnicott, 1960). This involves a third dynamic boundary, separating the mind's internal realm of desire, from its external projection as "appetite". Intrinsic to Spinoza's thought is his explicit linkage of willed desire, whether internally contained or directed externally, to its object of desire. Psychodynamic psychology, from its Spinozan inception, is object related.

Returning to observations of general behaviors experienced in Amsterdam's Jewish community among its world of Portuguese "men of the Nation" (Bodian, 1999), Spinoza discerns two conventional orientations. The first, in anticipation of later limited understanding of Freudian psychosexuality in terms of lust rather than biological determinism, is toward gratification of sensual desire. The criterion of pleasure is calibrated along an affective continuum between the basic emotions of "joy" and "sadness". Through active externalization, our intrinsic human striving transforms internal joy or sadness into the appetitive demonstration respectively, of love or hate. Neither in their internal nor external forms are these affects pure entities, but rather basic emotional elements in continuous conflict and compromise.

After sensual desire, Spinoza's second observed domain of generalized human striving, is the desire for economic wealth and social honor or reputation (Spinoza, 2002, p. 4), later compressed in his *Ethics* into the general category, "greed". Joining these, Spinoza discerns a third pathway reflective of his own experiences and instrumental in his transit between bewilderment and enlightenment. This is the psychological activity that Freud's teacher, Franz Brentano, will later term "internal", the original reflexive action of introspective psychology (Brentano, 1874, p. 29). Against sensuality and greed, Spinoza advises the cultivation of Reason's reflective thinking as our intrinsic human difference from other species.[3]

Oedipal Complexity

Spinoza's own dramatic break with the Jewish community entailed the repudiation of two fathers, real and symbolic. Through successful appeal in civil law for reclassification of his social status to "orphan", Spinoza functionally reengineered his socially perceived identity, releasing himself from the imperative of relieving his inherited paternal debt burden under the aegis of synagogue authority. Through his later confrontation with Rabbi Saul Morteira (Nadler, 1999, p. 153) himself a philosophically-minded exponent of Maimonidean Aristotelian thinking (Halbertal, 2014; Saperstein, 2005), Spinoza also repudiated the competent paternalism of his teacher,[4] redirecting Morteira's philosophically-imbued thinking beyond theology toward the secular domain of natural philosophy.

Through their reduction of the Oedipal situation to two dimensions of incest and parricide, both Aristotle and Freud highlight only tragic discontinuity between past and future through the radical shift of intergenerational differentiation. Indeed, as within the larger architectonic of the Freudian psychoanalytic model, such differentiation marks a significant hierarchical boundary (Grossman, 1992), with its attendant functional shift from Laius' generational experiences to those of Oedipus.

However, the tragic discontinuity of Oedipal differentiation is only part of the Oedipal story. The contrasting dimension of continuity is also reflected in Sophocles' drama. His chastened Oedipus, nearing death at Colonus, undergoes a new moment of *anagnorisis,* much as our analytic patients build foundationally upon transitory recognitions as the base for future recognitions. Not only does Oedipus reflect upon the earlier rash act of blinding himself, as well as its contingent effects upon his family, but also recognizes himself (and is recognized by the Gods), through his Jobian endurance, as a devout man of faith. In *Oedipus at Colonus*, Oedipus' consciously resolved self-reflection suggests an ancient literary depiction of the individual's arrival at Klein's "Depressive Position" with his dramatic working-through, painfully enacted and emotionally endured, reflective of this first illustration of the psychoanalytic struggle. So too, Spinoza. However, the indices of continuity in his Oedipal challenges toward the previous generation, may be indistinct for the modern reader. Its clue is in the first sentence of the *Treatise on the Emendation of the Intellect* as revealed by the term, "hollowness and futility". Even in its English translation from the Latin, "hollowness and futility" signals its original predecessor, the Hebrew superlative *hevel hevelim*, translated in the King James bible as "vanity of vanities", a term appearing in the first line of *Kohelet*, the Hebrew bible's book of Ecclesiastes. Spinoza's reference to continuity with biblical "Wisdom" literature (Alter, 2010) through the lens of natural philosophy is reflected in the parallelism between the first sentence of his first treatise and its Solomonic referent from Ecclesiastes. Spinoza's own practical utility to the world of Dutch Protestant Dissenters was in his command of Hebrew; and his famously heretical *Theological-Political Treatise*, relies heavily on Hebrew biblical commentary (Nadler, 2011; Wolfson, 1934) including explicit reference to the commentaries of Maimonides, Rabbi Shlomo Itzhaki (Rashi), David Kimchi, and Abraham ibn Ezra (Rudavsky, 2001, 2015; De Spinoza, 1996).

The trademark comment of the 12th-century biblical commentator, Abraham Ibn Ezra, first found in his commentary on Genesis1:1, concludes, *"v'hamaskil yavin"*, or "the philosophically inclined will know what I am alluding to" (my translation). This is itself, an implied doubling of scriptural meanings, directing readers to interpretation along the lines of Neoplatonic philosophy. From his outset in the first line of *TEI*, Spinoza winks broadly to *Kohelet* (Ecclesiastes) and specifically to Ibn Ezra's commentary,[5] linking biblical "Wisdom" literature to medieval "natural philosophy" in evolution to modern science (Gomez-Aranda, 2006; Rudavsky, 2015; Stitskin, 1962).

The literary form of multiple interpretive levels, as in the doubled meanings suggested by Abraham Ibn Ezra—recognizable to those who understand philosophy—finds later transformations in the philosophical writing of Spinoza as well as in Freud's literary demonstrations of unconscious meaning in dreams, parapraxes, and jokes. Doubling, representing the action of transformation or translation across conceptual boundaries, is also prominent both in Spinoza's and Freud's social-psychological experience, wherein aspects of personal identity are repressed, suppressed, dissociated, and denied under subjectively felt external pressures. Its literary prominence in Freud's writing is foreshadowed by the writing of Heinrich Heine, where doubling expresses the transfer or transformation of meanings and concepts across linguistic and cultural boundaries.

What is significant in Spinoza's introductory *TEI* statement is not simply his act of doubling, with allusion to a Hebrew literary reference in this Latin text, but also, his effective continuation of Abraham Ibn Ezra's 12th-century Neoplatonic construction through *Kohelet*, of the mind's multi-leveled organization. Ibn Ezra's commentary, written five hundred years before Spinoza's birth, was still vibrant within the curricular context of Spinoza's text-based Hebrew education.[6] Spinoza's transformation of these ideas in *TEI* shifts the categories of sensual desire, wealth, honor, and self-reflection embedded in medieval fantasy, from discrete "agencies" of mind to empirical observations of what people do, dependent upon the different dynamics imputed by him to be the elements involved in human thought.[7]

For Spinoza, the "philosophical" level of understanding, potentially unrecognized within the doubled meanings of human behavior, and beginning in a personal despair as old as that of the aged King Solomon, is away from the dubious, uncertain pleasures of sensuality, wealth, and social esteem. Rather, for Spinoza, pleasure inheres in the pursuit of reflexive thinking about how the mind thinks, in alignment with Nature. Additionally, and perhaps related directly to the public cruelty and humiliation of his own synagogue ban, Spinoza reflects on the unique joy of personal philosophical reflection against social forms of appetitive desire demanding the "drawback" of conformity in "that to attain it we must conduct our lives to suit other men, avoiding what the masses avoid and seeking what the masses seek" (Spinoza, 2002, p. 4).

Separating out the intellectual roots of Spinoza's thinking from what he achieves in this essay, the clinician-reader discerns a trajectory that begins in affective registration of personal experience, Spinoza's anxiety. Essentially, Spinoza spells out his presenting complaint: the world seems purposeless and sapped of value. Much like our patients, he looks at himself in the world and recognizes his anxious permeability within acts by individuals, institutions, and circumstances in his external world. He questions whether such events are the "source" of his suffering or perhaps, its "object", much as do others, from the Kleinian "Paranoid Position". From this perspective, as Spinoza is later to demonstrate in his *Ethics*, the anxious sufferer projects his fears onto external objects of his own creation (Spinoza, 2002, p. 26). But such projective action, as we recognize in contemporary clinical theory, only seeks to rid the individual of intolerable states of mind through expulsion (Bion, 1959). Its yield of pleasure and unpleasure is uncertain. Rather, the root of human suffering, as of joy, is within the individual's mind. Whether approaching psychology from a cognitive-behavioral or psychodynamic perspective, Spinoza's arrival by the end of the short paragraph introducing *TEI* is to what we know and practice today, that our subjective registrations and apperceptive resonances remain internal, yet instrumental in guiding our actions (Mead, 1922; Ferenczi, 1909; Tolman, 1932).

Finally, Spinoza presents yet another level of textual continuity with the tradition of his teacher, Rabbi Saul Morteira. Within Spinoza's general overview of mind, already present in the *TEI*, he sets out a variation on Aristotelian concepts directly aligned with the writing of Maimonides' *Eight Chapters*, a psychological and ethical introductory commentary on the section of *Mishna* called *Pirke Avot* [The "Sayings of the Fathers"] in which Maimonides construes five faculties for the functioning of the soul. These include: the "growing" faculty of obtaining and processing nutrients; the "feeling" category; the "imaginative" category; the "appetitive" category; and the category of "rationality" (Gorfinkle, 1912, pp. 38-45). It is possible to recognize these categories within the categorical assumptions of Spinoza's general model. Human striving, "conatus", assumes the vital role later assigned by Freud to libido and later, to Winnicott's *going on being*.[8] "Feeling" is addressed broadly in Spinoza's concentration both upon perception and upon the affective base of mental functioning; "imagination" operates as the base of associative awareness, in the realm of ideas; "appetite" is formally named relative to human extension of desire as action in the external world, with an internal aspect of appetite functioning as desire; "rationality" operates not only as an early correlate to Freudian "Ego", but directly within the Spinozan system as a check upon the generative capability of imagination, much as Id functions within Freud's dictum, "where Id was, Ego shall be".

Reading Spinoza from a psychodynamic clinical perspective, an orientation impossibly distant from the author's thought requires a willingness for rapid shifts in the reader's attention, necessary to follow his 17th-century philosophical argument. In this, as in the early essays of Freud (Freud, 1890; Miller & Sweet, 2018), the reader is conducted from observation to observation, curious to discern not only the argument's shape, but also the quality of its elements as well as their links to antecedent, received thought. It is in these elements that the observations of Spinoza align with contemporary clinical thought.

Spinoza's Model of Mind

TEI sets out a manifesto for a social order based in natural philosophy, the precursor to today's "science", which like Freud's, extends from the individual's private experience toward transformation of society. Beginning in philosophy, the transformations to be wrought by Reason are multidisciplinary, imbuing moral philosophy, education, medicine, and technology or "the science of mechanics".[9] Comprehensively, Spinoza foreshadows our 21st-century arrivals in applications of science capable of improving the lot of as many human lives as possible (Spinoza, 2002, p. 6). Yet by the same Spinozan criteria, our 21st-century fetishization of technology and acquisition fails the more comprehensive test of moderation. Psychological resolve—akin to the psychoanalytic formulation of the ego's moderating functions (Waelder, 2007)—is necessary in order to preside over our adaptive desires. Spinoza's articulation of a modern psychological model of mind is itself still practical both for making sense of our behaviors and toward therapeutic address of our psychological distortions or "deformations" and confusions. The *Ethics'* later Spinozan architectonic portrays the dynamic combination of elements across multiple, interactively functional continua. These include the axes: (1) pleasure-unpleasure; (2) internal perception[10]-external reality; (3) certainty-uncertainty; together with (4) elemental interactions both at single and multiple moments of time- past, present, and future, and all in the service of (5) desire, or appetite, (6) through the changing balance of the affects, joy and sadness.

In continuous movement, the interaction of these continua provides a "three dimensional" model of psychic functioning that foreshadows by three hundred years the three-dimensionality of dynamic models generated by Freud (Grossman, 1992), Bion (Miller & Sweet, 2018), and Lewin (Barranger & Barranger, 2008; Lewin, 1936; Stern 2013a, 2013b).

As shown above, Spinoza begins his writing in Oedipal differentiation and continuity, transforming his reception of Neoplatonic and Aristotelian conceptions concerning agencies of mind, to observations of what people do in a reduction of theological transcendence to the empirically discernable domain of immanence (Yovel, 1989a). The psychological domain of thinking or intellect is central to Spinoza's worldview. His critique of sensual, acquisitional, and social pleasures pivots not only upon their ultimate incapacity to satisfy, but also upon their destructive effect upon clear thought. Obsessed with these goals, individuals are left incapable of "thinking of anything else". When proximate goals are reached, it is often with a sense of confusion and depletion, inhibiting clear thought. Considering such goals, Spinoza observes that

> the more each of them is possessed, the more our joy is enhanced, and we are therefore more and more induced to increase them both. But if it should come about that our hopes are disappointed, there ensues a profound depression. (Spinoza, 2002, p. 4)

The act of presiding over one's own thinking is for Spinoza, a unique human capability. It facilitates each individual's development of uniqueness rather than mindless social conformity.

Spinoza, earlier a partner in a family import firm that lost multiple spice cargoes both to pirates and to military seizure of their sailing vessels, knew firsthand that such ambitious acts en route to wealth and social esteem were uncertain gambles (Israel, 2001). Indeed, his deconstruction of the affect, *gladness,* is an example of the larger array of complex emotions later detailed by Spinoza, which might be applied interpretively to the emotional vicissitudes of such ventures (de Spinoza, 1677, p. 81. III.P18. Schol 2).[11]

Considered from our contemporary psychoanalytic perspective, the Spinozan example of *gladness,* arrived at through self-reflection, anticipates Freud's integration of the evolutionary notion of "dependent concommitance", articulated by the mid-19th century British physician Hughlings Jackson (Grossman, 1992). It is an affective state that is in itself, complex and dependent upon evolution from earlier states. *Gladness*, in its dependency and transformation from other affective moments, requires the individual's conscious or unconscious undergoing of such earlier moments in order for registration of its own metamorphosis.

The trajectory of *gladness* begins at a time "n", now in the past, with the individual's experience of sadness, mentally contained in relation to the potential joy once hoped for upon successful completion of a desired business venture. This sadness exists as a present memory of the past, contained internally, and reflective of an even earlier internal joyous wish, now certain in its failure through extension into the external world. Time "n", while past, consolidates multiple moments of willed wish, joy, externalized appetite, external registration of certain failure, and internal registration of sadness.

The construction of *gladness* continues with the certainty at a later time (n+1) that the venture, desired and enacted at an earlier time, (n), has failed, causing a sense of disappointment in its painful yield of unpleasure. However, as time (n+1) shifts to time (n+2), the complete certainty of loss erodes. With this, the foreclosed conviction of painfully certain loss becomes transformed into hopeful uncertainty. Finally, at time (n+3), *gladness* emerges with the successful arrival of the anticipated cargo, earlier feared lost. Its emergence would have been impossible without mental processing of multiply experienced fusions in feeling and thinking, across multiple transformations, over time. However related to tangible events in the external world, the vicissitudes eventuating in Spinoza's *gladness* occur entirely within the mind.

This interpretive analysis of a single constellation of affect and thought, reflects the interaction of internal and externally projected psychological fields, of pleasure and pain, certainty and uncertainty, as well as momentary assessments at different temporal points, all intersecting within the realm of desire, or willing—this time in the service of a positive outcome in the domain of increased wealth and social standing.

The dynamics of *gladness* illustrate the Spinozan primacy of psychological analysis, enlisted in the service of necessarily adaptive human appetites contributory to material and social desire. Despite subordinating sensuous desire and social desire to philosophy, Spinoza recognizes the necessities: (1) "to enjoy pleasures just so far as suffices to preserve health"; and (2)

> to seek as much money or other goods as are sufficient for sustaining life and health and for conforming with those social customs that do not conflict with our aim (Spinoza, 2002, p. 6)

of improving the functioning of the intellect.

The Primacy of Love

Spinoza observes in *TEI*, that our psychological suffering concerns the objects of our love, noting how

> all happiness or unhappiness depends solely on the quality of the object to which we are bound by love. For strife will never arise on account of that which is not loved. (Spinoza, 2002, p. 5)

While Spinoza considers joy and sadness basic affects, with their projection into the external world called respectively, Love and Hate, the effective partner in a psychological binary with a loved object is absence. Unlike Freud's expansion from a single libidinal drive to consideration of the Love-Hate binary[12] first observed by Empedocles, the Spinozan opposition of Love with absence prefigures late 20th-century psychoanalytic thinking about developmental, relational lacunae and failures of attachment (Green, 1997; Stern, 1985). Here, the object summoned through love, like the preconception suggested by Bion or "created" by the Winnicottian baby, remains unmet in realization. The result is not successful relatedness in the external world, itself satisfactorily internalized, but rather the incorporation of absence, tincturing the experience of enacted desire.

Of unloved objects, Spinoza observes that: loss produces no sorrow; another's possession evokes no envy; that threat to them involves no sense of fear or hatred as it does to loved objects. Indeed "emotional agitation" occurs for Spinoza, only "in the case of the love of perishable things". In this regard, it is critical to remember that the now-absent object relation, unmet in loving desire, continues to cause emotional agitation in its absence because it remains at some level, loved.

Analyzing Perception & Method

Spinoza's observations of "perception" concern not the transformative act between body and mind, but rather the manner by which we interpret our perception, what later psychologists term "apperception". He divides these into four groups. The first derives from "hearsay, or from sign conventionally agreed upon" (Spinoza, 2002, p. 7). His example is the way we know the dates of our birthdays, having been informed by others. The second derives from "casual experience",

> that is, experience that is not determined by intellect, but is so called because it chances thus to occur, and we have experienced nothing else that contradicts it, so that it remains in our minds unchallenged. (Spinoza, 2002, p. 7)

Much of what we hear clinically from our patients, resides within these two categories in consequence of the Beckettian sequence "ill-said, ill-heard, ill-recaptured" (Beckett, 1964, p. 7). These form the unquestioned assumptive base of daily life, with fixed opinions, often foreclosed to further inquiry.

Spinoza now determines a third form of perception, one that operates regularly in clinical psychotherapeutic practice. This

> is the perception we have when the essence of a thing is inferred from another thing, but not adequately. This happens either when we infer a cause from some effect or when an inference is

made from some universal which is always accompanied by some property. (Spinoza, 2002, p. 7)

Spinoza's example begins with the observation of person (a) relative to person (b), followed by (a)'s imputation that (b)'s sensory apparatus links her body and mind. Further, is our assumption that this synthesis of soma and psyche is the cause of a particular sensation, experienced perceptively by the observed individual, (b). However, as with clinical interpretation, which has been called a "mythology" or "external fantasy" congruent with the hearer's "internal fantasy" (Bion, 1965; Grossman, 1992), Spinoza recognizes that from these generalizations, however accurate, "we cannot positively understand" the nature of the sensation experienced by another, and caused by that union of body and mind. Another example is our recognition of perspective in optics, where the same object appears smaller to the eye when beheld from afar than when it is near, but our understanding is that it is the same object.

Finally, Spinoza arrives at his fourth level of perceptual understanding

when a thing is perceived through its essence alone, or through knowledge of its proximate cause. (Spinoza, 2002, p. 8)

Clinically, we operate at this level, too. As when on the one hand, operating at the third level of perception, we intuit a patient's love both from her explicit narrative at the level of language and from the softness in her voice at the level of gesture; while at this fourth level, joined with the patient, the therapist (or patient) may also experience directly within the clinical interaction in what is today called "thirdness" (Benjamin, 2004; Green, 1975; Ogden, 1994). Spinoza's example is similar in recognizing "from the fact that I know something, I know what it is to know something" (Spinoza, 2002, p. 8).

Spinoza suggests that our knowledge of these perceptual forms is useful in facilitating our own discernments in thought. It is to be applied in choosing the perceptual mode that best fits the context of thinking, in order to achieve "the highest degree of perfection that man can attain". Spinoza sets out specific criteria for our choice of perceptual modality. The first is

To have an exact knowledge of our nature which we wish to
perfect, and at the same time to know as much of the nature of
things as is necessary. (Spinoza, 2002, p. 8)

Clinicians will appreciate that what is demanded under this consideration in the domain of applied psychology, is clarity in our
therapeutic task and method (including self-knowledge through personal therapeutic experience), as well as a commitment to understanding the specific nature and demands of the treatment situation.

Attention to this criterion facilitates the correct inferences relative
to the "differences, agreements, and oppositions of things" (p. 8). As
against such clarity, Spinoza anticipates late 20th-century constructions of the analytic relationship as an inquiry into a lived dream-
state, noting how adhesion to false ideas are "practically the same as
dreaming with one's eyes open or while wide awake" (Spinoza, 2002,
p. 19).[13]

The purpose of these Spinozan considerations, as with Bion's
considerations relative to his theory of thinking, is for reasoned
thought in order that we "conceive aright the extent to which things
can, and cannot, be acted upon" (Spinoza, 2002, p. 8). In psychoanalytic work, this is a reminder of the limitation of our professional
endeavors.

Spinoza cautions us in humility. In intuiting psychological causation, both in ourselves and others, there are causes and conditions we
simply cannot know. Freudian libido, for example, is seen as a correlate for Spinoza's conatus, or life's striving, by early 20th-century
psychologists (Bernard, 1946; Rathbun, 1934; Smith, 1925, 1926;
Tanner, 1907a). But narrowly imagined as a specific originating force
separate from the generalized idea of conatus or human striving, a
reified reception of libido falls into perception's hearsay category, the
result of an "enquiry extending to infinity" (Spinoza, 2002, p. 8).
Intuition however refined, must content itself with what it cannot
know. Spinoza's example is apposite, "analogous to that of material
tools, where the same kind of argument could be employed". His
argument goes as follows

to work iron, a hammer is needed, and to have a hammer, it must
be made. For this purpose there is need of another hammer and

other tools, and again to get these there is need of other tools and so on to infinity. In this way one might try to prove in vain, that men have no power to work iron. (Spinoza, 2002, p. 9)

Spinoza here articulates the developmental consideration of process, itself illustrative of what Hughlings Jackson will later construe as "dependent contingency" and beginning with the striving, intellect, and brawn, which are the "gifts" with which we begin.

But the fact is that at first, with the tools they were born with, men succeeded, however laboriously and imperfectly, in making some very simple things; and when these were made they made other more complex things with less labor and greater perfection; and thus advancing gradually from the simplest works to the making of tools, and from tools to other works and other tools, they have reached a point where they can make very many complex things with little labour. In just the same way, the intellect by its inborn power makes intellectual tools for itself by which it acquires other powers for other intellectual works, and from these works still other tools- or capacity for further investigation- and thus makes steady progress until it reaches the summit of wisdom. (Spinoza, 2002, p. 10)

It may be observed that this progression is analogous to the outcome of therapy, where absent an aspiration for the "summit" but instead for sufficient resolution, therapeutic process is traceable empirically through the repetitive workings of clinical method (Miller & Sweet, 2018).

Spinoza, who is famous for reliance upon mathematical models toward psychological understanding, proposes an idealized conceptual model for understanding a "true" idea, a preconception that fits in its externalized test of realization in external reality.

A true idea (for we do have a true idea) is something different from its object (ideatum). A circle is one thing, the idea of a circle another. For the idea of a circle is not something having a circumference and a center, as is a circle, nor is the idea of a body itself a body. And since it is something different from its object it will also be something intelligible through itself. That is, in respect of its formal essence the idea can be the object of another objective essence, which in return, regarded in itself, will also be something real and intelligible, and so on indefinitely. (Spinoza, 2002, pp. 10–11)

Spinoza turns here to method, not as reasoning or understanding itself, but as a concept of the "true idea". In clinical practice, this is the manner in which therapy is conducted. Method involves a training of the mind to a standard of "all that needs to be understood", with "rules as aids", and with limits, "ensuring that the mind does not waste its energy on useless pursuits" (Spinoza, 2002, p. 11). Here, Spinoza argues along the same lines as Freud, in differentiation of hierarchical levels and boundaries in psychoanalysis (Grossman, 1992). He suggests that method itself is "nothing but reflexive knowledge". That is, it is "the idea of an idea", itself dependent upon the original idea or conception (in the case of psychotherapy, the nature of the psyche and its possibility in attainment of its "greater perfection", aided by the mediation of another person).

The discoveries, for Spinoza, via method and conviction in the concept of a true idea, are toward differentiation between one perception and another. This too, is part of his method wherein "the more things the mind knows, the better it understands both its own powers" and from such understanding, "the more easily it can direct itself and lay down rules for its own guidance, restraining itself from useless pursuits". Here is Spinoza's compressed, nutshell anticipation of psychoanalytic psychotherapy. His guideline is

that what we cannot acquire by chance, we may yet acquire by deliberate planning, and also in order to make it clear that, for the validation of truth and sound reasoning, we need no other instruments than truth and sound reasoning. (Spinoza, 2002, p. 11)

The object, for us, as for Spinoza, is human thought, which through its prejudices and great difficulties in generating a "considerable capacity to make accurate distinctions" results in a "human condition, which, as has already been shown, is highly unstable (Spinoza, 2002, p. 12). Indeed, Spinoza tragically continues, musing on the tendency for mental foreclosure, as humans act as "automatons"

> men whose minds are also blinded either from birth or by reason of their prejudices, that is, through some accident that has befallen them. For they are not even aware of their own selves. If they affirm or doubt something, they do not know they are doubting or affirming. They say they know nothing, and they say that they are ignorant of this very fact of knowing nothing. And they do not even say this without qualification; for they are afraid that, in saying they know nothing, they are declaring that they exist, so that in the end they have to maintain silence lest they should perchance say something that has the savour of truth. (Spinoza, 2002, p. 12)

Yet again, Spinoza's writing seems to echo *Kohelet*, which reminds the reader of a similar ignorance, in "eyes that do not see and ears that do not hear" (Ecclesiastes 1:8).

Finally, Spinoza adds the dimension of verbal expression to our psychological capacity for ignorance. He observes

> since words are a part of the imagination- that is, since many of our concepts are formed according to the haphazard composition of words in memory from some disposition of the body- there can be no doubt that words no less than imagination can bring about many grave errors unless we exercise great caution in that respect. Add to this that words owe their formation to the whim and understanding of the common people, so that they are merely symbols of things as they are in the imagination, not in the intellect. (Spinoza, 2002, p. 24)

Much of progressive development in psychoanalysis begins with concepts that reverse the direction of earlier concepts. Ferenczi's "introjection", for example, reverses the action of Freud's "transference" (1909). The idea of present maternal absence preceding Green's "dead mother", reverses the presence of a vibrantly living internal object (Green, 1997). Spinoza cautions about the ease with which words may be inverted into their negatives. In discerning psychological observations, the necessary test of such possibilities as viable general ideas, is in the testing of clinical hypothesis, lest

> we affirm and deny many things because the nature of words, not the nature of things, suffers us to do so; and in our ignorance of the latter, we may easily take the false to be true. (Spinoza, 2002, footnote d, p. 24)

The demand of Spinoza's rigorous analysis, still elusive within clinical psychoanalysis, is that conceptions must be crystal clear, with

> all the properties of the thing, when regarded by itself and not in conjunction with other things, can be deduced from it, as can be seen in the case of this definition of a circle. (Spinoza, 2002, p. 26)

Conclusion

Spinoza's TEI, while a brief, early essay, is forceful in setting out his method of therapeutically addressing distorted perceptions, and so, their misguided contingent extension from individually contained psychological experience, into the external world.

His observations foreshadow psychoanalytic discernment of associative process, memory, transference, projection, reality testing, and the psychic presence of the negative, as well as defensive forms including parataxic distortion, dissociation, and the foreclosure of ideas. Additionally, his careful discernment of psychological experience along the lines of plausibility within daily life—such as in the interaction of the binaries pleasure/pain, certainty/uncertainty, internal/external, across different periods of time and in changing temporal forms of affect and awareness, is an early foreshadowing of contemporary therapeutic models. Remarkably, Spinoza's clear examples through observation and reflection upon what people do, as in his analysis of the complicated levels of awareness in *gladness*, is a foreshadowing of psychoanalytic behavioral analysis. The form of this essay in early modern psychology links aspects of medieval psychological constructs and literature, with extension of thought beyond the imaginary into the empirically discernable realm of what we do when we think, whether through imagination or intellection, guided by Reason.

Like the Freudian model (and indeed, the earlier Lucretian), extending from individual functioning to social and civilizational consideration, Spinoza also forwards a broad model, meant to transform science, education, as well as individual capability in practicing a method toward generation both of clear thinking as well as doubtful admission of what we do not understand.

For us as for Freud, continuing in the "atmosphere" envisioned by Spinoza in the domain of understanding human nature, Spinoza's reflections on psychology from reflection upon his own experience, are extraordinary precursors of what in our time, have become testable elements vital within clinical practice.

Notes

1　See footnote 7 below for the possible textual transformation of Spinoza's thought from Maimonides' 12th-century ethical writings. As noted both in 20th century and contemporary scholarship (Adler, 2012, 2013; Wolfson, 1934) Spinozan thought is located both within the broad nexus of medieval Jewish philosophy and also traceable to the formulations of specific writers. In this regard, from the time of Saadia Gaon (9th century) through Yehuda HaLevi (11th century) through Maimonides, the idea that the soul or mind operated as the "craftsman" relative to the body or limbs as "tool" had already become commonplace in Jewish philosophical thought (Malter, 1912, p. 459). The statement that "all the things which were the source and object of my anxiety held nothing of good or evil in themselves insofar as the mind was influenced by them" may be read as Spinoza's modern transformation of this by-now, accepted notion in Jewish ethical literature.

2　This is the first significant **d**, or elemental landmark (Miller & Sweet, 2018) in the history of modern psychology—the idea of the psyche recognized in its functionality as separate from its somatic determinants; and in itself, the arbiter of external reality's effects upon the body. It is this notion that Lou Andreas-Salomé credits as Spinoza's brilliant accomplishment in modeling an immediately recognizable, functionally plausible, conception of psychology (Andreas-Salomé, 1964, p. 75).

3　Early 20th-century "Chicago" social science theory (James, 1904), linking the individual with her environment, and based on qualitative research, locates "four wishes" corresponding to categories of human endeavor earlier discerned by Spinoza. These include: (1) the basic desire for security, which becomes the foundational grounding for Sullivanian "security operations" (Sullivan, 1953); (2) the desire for intimate relatedness with others; (3) the desire for social recognition; and, as with Spinoza's new horizon of "thinking", (4) the desire for "new experience" (Colyer, 2015; Thomas, 1917).

4 David Bakan's posthumous work attempts linkage between Freudian thought and the medieval Aristotelian thought of Maimonides (Bakan, Merkur, & Weiss, 2009). Given the very different linguistic and textual bases of Spinoza's and Freud's educations, the idea is fruitful but unlikely within direct textual transmission. Spinoza's education was in a traditionally rabbinic Hebrew language textual curriculum (Fisher, 2020; Nadler, 1999; Wolfson, 1934). Freud's early acquaintance with Hebrew was through his father's home schooling in a bible supplemented by German language commentary (Gillman, 2018), followed by a secular German gymnasium education, based in Latin and Greek classics (Winter, 1997). Freudian thought is mediated by Spinoza's secularizing trajectory of natural philosophy rather than the direct result of Maimonidean scholarship. Spinoza, on the other hand, knew his Maimonides, as indicated in his *Theologica-Political Tractate* and *Ethics* (Rudavsky, 2001; Spinoza, 1670; Wolfson, 1934). See footnote 7.

5 The medieval depiction of mind portrays interactive conflict imagined between three competing agencies of mind or soul, corresponding to different embodied terms. The first is the vegetative level of *Nefesh*, the second is the perceptive level of *Ruah*; the third is the reflective-intuitive level of *Neshama*, guided by the *Lev*, or heart—itself a category of guidance for the body's limbs as discerned by another Judeo-Arabic Spanish author, Bahya ibn Pakuda (Mansoor, 1973).

6 The composition of commentaries upon an earlier "scriptural" object, requires the continued integrity of the primary text, without revision. Commentaries and later, supercommentaries both upon the earlier scripture and subsequent commentaries, reflect standard literary form in rabbinic tradition (Simon, 1993). The annotated printed form of the Hebrew bible, the Mikraot Gedolot, as well as Freud's Philipson bible are presented as texts with commentary (Gillman, 2018). The formal aspect of Freud's own written composition—with earlier work standing together in agreement and disagreement in relation to later work, together with interpretive elaborations upon the entire set of arguments, is further supplemented by post-Freudian supercommentaries. This literary form, now transformatively repurposed both in the literary and oral traditions representative of psychoanalysis, replicates the formal shape of intellectual discourse continuously engaged in thinking, dispute, and expansion of thought in its classical rabbinic presentational form.

7 Just as the organization of soul traceable to Ibn Ezra is notable in *TEI*, so too is Maimonides' interpretation of Aristotelian categories regarding the soul's functionality. These include: the physical vegetative faculty, the faculty of feeling, the faculty of imagination, and the faculty of rationality (Gorfinkle, 1912, pp. 38–39). Spinoza unlinks these Maimonidean concepts from a framework of religious duty (Gorfinkle, 1912, p. 47), but maintains mind's

unconscious physical drive in his conatus, its feeling capabilities in description of perception and the affective ground of his psychology, and its unconscious and ongoing faculty of imagination in relation to the mediation of intellection, presided over by rationality. In this way, the specificity of Maimonidean categories is transformed through Spinozan reconstruction, just as Maimonides transforms Aristotelian categories already mediated by the 9th century Arabic scholar, al-Farabi (Gorfinkle, 1912, p. 39, ft 1; Strauss, 1952).

8   It should be observed that Spinoza's philosophical orientation is monistic, differing both from Descartes' and later, Freud's dualism. In its monistic form, Spinoza's orientation also departs from the rabbinic dichotomy between "good" and "evil" instincts (Malter, 1912).

9   While this is historically congruent with the mechanisms of the Cartesian era, it is also congruent with Maimonides' characterization of intellect, in theoretical and practical aspects. Included in the latter are considerations of mechanics such as those found in Maimonides' *Eight Chapters* (Gorfinkle, 1912, p. 43).

10   Jacob Adler (2012) describes an evolution in Spinoza's thinking from *TEI* to his *Short Treatise* to the *Ethics,* arranging and rearranging the concepts of hearsay or opinion, reasoned thought, and intuition, toward their final form in the *Ethics,* Part II, which resembles a model generated by Solomon Delmidego, a student of Galileo and a rabbi resident in Amsterdam until the time of Spinoza's birth, whose work, *Sefer Elim,* published by the press of Rabbi Menasseh ben Israel, one of Spinoza's teachers, was present in Spinoza's library.

11   The emotional journey across affective moments is recounted here by Spinoza, explaining that "*hope* is nothing but *an inconstant joy which has arisen from the image of a future or past thing whose outcome we doubt*; fear, on the other hand, is *an inconstant sadness, which has also arisen from the image of a doubtful thing.* Next, if the doubt involved in these affects is removed, hope becomes *confidence,* and fear *despair-* namely, *a joy or sadness which has arisen from the image of a thing we feared or hoped for.* Finally, *gladness is a joy which has arisen from the image of a past thing whose outcome we doubted,* while *remorse is a sadness which is opposite to gladness".* The reader notes too, that the language of the Curley translation (De Spinoza, 1996) varies from the Shirley translation of *Ethics* (Spinoza, 2002). In this essay, I rely upon the Curley, whereas in my later reading of *Ethics,* I generally use the Shirley, as I have also in this reading of the *Treatise on the Emendation of the Intellect.*

12   Curiously, Empedocles' binary of love-hate has also been understood as love-strife (Farrell, 2007, p. 88). If understood as strife, both the Spinozan and Freudian models contain this binary polarity in their respective constructions of ongoing affective change in intellection and the centrality to Freud of psychic conflict.

13   While the contemporary reader observes allusion to *Kohelet* in Spinoza's early modern philosophical tractate, his reference to a human waking dream-state is

also congruent with the Latin, Epicurean poetry of Lucretius, written in the first century, BC,

> Whilst yet thou livest and lookest?—who in sleep
> Wastest thy life—time's major part, and snorest
> Even when awake, and ceasest not to see
> The stuff of dreams, and bearest a mind beset
> By baseless terror, nor discoverest oft
> What's wrong with thee, when, like a sotted wretch,
> Thou'rt jostled along by many crowding cares,
> And wanderest reeling round, with mind aswim.
>   (Lucretius, Project Gutenberg, 2008)

In *Ethics*, this idea of snoring through life, seeing only "the stuff of dreams" will be linked with narcissistic grandiosity and omnipotence.

Part III

Chapter 6

Ethics, Part I

The present chapter is the first of two, corresponding to the first two of *Ethics*' five parts, read closely toward consolidation of a Spinozan psychodynamic model. These are followed next by two chapters addressing Spinoza's development of a therapeutically applicable model in *Ethics* III; and then, by two later chapters, summarizing our *clinical Spinoza*, the integration of Spinoza's thinking within contemporary psychoanalytic practice. My reading of *Ethics* Part I is divided into four sections: Introduction; Some Contextual Background; Addressing the Text; and Tools of Inquiry.

Introduction

Knowledge of Spinoza differs from acquaintance with Spinoza. What drops away from our understanding under the condition of mere acquaintance is experience; and it is the experiential loss of Spinoza toward understanding his place in psychology, that causes Spinoza to vanish, absorbed into the advancing flux of psychoanalysis. This disappearance occurs to the degree that we do not read Spinoza. For it is only in experiencing the argumentative force of reading, that one truly encounters Spinoza.

Fortunately, our psychoanalytically informed commentaries have prepared us for such encounter. Perspectival differences remain in observers' attitudes and emphasis, but as remarked by Lou Andreas-Salomé, Spinoza meets us all on our journeys. One such contrast is in the tension between Spinoza's holistic monism, a theme later underlined in consolidating the American humanistic

DOI: 10.4324/9781003246404-10

critique of psychoanalysis as against Tanner's narrower behavioral reading of Spinoza, focused upon a psychology of effects (Tanner, 1907a). Each of these perspectives is legitimate, claiming strong general or universal power, within context. As Spinoza reminds us in Part II, what we term universals are themselves variable and multiple, in that they are subject to consensual validation, education, and experience. Spinoza anticipates what Bion terms the "selected fact": a universal recognized interpretively, on intuitive emergence from within the experiential flux, tolerant or clashing with other selected facts, themselves contrasting both in their universality and in the contexts of their recognition. At the same time, if taken without their necessary conjunction, these remain partial observations at best, subsets of the whole.[1] In *Ethics*, interpretive multiplicity trumps singularity.

Similarly, without direct experience, the same kind that Freud could recognize in citing Spinoza's mode of thinking relative to Leonardo's artistry, we lose the experiential edge that generates aliveness in conceptual parallels between Spinoza and psychoanalysis. These clinical readings of *Ethics* attempt to follow this edge. Such experiential recognition bears comment: starting my research with straightforward readings of *Ethics*, I began to discern repetitive underlying currents in Spinoza's writing that seemed discontinuous in their emergence and disappearance. As I followed Spinoza's thinking off-piste, attempting clear understanding, I found philosophical and literary references that further shaped my reading. One such diversion, provoked by Spinoza's scholium at II. Proposition 7, led me to Maimonides' 13th-century *Guide of the Perplexed,* a classic text in Jewish philosophy, well known to Spinoza and contained in his personal library (Green, 2015; Harvey, 1981; Offenberg, 1973; Wolfson, 1934).

The specific citation reads,

> some of the Hebrews seem to have seen this, as if through a cloud, when they maintained that God, God's intellect, and the things understood by him are one and the same. (De Spinoza, 1996, p. 35)[2]

This narrative was followed by Spinoza's brilliant illustration concerning the rays of a circle, describing an infinite range of imagined rectangles. The clash of these two descriptions, one indistinct and changeable, while the other logically demonstrated an unlimited unconscious realm beneath the empirical fact, felt immediately illuminative.

Turning to Maimonides' *Guide* in the hope of explanation, I was led to another analogy for the doublings of unconscious apprehension, illustrated by Spinoza through his geometric example of the circle and rectangles. Elaborating the scriptural verse, Proverbs 25:11, "Like golden apples in silver showpieces" (Tanakh, 1985, p. 1327), Maimonides describes a silver filigreed apple

> in which there are apertures with very small eyelets, like the handiwork of silversmiths. They are so called because a glance penetrates between them. (Maimonides, 1963, V 1, p. 12)

Maimonides links this image, with its silver apertures disclosing hints of a golden interior, to the doubled meanings inherent in well-constructed parables,[3] in which External meaning contains wisdom that is useful in many respects, among which is the welfare of human societies, as is shown by the external meaning of *Proverbs* and of similar sayings. Their internal meaning, on the other hand, contains wisdom that is useful for beliefs concerned with the truth as it is (ibid, p. 12).

Immediately, I recognized that Spinoza's circle, with its imagined, unlimited range of interior rectangles, corresponded to the doubled aspect of Maimonides' silver filigreed apple, with its contrasting realms of social consensus and private philosophical understandings. Later, I would come to recognize how Spinoza, too, in his differentiation between *knowledge of the second kind* and *knowledge of the third kind*, extends the doubled notion of socially consensual understanding and intuited truths. I recognized too, in linkage forward, how our daily clinical recognitions of the unconscious are the yield of enormous cultural change in the centuries since Maimonides and Spinoza. Indeed, today, the Freudian legacy of the unconscious as assumptive truth endures within popular culture. More ironically than Maimonides could ever know and more destructive to human privacy than Freud could imagine, the disclosing of internal gold continues to be an apt image for the unconscious data that contemporary society accepts as a corporately monetizable, daily fact of life.[4]

What became distilled for me from this experiential reading of Spinoza, was a single idea, to be expanded as I read: the synthesis of a cloud's indeterminacy together with the precision of geometric illustration, disclosing the unseen through what is observable. As I read forward, I realized that I had begun to conceive of Spinoza's thinking as reflecting what I construed as a *cloudy mathematics.*[5]

Both Maimonides and Spinoza are explicit in pointing to the simultaneity of multiple meanings and possibilities within an ostensibly singular occurrence.[6] Indeed, according to Spinoza, this is regularly mirrored in the form of Nature's attributes, thought and extension, categories borrowed from Descartes and transformed by Spinoza into simultaneous operation as parallel aspects of the same substance, in *Ethics* Part I.

Discovering Gilles Deleuze's commentary, *Spinoza. Practical Philosophy*, published in English in 1988, I was thrilled to see his recognition of similar doublings in *Ethics'* presentational form. Against *Ethics'* linear order that so frustrates integration with modern psychoanalytic thinking, but detached from which, gems of concordance are clearly present, Deleuze observes a "broken" progression of scholia. Together with prefaces and appendices, these scholia act as Spinozan opinion pieces: explanatory essays that double in their commentary, the classic philosophical demonstration of the larger text.[7]

It is through his reading of scholia that Deleuze finds the same quality that I also locate in Spinoza: a passionate, argumentative, carefully descriptive Spinoza, independently opining, often chastening, while doing so within his strictly imposed confines of chosen, philosophical scaffolding. Freud would later accomplish the same kind of doubled contrast in his writing, by preserving earlier versions of his thinking, together with later versions, in the *Standard Edition*. Essentially, this essay form recapitulates the medieval *super-commentary*, familiar both in the study of Scripture and philosophy, itself an emergent and transformational force in the medieval Jewish thought that was Spinoza's intellectual foundation (Rudavsky, 2018; Simon, 1993).

Perhaps the most psychoanalytically attuned approach toward apprehending what Freud accurately terms Spinoza's *doctrine* (II. Appendix, p. 277), is provided in commentary by the mid-20th century Spinoza scholar, Harry Austryn Wolfson. Referring to the "apperceptive mass" which is our experiential base in reading *Ethics,* we find

> at first, these encrustations are indistinguishable and shapeless clumps, clinging to the propositions as bits of scrap-iron cling to a magnet. But let our mind play upon them- to scrutinize them and to study them. By the catalytic action of the mind these indistinguishable and shapeless clumps begin to dissolve; they begin to group themselves, to solidify themselves into larger units, to become differentiated from each another, to assume form, and ultimately to crystallize themselves into distinct topics of recognizable historical problems of psychology. (Wolfson, 1934, p. 5)

In the 20th century rush to locate conceptual parallelism between *Ethics* and psychoanalysis, such leisurely, associative play, itself confident in creativity, has been lost.[8] Yet, certainty of historical reception has been affirmed. Reading through distortion, repetition, amplification, and affirmation, clear familial links and patterns are discernable between Spinoza's *Ethics* and psychoanalytic development.

Oriented now to our focus upon clinical practice, dependent on association between what we know subjectively through our work and what we read, Spinoza enlivens by what he evokes: as Wolfson's "bits of scrap iron" are shaped by the clinical magnet of experience.

Beginning Part I: Some Contextual Background

Today, with our educational and cultural assumptions based in modern natural science, Part I of Spinoza's *Ethics* seems arcane and difficult. Certainly, it did to early 20th-century psychologists, recognizing Spinoza's anticipation of modern psychodynamic psychology (Smith, 1925, 1926; Tanner, 1907a).

Founded on 17th-century thinking, Spinoza accomplishes in human psychology what Copernicus and Galileo earlier accomplished in relation to our place in the cosmos.[9] We are construed as finite, overdetermined, creations, within the natural order. This is contrasted with Spinoza's construction of how earlier cultures arrived at their anthropomorphic concept of God: through a mechanism, detailed in the Appendix to Part I, resembling what today's psychoanalytic clinicians recognize as projective identification. It might be said that modern psychology, therefore, begins with Spinoza's observation of human projective identification as a means of ensuring fictional, if socially accepted, security.

However, to arrive at this Appendix reading, the reader must traverse thirty-six propositions with their attendant explanations and commentaries. Like the Freudian *nachtraglichkeit*, our retrospective reading compels the reshaping of what we have read, discerning what seems significant in order to form hypotheses that lead to a more cohesive understanding. Like Amy Tanner (1907a), our lack of pre-paration for Spinoza's geometric demonstration allows a certain wide-eyed naivete; but like M. Hamblin Smith (1925), we recognize its importance, if in the service of broadening our historical, cultural contextual understanding of *Ethics'* transition from late medieval times to modernity.

Reading *Ethics* in this way, our clinical antennae are receptive to whatever seems to come, mindful that Spinoza functions as a guide to our perplexity. We find, through this approach, that our linear reading through the Parts approximates tutorials, with similarity to psychotherapeutic sessions in their immediacy of focus. Joined in argument, like it or not, we also experience different accents, transformations, and repetitions of earlier thematic material; and are reminded of Giles Deleuze's accuracy in recognizing that one discovers Spinoza, always from the *middle*, from our engagement with him.

Perhaps the most difficult of such middles for the 21st-century clinician to imagine is the socio-cultural moment in time, from which Spinoza wrote. While Smith (1925), comments that like Freud, Spinoza was Jewish, his reductive comment is unclear in specifying meaningful challenges within the Jewishness either of Freud or Spinoza. Recognizing the specific nature and chal-lenges within Spinoza's Jewishness are necessary to contextualize his work.

Baruch Spinoza's Hebrew language education occurred in the *Talmud Torah* synagogue community of Amsterdam in an atmosphere of enthusiasm, relief, and challenge with great hopes for Spinoza's own generation. Spinoza, born in Amsterdam in 1632, was raised in a freedom of Jewish practice and education that had been an impossibly distant hope of his immediate forbearers (Nadler, 1999; Kaplan, 1989; Yerushalmi, 1980). Yet, the heightened emphasis on Hebrew bible study in the Amsterdam community, as against more traditional study of rabbinic texts, was itself, the transformative effect of the bible's importance to former Iberian *New Christians*, focused through the lens of Catholic intolerance upon a Judaism reduced in fantasy to the "law of Moses" (Fisher, 2020, p. 28).[10]

In contrast to the Amsterdam-born Spinoza, most of Spinoza's community had been born in Portugal or Spain, where their families had endured the five or six generations since 1492, under the persecutory reign of the Inquisition (Kaplan, 1989; Yerushalmi, 1971, 1980). Attempting to maintain links with their proscribed heritage, they had functioned as crypto-Jews, called *conversos*, or the more greatly deprecatory *marrano* or "pig" (the Hebrew term is *anusim*, or "forcibly coerced") now practicing Christians, but tainted by suspicions of their blood impurity under the racial standard of the *limpieza de sangre* (Gilman, 1972; Yovel, 1989a).

Flight from the Iberian Peninsula did not entail a simple transfer of faith from Catholicism to Judaism. It involved both the acquisition of new and problematic worldviews entwined with ritual practice, as well as fundamental shifts in identity. Arriving in cities like Hamburg or Amsterdam, tolerant of Jewish communal practice, the individual problem was that adjustment

> to their new lives within the Jewish community was truly enormous. The Marrano who arrived as an adult had not only to undergo circumcision, but also to acquire rapidly a large fund of Jewish skills and knowledge without which even minimal participation in the life of the community would be impossible. The habits, ideas, and attitudes which other Jews had inherited naturally, and in which they had been educated during their former years, had now to be compressed and assimilated by mature men in a very short time. (Yerushalmi, 1971, p. 47)

The problem, Yerushalmi explains

> was not that they knew nothing of Judaism, but that what they knew was often a pastiche of fragments inherited from parents, gleaned haphazardly from books, disorganized, with significant gaps, sometimes distorted. (Yerushalmi, 1980, p. 165)

This heterodox, haphazard, and distorting clash of cultures and doctrines led to great difficulties within the Amsterdam community, including the community ban of *herem*, or separation, itself exposing the individual to a lack of social, vocational, and economic supports in a larger society definitive of the individual through association with faith communities.

It is possible to trace certain of the themes emergent in *Ethics*, from the ferment of this rich social matrix. For example, determined to expose New Christian heresy under the Inquisition, Old Christian writers discerned philosophical currents indicative of religious heterodoxy including an

> Averroeism and skepticism that had been spreading amongst the Jews of Spain even before the expulsion of 1492 and which were adopted by many a 'New Christian' in the sixteenth and seventeenth centuries. (Kaplan, 1989, p. 162)

Specifically, these included four general themes represented in *Ethics*, in

> (*a*) the autonomy of the understanding in matters speculative and ethical; (*b*) repudiation of the conventional forms in which divine revelation was conceived; (*c*) insistence on the immutability of the natural order since creation, its laws having been determined by God in perpetuity and (*d*) the belief in a natural law, common to humanity from its outset, and having a moral rather than a religious quality. (Kaplan, 1989, p. 163)

Additionally, there were currents of deep unrest within the synagogue itself. One such issue concerned the heavenly fate of family left in Spain, relative to contemporary belief in immortality, a theological issue focusing on eternal life, differentiating Amsterdam's New Jews from their New Christian friends and relatives in the Iberian Peninsula (Altmann, 1972; Nadler, 1999, 2001), that was effectively negated by Spinoza's *Ethics*, by placing all souls on the same footing within the immanent fact of their mortality.

Another deep current of unrest is underlined by contemporary scholarship. As within Inquisitional practice in Spain, the synagogue also relied on community informants to confirm charges of heresy (Kaplan, 1989; Nadler, 1999). One such report, relative to Spinoza's colleague, Juan de Prado,[11] portrays despair akin to traumatized survivors of the *Shoah* three hundred years later. Prado, having escaped inquisitional imprisonment and torture, would declare of his situation relative to the *Ma'amad*, the lay administrative board of the synagogue, that

> these absurd Jews seem to want to set up an inquisition here, God help us. (Kaplan, 1989, p. 139)

Despairing of a deity recognizable through human anthropomorphic imagination, this New Christian who had fled Spain to become a New Jew in Amsterdam would claim, in light of his own suffering, that

> God is powerless: If He had any power, He would save his people from Inquisition; since He does not, it would seem that He is powerless. (Kaplan, 1989, p. 144)

Added to this rich matrix of hopeful if upsetting, societal upheavals, are the complex textual parallels in *Ethics*, relative to traditional commentators on Scripture in Jewish philosophy including Maimonides and Hasdai Crescas, each separately referenced in Spinoza's writing and interwoven with more modern themes of philosophy and science, including Galileo and Descartes. Largely unattributed, if present either as provocative question or underlying argument, these were drawn from Spinoza's broad

> fund of knowledge acquired through miscellaneous reading which in his mind formed itself into a composite picture of the salient features of traditional philosophy. (Wolfson, 1934, p. 4)

Wolfson elaborates, writing that

> we do not know nor can we ascertain exactly what books
> Spinoza had actually read, what quotations he had come across
> in the course of his readings, or what casual information he had
> gathered from conversations with friends. (Wolfson, 1934, p. 4)

To this, the reader must also allow for Spinoza's

> aggregation of notes swarming with references to sources of texts,
> to parentages of ideas, to conflicts of opinions, and to diversities
> of interpretations, all of them ready to come up to the surface,
> whenever the occasion arose, and take their place in the picture.
> (Wolfson, 1934, p. 5)

Still, the contemporary clinical reader must not be entirely seduced
by the creatively integrative associational history of Spinoza's
thought, but remain focused upon what it offers to our clinical
psychoanalytic practice.

Addressing the Text

Psychoanalytic Spinoza commentators have all negotiated *Ethics*
Part I at arms-length, disposing quickly of the problematic seam
between theology and philosophy en route to psychology. From this
perspective, Part I functions as a complicated philosophical gateway
foundational: to the basic laws of psychology discussed in Part II; to
the observable cause-and-effect behaviors of psychology discussed in
Part III; and to the ethical problems of our limited, human choice,
which in Parts IV and V, validate the results-based similarity of
Freudian and Spinozan systems[12] as well as the values implicit in
psychoanalytic humanism.

Having the benefit of such foundational observations, our present
clinical reading of Spinoza proceeds from a sharper angle, the
standpoint of contemporary clinical psychoanalysis (Miller, 2016).
What might a clinical reading of *Ethics* contribute toward our present
vernacular understanding? How are we affected as we read *Ethics*?

What thoughts shape themselves in our thinking; and what we can draw from this experience in application to our work?

Spinoza's arrival at a narrative observation resembling the modern form of projective identification, in the Appendix concluding Part I, represents the clinical starting point of *Ethics*. Brilliantly rich, it is a formulation narrated in forceful argument against our human *fallacy of understanding* (Levenson, 1978). Spinoza writes,

> it will suffice at this point if I take as my basis what must be universally admitted, that all men are born ignorant of the causes of things, that they all have a desire to seek their own advantage, a desire of which they are conscious. From this it follows, firstly, that men believe that they are free, precisely because they are conscious of their volitions and desires; yet, concerning the causes that have determined them to desire and will they do not think, not even dream about, because they are ignorant of them. (I. Appendix, p. 239)

The conscious desire to seek one's own advantage is what Spinoza will later call *Desire*. Underlying desire are two unconscious fields, noted clearly among our psychological commentators only by Amy Tanner (1907a, p. 514). These are: (1) the internal psychological field of *willing*, and (2) the transformation of *willing* in extension through action from the individual's internal functioning into the external world, which Spinoza terms *appetite*. The fundamental confound is that human consciousness is extremely limited, but that narcissistically, we take it to be complete, arrogant in our belief in complete freedom. All of our psychological commentators recognize that it is in the becoming conscious of our limitations, and the re-cognizing further of what we are capable of thinking and doing, given the scope of our ignorance and our determinate limitations, are at the root both of *Ethics* and psychoanalysis. This is the "complete adaptation to reality" noted by M. Hamblin Smith (1925, p. 257) as well as the striking "congruence in essential elements" both of "mood and direction" in Spinoza and Freud (Bernard, 1946, p. 99). Fromm condenses this passage from Part I Appendix, writing of Spinoza's idea that man is guided by forces he is not aware of. As he put it, man believes himself to be free because he knows his desire, but he is not aware of the causes for his desires. (Fromm, 1964a, p. 71)

But none of our commentators convey the sharp bite of Spinoza's observation as he continues

Secondly, men act always with an end in view, to wit, the advantage they seek. Hence it happens that they are always looking only for the final cause of things done, and are satisfied when they find them, having, of course, no reason for further doubt. But if they fail to discover them from some external source, they have no recourse but to turn to themselves, and to reflect on what ends would normally determine them to similar actions, and so they necessarily judge other minds by their own. (I. Appendix, p. 239)

Here, Spinoza outlines two sets of conditions. The first is the simple action of desiring, acting, and achieving gratification, with ample certainty in external circumstances. The second causes anxiety in the failure to locate external causality; and here, Spinoza articulates what William James will later call the *psychologist's fallacy* (James, 1981, p. 195).[13] It is likely that from such recognition, Tanner (1907a) recognized Spinoza as a proto-Jamesian. Simply put, this fallacy of understanding substitutes one's own viewpoint for the viewpoint of another.

Spinoza continues, having set up this Jamesian condition for projection of one's own thought/feeling constellation upon another. He writes,

further, since they find within themselves and outside themselves a considerable number of means very convenient for the pursuit of their own advantage- as for instance, eyes for seeing, teeth for chewing, cereals and living creatures for food, the sun for giving light, the sea for breeding fish- the result is that they look on all the things of Nature as means to their own advantage. (Spinoza, 2002, I. Appendix, p. 239)

That is, already primed to project our inner convictions of imagination and feeling onto the external world, we locate actual proofs in Nature in what today we call the "commons", freely given natural benefits, both individual and social, convincing us of our fantasies. And from this faulty assumption, we make a wild assertion (that at least dispels anxiety) in

> realizing that these were found, not produced by them, they come to believe that there is someone else who produced these means for their use. For looking on things as means, they could not believe them to be self-created, but on the analogy of the means which they are accustomed to produce for themselves, they were bound to conclude that there was some governor or governors of Nature, endowed with human freedom, who have attended to all their needs, and made everything for their use. And having no information of the subject, they also had to estimate the character of these rulers by their own, and so they asserted that the gods direct everything for man's use so that they may bind men to them and be held in the highest honor by them. (ibid, p. 239)

Having created gods, imbued anthropomorphically with the projected psychologies of man, Spinoza now describes how we identity in our gods, the products of our own projections,

> so it came about that every individual devised different methods of worshipping God as he thought fit in order that God should love him beyond others and direct the whole of Nature so as to serve his blind cupidity and insatiable greed. Thus it was that this misconception developed into superstition and became deep-rooted in the minds of men, and it was for this reason that every man strove most earnestly to understand and to explain the final causes of all things. 'but in seeking to show that Nature does nothing in vain- that is, nothing that is not to man's advantage- they seem to have shown only this, that nature and the gods are as crazy as mankind. (I. Appendix, pp. 239–240)

Spinoza rests his case with the concluding movement of projective identification: the internalization of the projected contents, marked not as one's own but rather as an imposition of the Other's psychology, writing

> consider, I pray, what has been the upshot. Among so many of Nature's blessings, they were bound to discover quite a number of disaster, such as storms, earthquakes, diseases and so forth, and they maintained that these occurred because the gods were angry at the wrongs done to them by men, or the faults committed in the course of their worship. And although daily experience cried out against this and showed by any number of examples that blessings and disasters befall the godly and the ungodly alike without discrimination, they did not on that account abandon their ingrained prejudice. For they found it easier to regard this fact as one among other mysteries they could not understand and thus maintain their innate condition of ignorance rather than to demolish in its entirely the theory they had constructed and devise a new one. Hence they made it axiomatic that the judgment of the gods is far beyond man's understanding. Indeed, it is for this reason, and this reason only, that truth might have evaded mankind forever had not Mathematics, which is concerned not with ends but only with the essences and properties of figures, revealed to men a different standard of truth. (ibid, p. 240)

Having achieved both projection and internalization of those projections, Spinoza's illustration of faith in anthropomorphic gods recognizes the defensive necessity to armor belief against further inquiry, lest the "theory they had constructed" become challenged.

Narratively, Spinoza has traced the dynamic pathway from (1) human anxiety and dread, (2) through projection and (3) identification with the externalized action of projection; to (4) anxious conformity with the imagined conscious demands of gods, (5) validated erroneously by reference to positive and negative life experiences. Finally, (6) this psychological construction is aggressively defended by the conviction that such mysteries are beyond human comprehension.

Here, our psychoanalytic commentators have mistaken *Ethics'* geometrical demonstration itself, either as a hindrance to understanding

(Tanner, 1907a) or as the echo of an ancient philosophical form (Smith, 1925). Rather, as Spinoza argues in Part I Appendix, such mathematical procedure is the necessary tool for clarifying humanity's "widespread misconceptions" (p. 240). The geometric format through which Spinoza famously reduces human psychology to lines and planes, is only mechanistic at its surface. Its wisdom is in Spinoza's demonstration of method, correctly apprehended by Lou Andreas-Salomé, as endorsing a replicable process for thinking.

The next section views Part I from the psychological perspective of this Appendix. It explores Spinoza's generation of conceptual tools useful in inquiry.

Tools of Inquiry

The clinical method bequeathed to us by Spinoza is informed not only by the forward progression of his argument, but also shaped by retrospective recognition of transformations, apparent only through later thought, Freud's *nachtraglichkeit*. To arrive at understanding of such "deferred action" in *Ethics* Part I, it is necessary to traverse 36 propositions, 34 proofs, 15 corollaries, 14 scholia, 7 axioms, 6 definitions, and 2 explications. In this way, the reader arrives at the Part I Appendix, with Spinoza's 17th-century prototype of projective identification as the mechanism allaying our human anxieties about Nature's freely given beneficence. Reading *Ethics* forward again, we are reminded of another Spinozan observation, encountered in his earlier *Treatise on the Emendation of the Intellect,* reflected above. There, Spinoza proposes the difficulty of creating a hammer with tools themselves requiring the use of a hammer, a logical impossibility, if empirical reality were not more compelling than logic. He reasons

but the fact is that at first, with the tools they were born with, men succeeded, however laboriously and imperfectly, in making some very simple things; and when these were made they made other more complex things with less labor and greater perfection; and thus advancing gradually from the simplest works to the making of tools, and from tools to other works and other tools, they have reached a point where they can make very many complex things with little labor. In just the same way, the intellect by its inborn power makes intellectual tools for itself by which it acquires other powers for other intellectual works, and from these works still other tools—or capacity for further investigation—and thus makes steady progress until it reaches the summit of wisdom. (Spinoza, 2002, p. 10)

Two hundred and fifty years later, Alfred North Whitehead would describe the intellectual tool of insight as emergent through a similar process, writing that

the true method of discovery is like the flight of an aeroplane. It starts from the ground of particular observation; it makes a flight in the thin air of imaginative generalization; and it again lands for renewed observation rendered acute by rational inter-pretation. The reason for the success of this method of imaginative rationalization is that, when the method of difference fails, factors which are constantly present may yet be observed under the influence of imaginative thought. Such thought supplies the differences which the direct observation lacks, It can even play with the inconsistency; and can thus throw light on the consistent, and persistent, elements in experience by comparison with what in imagination is inconsistent with them. (Whitehead, 1978, p. 5)

Ethics Part I supplies us with a conceptual toolbox, considerations in negotiating our thinking-through both the essentials of human psy-chology and the dynamic operations of human action. These in-tellectual tools are generated in the heat stoked between two currents of thought. We are already prepared for the first, as it culminates in behavioral observation of projective identification; and concerns opinionated distortions of thought linked both to human dread and belief in narcissistic omnipotence masquerading as truth, the very ideas that will follow *Ethics* through Part V and later inform hu-manistic psychoanalysis (Weiss, 1952; Fromm, 1964a, 1964b).

The second is in the transformation of ancient and medieval philosophical categories into tools for clearly structured, modern inquiry in the human sciences. These begin as ambiguously as the Hebrew Bible's *In the beginning*, not as a given point in time, but as the beginning of creative process in contemplation of God's infinity. So too, does Spinoza's philosophical recognition of God's *substance*, plunk the reader into a Deleuzian *middle* (Deleuze, 1988, p. 129); because under Spinoza's reckoning, full knowledge of God's infinity is impossible (I P11, Schol). As if contemplating what is fully impossible to contemplate were not difficult enough, Spinoza adds the additional dimension of language: when he writes *God,* he means *Nature.* Spinoza explains to his correspondent, Henry Oldenburg, of London's Royal Society that

> I do not differentiate between God and Nature in the way all those known to me have done. (Spinoza, 2002, Letter 6, p. 776)

Indeed, the significant fact of *Ethics* Part I might be interpreted as the fallacy in human construction of God in our own image, our anthropocentric opinions.

In the beginning of Part I is God's *substance,*

> by substance I mean that which is in itself and is conceived through itself; that is, that the conception of which does not require the conception of another thing from which it has to be formed. (I. Definition 3, p. 217)

If substance as God or Nature is eternal, unknowable in its self-generated fullness, derivative aspects of the Eternal are knowable as *attributes*, parallel qualities of *thought* and *extension*. Building upon medieval philosophical inquiry into divine attributes, explored by Hasdai Crescas, a 15th-century Jewish philosopher cited by Spinoza (Spinoza, 2002, letter 12, p. 791; also, Harvey, 1998; Wolfson, 1916), but reduced to two dimensions under the Cartesian focus upon *thought* and *extension*, Spinoza provides clinicians with twinned conceptual fields (as well as their relationships with one another) made clinically explicit through WR Bion's psychoanalytic study of thinking, three hundred years later (Bion, 1962).

As Spinoza explains to Henry Oldenburg, he defines God

> as a being consisting of infinite attributes, each of which is infinite or supremely perfect in its own kind. Here it should

be observed that by attribute I mean every thing that is conceived in itself and through itself, so that its conception does not involve the conception of any other thing. For example, extension is conceived through itself and in itself, but not so motion; for the latter is conceived in something else, and its conception involves extension. (Spinoza, 2002, Letter 2, pp. 762–763; also I.P11)

Attributes are fundamental natural functions partaking of Nature's substance, which we have seen is similarly

in itself and is conceived through itself; that is, that the conception of which does not require the conception of another thing from which it has to be formed. (I. Definition 3, p. 217)

But, just as attributes are fundamentally linked to the substance of Nature,

all the attributes it possesses have always been in it simultaneously and one could not have been produced by another; but each expresses the reality or being of substance. (I. Proposition 10, Scholium, p. 221)

Recognizing that each entity, everything, must be "conceived under some attribute" (I. Proposition 10, Scholium, p. 222) some dimension of its being, Spinoza affirms the bold Aristotelian project of searching for greater perfection,[14] writing that,

the greater the degree of reality that belongs to the nature of a thing, the greater amount of energy it has for existence.[15] (I. Proposition 11, Scholium, p. 223)

Applying this idea therapeutically, we recognize that our clinical work generates greater and greater articulations of differentiated thought, allowing both therapist and patient the developing appreciation of her psychological reality (Bollas, 2006). This includes, of course, the progressive correction of earlier, distorted, and unformulated ideas.

At this point, with the inclusion of my own therapeutic parallels to Spinoza's Part I, it would be prudent to comment on another clinical concept that becomes necessary in reading Spinoza, the idea of *containment*. The containment required in reading *Ethics* concerns the terrific jostling of complex ideas, linked to its complicated presentational form rather than the intrapsychic and interpersonal anxieties generated in the consultation room. Addressing the reader's perplexities early in Part II, Spinoza adopts a therapeutic stance, encouraging the reader to proceed with him slowly, step by step in testing his thinking,

> at this point our readers will no doubt find themselves in some difficulty and will think of many things that will give them pause. So I ask them to proceed slowly step by step with me, and to postpose judgment until they have read to the end. (II. Proposition 11, Scholium, pp. 250–251)

But, in order to contain, one must also negotiate the clarities and confusions of 115 different segments in Part I, both repetitive of earlier points, and elaborative. Part of the difficulty bedeviling 20th-century psychoanalytic writers on *Ethics* is the sheer vastness of Spinoza's generated thought. Juggling these into cohesive form approaches the ease of herding cats. Each reader of *Ethics* must determine her own compass points, and contain the items, as Wolfson tells us, as they begin to cluster into larger formations, not unlike the process of discovery narrated by Spinoza himself and elaborated by Whitehead, itself impressionistic and intuitive (Whitehead, 1978, p. 5; Wolfson, 1934, p. 4). The reading of *Ethics'* scholia as the whispering of such underlying coherence facilitates interpretation of our clinical psychological viewpoint.

Substance and its attributes are exemplary of causal relationship in Spinoza's presentation. Substance operates as a particular kind of terminus, self-formed and self-originating, behind which we can discern nothing else. Philosophers know this condition as the *first cause* (I. Definition 3, p. 217; I. P28, Schol, p. 232), following which all causation is termed, *efficient* or *proximate*.[16] Clinically, our judgments of causality are based on efficient cause: that which best satisfies explanation of the empirical outcome. This process of explanation works backward, both in Spinoza's understanding and from our clinical perspective, from behavioral effect to the most likely efficient cause. We know from clinical process that what is originally hypothesized as causal relative to our patients' distress becomes subject to change, elaboration and subtraction through dyadic process, as the constructively interpretative process of analysis moves toward what Spinoza and philosophers before him, termed "a greater perfection", the more refined rational understanding of specific, efficient causality.[17]

Cleverly, Spinoza deploys *substance* and its *attributes*, thought and extension, as his first pivot toward later recognition of projective identification. Passionately, he focuses upon those who are convinced in their substitution of fictive certainty for inquiry, writing that

> they neither distinguish between the modification of substances and substances themselves, nor do they know how things are produced. (I. Proposition 8, Scholium 2, p. 220)

Arrogant in our projective claims, we confuse the substantive with its modified forms in the attributes of thinking and extension. This dynamic relationship of substance to its own modified forms illustrates the essential process psychology underlying Spinozan thought. Within human psychology, the relation of substance and its modifications will be paralleled by the idea of what is essential or necessary to the person, so shared by each of us as in the *one genus* postulate of Sullivan (1953, pp. 32–33), in relation to the accidents or traumata which befall us: the latter being the particular experiences that shape our becoming who we are.

By contrast, human ignorance is reflected by those who, after the tales of Ovid, an ancient author quoted by Spinoza in Part III,

> without any hesitation they imagine trees as well as men talking and stones as well as men being formed from seeds; indeed, any forms whatsoever are imagined to change into other forms. So too, those who confuse the divine nature with human nature easily ascribe to God human emotions, especially so long as they are ignorant of how the latter are produced in the mind. (I. Proposition 8, Scholium 2, p. 220)

Spinoza here describes a narrow range of what we would term *fantasy*, shared consensually within social groups. His recognition is that such imagination, while creatively generative,[18] does not represent the truth which it imputes to itself. Instead, Spinoza proposes transition from this anthropomorphic concept of God to an early scientific conception of human action subordinate to the vastness and indivisibility of Nature (I. Proposition 13. Scholium).

Spinoza's argument in Part I is that Nature is eternal and infinite, requiring only itself in its own creation. Nature, by doing what it does (*Natura Naturans*) creates a hierarchy of living things (*Natura Naturata*) through the attributes of thought and extension, wherein we locate the determined nature of human beings, with every finite generation resulting from the preceding generation's efficient causation within a chain of transmission (I. Proposition 11, Scholium, p. 223; I. Proposition 29, Scholium, p. 234). At the same time, this modern conception of natural systemic function is opposed to the common anthropocentric fallacy construing God from within the mind's imaginings. In this regard, Spinozan influence in the early development of psychoanalysis is limited. Theoretical corrections of anthropomorphic representation within psychoanalytic thought and action are only attempted a century into its conceptual development (Grossman & Simon, 1969; Schafer, 1976, 1999).

Again and again in Part I, Spinoza accentuates the emergence of conceptual tools including *substance*, *essence*, *thought*, and *extension* in relation to Nature's laws, arrayed in contrast to the errors of anthropocentric opinion. His pursuit is relentless, arguing against the impossibility that Nature might be apprehended "in the likeness of man, consisting of mind and body, subject to passions" (I. Proposition 15, Scholium, p. 224). At the same time, the reader is encouraged to reach beyond current opinion toward greater perfection in rational thinking, to recognize that "whatever is" in the natural, living world, is in Nature, under its abiding and determinative laws, inconceivable outside of Nature (I. Proposition 15, Scholium, pp. 224–225).

As Spinoza's ideas surface, they are recursively joined with earlier ideas; and these conjunctions are carried forward both as elaboration and as difference. For example, returning to the idea of

Nature's unity in that "absolute infinite substance is indivisible" (I. Proposition 13, p. 224), Spinoza rejects a partial, finite view of any of Nature's dimensions, despite our human capability to imagine such a position. Extending this notion to clinical inquiry, as Rathbun (1934) and Weiss (1952) recognize, our capability to focus on small details, discrete dynamics, must not confuse the dynamically alive fabric of the whole, functioning individual within the systemic fabric of the universe.

The essay form of Spinoza's scholium both constructs and disrupts. Disruption is achieved in the manner clinically discerned by Ferenczi and Rank (1923, p. 9), in piercing the fixity of narcissistic belief. As Spinoza will explain dynamically in Part III, such negation of a fixed idea engenders doubt, itself undermining certainty. His illustrative examples range vividly from the mathematical or geometrical to the fanciful (for example, I. Proposition 15, Scholium; I Proposition 17, Scholium). Oddly, this persuasive dimension of Spinoza's presentation goes unnoted by commentators of Spinoza's psychoanalytic foreshadowing. Yet, the persuasive, ironic, force of these examples reminds the reader of Freud's own stylistic power as essayist (Freud, 1890; Miller & Sweet, 2018). For example, arguing against our misguided anthropomorphism relative to conceptions of God, Spinoza writes that this is

> just like one who, having made the supposition that a circle has the properties of a square, deduces therefrom that a circle does not have a center from which all lines drawn to the circumference are equal. (I. Proposition 15, Scholium, p. 226)

Returning again to geometric analogy in arguing that natural laws themselves are enduring, he suggests the absurdity of attempting to prove either that a triangle's three angles are not equal to two right angles, or that a given cause does not give rise to a specified effect (I. Proposition 17, Scholium, p. 228).

Approaching the same target from another angle, Spinoza observes that our "natural inclination to divide quantity" through imagination distorts the fact of Nature's infinity, "one and indivisible" (I. Proposition 15, Scholium, p. 227). Bringing an example from 17th-century chemistry, the reader is reminded of the relentless progression of science. For Spinoza is correct in his present historical moment that water droplets are divisible, but that the material nature of water is not. A century later however, his argument will collapse under Henry Cavendish's discovery of water's chemical composition, H2O! (I. Proposition 15, Scholium, p. 227).

Shifting gears to distortion in our use of language, Spinoza argues that our imaginative construction of God or Nature in our own image "could be no more alike than the celestial constellation of the Dog and the dog that barks" (I. Proposition 17, p. 229).[19] Just as earlier, Spinoza observes the disconnect between our imaginative capability to divide whole objects into parts and the actual facts of Nature, here, he gestures to the confusions of language, instrumental in distorting thought. A dog is a dog is a dog just as a rose is a rose is a rose (Stein, 1913); except when they are not. Symbolic meaning must be differentiated from material meaning. Just because we imagine it, it may not be so, underlying Spinoza's agreement with Freud's later *reality principle* (Federn, 1915).

Continuing his argument on Nature's eternality in the Scholium at Proposition 19, Spinoza points out that the reader might find an alternative proof to the one supplied by Spinoza in his earlier work, *Descartes's Principles of Philosophy*, dismissing further "need here to go over that ground again" (I. Proposition 19, Scholium, p. 230). Momentarily, his argument rests completed.

As *Ethics* Part I proceeds to its Appendix conclusion, Spinoza's pace seems to accelerate, setting out layered conceptual tools that foreshadow later considerations in Part II. Considering the nature of a "finite thing with determined existence" (I. Proposition 28, Scholium, p. 232) such as the human being, he reaffirms efficient or proximate causation, observing that such an entity

> cannot exist or be determined to act unless it be determined to exist and to act by another cause which is also finite and has a determinate existence, and this cause again cannot exist or be determined to act unless it be determined to exist and to act by another cause which is also finite and has a determinate existence, and so ad infinitum. (I. Proposition 28, p. 233)[20]

Affirming that Nature or God is "absolutely the proximate cause of things produced from him", a chain of intergenerational transmission is imagined, proceeding from Nature in the creation of primary things which themselves become the medium for the next iteration of such entities, with the first in a causal chain engendering the next.

The reader is now positioned to glimpse a foreshadowing of *Ethics* Part III in the intertwining of Propositions 29, 30, and 31. First, Spinoza articulates the strict, determinist relation between *Natura naturans* (*that which is in itself, and is conceived by itself*) and *Natura naturata*[21] (*all that follows from the necessity of God's nature*) (I. Proposition 29, Scholium, p. 234).

Next, Proposition 30 claims that

> the finite intellect in act or the infinite intellect in act must comprehend the attributes of God and the affections of God, and nothing else. (p. 234)

Here is the linkage in comprehension, to deterministic action. All action, according to Spinoza, is subordinate to God's attributes and affections. With Proposition 31, Spinoza states too, that the human actions of will, desire, and love, are related to *Natura Naturata*. In the same moment, the reader glimpses the link between infinite Nature and the humanly finite, expressed in the philosophic language of the *intellect*. Continuing, Proposition 31 claims

> The intellect in act, whether it be finite or infinite, as also will, desire, love, etc, must be related to *Natura naturata*, not to *Natura naturans*.

Continuing in the scholium to I.P31, Spinoza writes,

> the reason for my here speaking of the intellect in act is not that I grant that there can be any intellect in potentiality, but that, wishing to avoid any confusion, I want to confine myself to what we perceive with the utmost clarity, to wit, the very act of understanding, than which nothing is more clearly apprehended by us. For now we can understand nothing that does not lead to

a more perfect cognition of the understanding. (I. Proposition 31, Scholium, p. 235)

Our clearest apprehension is in the *act of understanding*; and in this apprehension, we necessarily proceed a step along the path of greater perfection within our understanding! For the moment, given the high enthusiasm of this recognition, along with Spinoza, the reader can be forgiven for not reckoning with the possibility, given our capacity for imagination, for distortion in understanding, and so, a backward step toward lesser perfection. Spinoza will have more to say about this later.

Such recognition in reading illustrates the momentary *illumination* referred to by Deleuze in the reader's recognition of herself, as if in flash, as a Spinozist (p. 129). For clinicians, this is recognizable within the repetitive method and rhythm of therapy (Civitarese, 2008), in the singularity of the intuitive moment, itself a building block in the developing experience of psychotherapy as a succession of clear and hard-won understandings, transforming across time (Miller & Sweet, 2018).[22]

Continuing on, Spinoza explains the meaning of *will,* proposing that "will cannot be called a free cause, but only a necessary cause" (I. Proposition 32, page 235). He explains, by proof, that

> Will, like intellect, is only a definite mode of thinking, and so (Pr 28) no single volition can exist or be determined to act unless it is determined by another cause, and this cause again by another, and so ad infinitum. Now if will be supposed infinite, it must also be determined to exist and to act by God, not insofar as he is absolutely infinite substance, but insofar as he possesses an attribute which expresses the infinite and eternal essence of Thought (Pr 23). Therefore, in whatever way will is conceived whether finite or infinite, it requires a cause by which it is determined to exist and to act; and so (Def 7.) it cannot be said to be a free cause, but only a necessary or constrained cause. (I. Proposition 32, Proof, p. 235)

The clinical reader now remembers Freud's remark about Spinoza's *mode* of thought. And considers, juggling all these conceptual terms, tools for thought, how we begin: (1) with Nature's infinite *substance*; (2) expressed as an *attribute* (*thought and extension*), (3) expressed further as a *mode*, such as will or intellect, within thinking.

Writing of this orderly hierarchy wherein *will* and *intellect* are themselves necessary modes of the intrinsic natural attributes, thought and extension, Spinoza moves toward the conclusion of Part I with Proposition 33, expressing in modern terms, "it is what it is". The proposition simply states, "Things could not have been produced by God in any other way or in any other order than is the case" (p. 235).

But there is more work to be done, more thinking to be extended. Spinoza illustrates a clear binary that clinicians apprehend intuitively. He differentiates between the necessary and the impossible, writing

> since I have here shown more clearly than the midday sun that in things there is absolutely nothing by virtue of which they can be said to be 'contingent'; but I must first deal with 'necessary' and 'impossible' (I. Proposition 33. Scholium 1, p. 236)

Spinoza explains further that by "contingent", he means only that "the chain of causes is hidden from us". Therefore, a thing is or is not. But clinically, things are not so clear because the Spinozan definition of contingent describes the discursive and emotional ground upon which we often function. Here, we might refer to the Kleinian Paranoid/Schizoid position relative to the Depressive position. In-between the pure conception of the P/S and the pure conception of the D, we have Bion's notation of the P/S in its transient movements toward D (Miller & Sweet, 2018). Experientially, whether as registered by the patient or as observed by the therapist, these are lived, often confused moments of Spinozan contingency. Complete understanding, as in the resolution after a period of mourning, represents clear arrival at the Spinozan "impossible". Where love once was as necessity, the mourner traverses the middle ground of loss, so elegantly detailed by Freud (1917), only to arrive at an impossibility: one's love has gone, if not the memory of having loved and having been loved. Clinically, the Spinozan clarity between necessity and impossibility highlights the process between initial presentation and therapeutic resolution; whereas contingency as lived experience in clinical practice really does represent the excluded middle.

Finally, in the last proposition before the Appendix, Spinoza leaves the reader with food for thought, that, "nothing exists from whose nature an effect does not follow" (I. Proposition 26, p. 238).

Clinically, this proposition echoes Lou Andreas-Salomé's attention to multiple connections. It is the nature of interpersonal engagement that effects follow, both from individual participants and from their interactions. However, for Spinoza, this is affirmed through a proof in reference to the deterministic nature of Nature's system

> whatever exists expresses God's nature or essence in a definite and determinate way (Cor. Pr 25). That is (Pr 34), whatever exists expresses God's power, which is the cause of all things, in a definite and determinate way, and so (Pr 16), some effect must follow from it. (I. Proposition 36, Proof, p. 238)

This is a wonderful stepping off point toward Part II; and reflects the conceptual tools generated through Part I as proximate in causing the effects of thinking, detailed in Part II. But first, a momentary detour to the Appendix, where Spinoza's forward-looking argument against the fallacy of our anthropocentrism, finds dynamic expression in the depiction of projective identification with which we began this essay, beginning with our own anxious perplexity at all the good things with which we, as a species, have been provided.

Notes

1 Whitehead's process or *organic* philosophy, anticipating Bion's psychoanalytic terminology of preconception en route to realization with the idea of "prehension" en route to consolidation of an "actual entity", extends Spinozan 17th-century monism through 20th-century mathematics and science (Whitehead, 1978). Whitehead suggests two "species" of prehension: (1) the "positive", which will inhere in the "actual entity as felt" or "objectified for that subject"; and (2) the "negative", which is the "definite exclusion of that item from positive contribution to the subject's own real internal constitution" (Whitehead, 1978, p. 41), that is, that which is "not" in contrast to what "is", the "not-me" in contrast to "me" in Sullivanian terms (Sullivan, 1953, p. 161).

2 Rereading *Ethics* through the lens of a different translator (Spinoza, 2002), I realized that this cloud image had vanished! However, the second version offered what would prove to be a very useful footnote, directing me to Maimonides' *Guide of the Perplexed*. I was reminded that translation itself,

within the receptive history of ideas, is a vehicle for understanding; and that had I not encountered that first translation, it is likely that an idea which would become significant to me, linking Spinoza with algorithmic method in clinical psychoanalysis, might not have occurred in the same way.

3 Stern (2013) brilliantly elaborates Maimonides' interpretive layering of parables, recognizing too, the vivid imagery of this particular scriptural interpretation.

4 Perhaps the most striking developments in this regard are the findings of behavioral economics in application to politics and corporate utility, as in (1) the recent political controversies over Cambridge Analytica (Lapovsky, 2019) and (2) the monetization of unobserved, daily behavior in the service of corporate gain, through "surveillance capitalism" (Zuboff, 2021). In each of these instances, the formerly private psychoanalytic *unconscious* through data aggregation, has become the wealthy center of manipulative predation.

5 By generating dynamic consolidations of commonly observed character traits and behavioral attitudes (III. Proposition 18, Scholium 2 through III. Proposition 59), Spinoza provides data to support my construction. Underlying such observations is a generalizable clinical matrix or algorithm, much like Bion's, indeterminate or cloudy in immediate, interpretive discernment of particular conditions (Miller & Sweet, 2018).

6 Maimonides, for example, precedes Spinoza in describing the psyche as a singularity, itself operative only through the conjunction of five functional categories, received and transformed from Aristotle's original formulation. He writes

by the word 'parts', however, they do not intend to imply that the soul is divided into parts as are bodies, but they merely enumerate the different activities of the soul as being parts of a whole, the union of which makes up the soul.

(Gorfinkle, 1912, p. 38)

7 Similar to the *doubling* referenced above in Maimonides, Deleuze comments on Spinoza's doubling in the very character of his writing, with linear surface description through which the *broken* essays disclose "a second version underneath the first, expressing all the angers of the heart and setting forth the practical theses of denunciation and liberation" (1988, p. 29). Deleuze clarifies further, in a footnote, noting that it was common early modern procedure to conceal unorthodox arguments. He cites Bayles' dictionary as a later example. David Ruderman observes that a similarly equivocal voice had been common among Jewish intellectuals during the Renaissance, "cultural intermediaries" (2004, p. 10) bridging gentile and Jewish worlds. Additionally, multi-leveled communications, concealing as much as revealing, have long been a rhetorical tool (Zagorin, 1990), especially under the harsh press of societal persecution (Strauss, 1952).

8 However in the more generalized development of psychoanalysis from its classical origins to its contemporary vernacular expression (Miller, 2016), such leisure, play, and generative creativity is frequently encountered. Reading H.A.

Wolfson's dynamic formulation of the Spinozan 'apperceptive mass', the reader becomes immediately mindful of the late clinical consolidations of W.R. Bion in his Tavistock and Italian seminar series (Bion, 2005a, 2005b). Bion's descriptions of "intuitive speculation" through the illumination of creatively conjoined 'wild thoughts' conveys a process of imagination, feeling, and self-generated reflection in relation to the perceived object (the patient) much in the way that Wolfson describes his perceptual, feeling, imagination, and reasoning, relative to Spinoza as inquiry's object.

9   Adler (2012) comments on Spinoza's reception of Galileo's thought through reading the *Sefer Elim* of Joseph Delmedigo, a peripatetic rabbi and physician, himself a student of Galileo, whose work was published in Amsterdam, by the press of Menasseh ben Israel, one of the three rabbis in Spinoza's Talmud Torah congregation. Spinoza's personal library contained this volume (Offenberg, 1973).

10 When Spinoza was 8 years old, the heresy, ostracization by the Amsterdam *Ma'amad*, and resultant suicide of a *New Jew*, Uriel de Costa, gripped the Amsterdam Jewish community It has been observed that part of de Costa's tragedy was related to his disillusionment that 17th-century Jewish practice differed greatly from his idealized conception of biblical law, imaginatively elaborated from conversos' fragmentary oral histories and inversions of Catholic conceptions of the "Law of Moses" (Feuer, 1957, pp. 235–236; Fisher, 2020, p. 28).

11 At the same time that Spinoza was issued the ban of separation from the community, at the age of 22 in 1654, the physician Juan de Prado, was also ostracized for similar reasons. Complications involved both Prado's and Spinoza's effective challenge not only toward religious doctrine but also toward the administrative authority of the *Ma'amad*, or lay, governing body of the synagogue (Kaplan, 1989; Nadler 1999).

Contrasting the situation of Prado and Spinoza, Kaplan observes that Prado's "situation was an extremely serious one. Unlike the young Spinoza who had been born in Amsterdam, knew the local vernacular, and had found a place for himself in non-Jewish circles that displayed an interest in his scholarship and views, Prado—more than half of whose life lay behind him—had no roots in Holland and only a very tenuous economic basis on which to eke out an existence" (Kaplan, 1989, p. 135).

12 For example, Constance Rathbun comments that

The object of these methods is identical; to strengthen the ego, to modify the super-ego, to bring as much of the unconscious material into consciousness as is possible, and so to enable the individual to achieve a satisfactory adjustment to reality through insight into his own character. (Rathbun, 1934, p. 13)

13 In part, James writes,

The great snare of the psychologist is the confusion of his own standpoint with that of the mental fact about which he is making his report. ... The psychologist, as we remarked above (p. 183) stands outside of the mental state he speaks of. Both itself and its object are objects for him. (James, 1981, p. 195)

Here, the reader recognizes James' Spinoza-like recognition of the doubled mental state under observation with "both itself and its objects" operating as conjoined.

14 Martha Nussbaum observes in relation to clarification of distortion that

> Recognition of error is intimately related to the grasp of truth. Thus philosophical procedure tends in its very nature to make things better, given this diagnosis of the problem. Of course, each patient must see her errors, and the truth individually. (Nussbaum, 1994, p. 34)

15 As a precursor notion to Freud's mechanistic idea of "psychic energy", Spinoza's presents *conatus* or the intrinsic human power of self-preservative striving, our ability to exist. For Spinoza, such power transforms classical philosophy's conception of "virtue", reorienting the judgmental divide between virtue and vice to the contemplation of dynamic psychological mechanisms. He writes, "By virtue and power I mean the same thing (IV. Definitions, 8, p. 323). Referencing description of *conatus* at III, Proposition 7, Spinoza continues, "virtue, insofar as it is related to man, is man's very essence, or nature, insofar as he has power to bring about that which can be understood solely through the laws of his own nature" (IV. Definitions, 8, p. 323).

16 While psychotherapists might have little acquaintance with *efficient cause*, it was well-known within medieval philosophy. Maimonides' *Eight Chapters*, for example, a primer on ethics harmonizing rabbinic and Aristotelian thinking, assumes knowledge of efficient cause. Writing about the unique mental forms within different animals, a topic also addressed by Spinoza in *Ethics* (II. Proposition 13, Scholium). Efficient causation results in the fact that, "each species has its own characteristic soul distinct from every other, with the result that there necessarily arises from each soul activities peculiar to itself" (Gorfinkle, 1912, p. 40).

17 Later, we shall see that this distinction between first and efficient causality, together with the difference between Spinoza's monism and Freud's dualism, are two areas of difference in reading Spinoza today as critique of classical psychoanalysis.

The Freudian idea of libido locates motivation "behind" the efficient Spinozan cause of *conatus* or self-preservative psychological striving. While both Freud and Spinoza would agree upon Freud's mobilization of Hughlings Jackson's premise of dependent concomitance (Grossman, 1992) in which the function of a parallel system such as mind, depends upon the fact of another system, such as body, Freud's embodied libido (even before the dualistic expansion of libido into two drives, of loving and destroying) proclaims a physical starting-point, imputing a biologized first cause. Libido, of course, is just as speculative (and Latinized) a motivational idea as *conatus*: and indeed, both

M. Hamblin Smith (1925) and Erich Fromm (1964b), find Spinoza's *conatus* as human striving, preferable in its greater generality.

Benjamin Wolstein's late 20th-century reinterpretation of ego as consolidating and internalizing the effects of interpersonal relations, both reorients the physical origins of the Freudian ego and instantiates the privacy of the self against a mid-century Sullivanism opposed to the uniqueness of individual experience (Wolstein, 1987). The back-and-forth action of such *going on being*, both extending toward and internalizing consequential effects of interpersonal relations, recapitulates in Wolstein's model, Spinozan demonstration of efficient cause in psychological functioning.

18 While unattributed in Part I, this reflection of fantasy content bears the imprint of Ovid, later cited by Spinoza in Part IV, Proposition 17, Scholium, p. 330.
19 This topic of homonymous terms is also addressed by Maimonides, who writes in the same vein,

> let us imagine that three dark places are illumined, one lit up by the sun shining upon it, the second by the moon, and the third by a flame. Now, in each of these places there is light, but the efficient cause in the one case is the sun, in the other the moon, and in the third the fire. So it is with sensation and its causes. In man it is the human soul, in the ass it is the soul of the ass, and in the eagle, the soul of the eagle. These sensations have, moreover, nothing in common, except the homonymous term which is applied to them. (Gorfinkle, 1912, p. 40)

20 The reader is reminded of the infinite regress in Spinoza's example of working iron in the *Treatise on the Emendation of the Intellect.*
21 Wolfson suggests "with reasonable certainty" that the natura naturans/natura naturata distinction of I P29, was derived by Spinoza from Thomas Aquinas (Wolfson, 1934, p. 254).
22 The reader is reminded too, of Maimonides' *Guide* on moments of illumination in textual study when the interior or esoteric meaning of a parable becomes clear, relative to its external or exoteric meaning (Stern, 2013, p. 42).

Chapter 7

Ethics, Part II

Definitions and Axioms

Clinical readers have prepared for the experience of *Ethics* Part II through the lens ground by Spinoza in Part I: on the one hand, clarifying our fallacy of understanding in the human projection of internal psychological processes upon the external, material world, functioning as an obstacle to rational thought; and on the other hand, clarifying the possibility of perfecting our understanding through clear focus on the lawful, deterministic, operations of Nature, expressed by Spinoza in theological language, as God.

Beginning with the Definitions and Axioms of Part II, the reader engages with Spinoza's rapid-fire provisioning of conceptual ideas foundational to psychology.[1] In this, the action of reading might be compared to a shopper's removal of an item from a well-ordered shelf, to be thrown into the disorder of a grocery cart bound for the cashier. Although the ultimate goal is to re-stock our shelves at home, that task will have to wait for later. Almost immediately in engaging with *Ethics* II, the reader registers a sense of repetition as ideas addressed earlier are restated in other contexts. The effect of this repetition is for the reader to think, "of course", as what is stated or remembered becomes affirmed again in passing, enhancing its familiarity and plausibility, much as in the generative process of therapeutic conviction. However, in the formulation of his extended thought in *Ethics*, Spinoza's claim upon the reader's attention also generates conflict and confusion.

DOI: 10.4324/9781003246404-11

This process is not unlike the therapist's gathering of a patient's narrative, with the clinician capable of integrating certain elements, while other strands are repeated and transformed, awaiting possible later integration. In the same moment that we recognize repetition, we also sense the new together with a falling away of thought, transiently generated, such that from time to time, the earlier idea must be recovered through review. A similar process occurs almost immediately, within Part II Definitions.

Spinoza's preliminary definitions begin with the idea of *body*, defined as an expressive and determinate mode, reflective of God's essence in the form of an "extended thing" (II. Definition 1, p. 244). Immediately, the reader jumps the gap between Nature itself and the human body, imbued with natural characteristics or *essence*, explained in II. Definition 2 as

> that which, when granted, the thing is necessarily posited, and by the annulling of which the thing is necessarily annulled; or that without which the thing can neither be nor be conceived, and vice versa, that which cannot be or be conceived without the thing. (II. Definition 2, p. 244)

Here is the philosophical seam that conjoins Part I with Part II, fusing the antique conception of Divine Science within the immanent facts of Natural Science,[2] represented in formal demonstration through its historical emissary, Mathematics.

Next, as if in fundamental contrast and linkage, Spinoza defines the term *idea* in a form we shall see repeated in II.Axiom 2 and II.Axiom 3, as "a conception of the mind which the mind forms because it is a thinking thing" (II. Definition 3, p. 244). That is, an idea is a necessarily subjective formation in the embodied process of the mind's thinking. Spinoza also clarifies his use of the term *conception* in an Explication, writing,

> I say "conception" rather than "perception" because the term perception seems to indicate that the Mind is passive to its object whereas conception[3] seems to express an activity of the mind. (II.Definition 3. Explication, p. 244)

Having differentiated the passive modality of perceiving from the active modality of conceiving, Spinoza proceeds with his fourth definition, now differentiating the adequacy of an idea from what will later be recognized as its partiality or inadequacy. He writes,

> by an adequate idea I mean an idea which, insofar as it is considered in itself without relation to its object, has all the properties, that is, intrinsic characteristics of a true idea. (II. Definition 4, p. 244)

He then qualifies this definition, distinguishing between what is intrinsic and what is extrinsic, with the intrinsic agreeing both with the idea itself and that "of which it is an idea" (II. Definition 4, Explication, p. 244).

Already confused, the reader experiences panic; and consults his psychic grocery list to see what is present and what is not. Reviewing only the first four of Part II's seven Definitions, generates the following conjunction: (1) of a body, imbued with the essential aliveness of nature; (2) of a mind dependent upon body, necessarily generative both of thinking as process and of ideas as contents; (3) of the mind's active capability in generating conceptions together with its passive, receptive capability in registering perceptions; and (4) of the adequacy or completeness of any given idea in relation to its intrinsically generated object of thought.

Beginning with these Definitions of *Ethics* Part II, Spinoza generates a model of process-psychology complete with the dependent concomitance of mind upon body. Within mind are intrinsic processes of thinking always engaged with discrete objects-of-thinking. These properties operate together with perceptual receptivity, as the mind's gateway to the body's external relations. And, in application to this entire system in portraying the true nature of mind, the question of an ideas' adequacy or inadequacy gestures to the development of psychology not only as a conceptual field but also as rational practice, discerning clarity from confusion and fragmentary, deformed, emotion-imbued thought.

If *definition* concerns what a thing is, then an *axiom* extends definition more broadly to a generally recognized fact or law. As the reader shifts from Spinoza's Definitions to the Axioms of Part II, the 21st century reader remembers that even in Spinoza's time, contemporary readers were puzzled by his terminology. Henry Oldenburg, of London's Royal Society, for example, writes of Spinoza's explanations that

> your last letter did indeed shed a great deal of light for me, but not so much as to dispel all the darkness. This will, I hope, be the happy outcome when you have clearly and distinctly furnished me with your views on the true and primary origin of things. For as long as it is not quite clear to me from what cause and in what manner things began to be, and by what connection they depend on the first cause, if there be such a thing, then all that I hear and all that I read seems to me quite incoherent. (Spinoza, 2002, Letter 5, p. 767)

A letter from Spinoza's student, Simon de Vries, similarly puzzles at the difference in meaning between definition, axiom, and postulate, citing two contemporary mathematicians with conflicting views, and requesting of Spinoza that his students

> would very much like you, Sir, to write to us (if we are not giving you too much trouble and your time allows) giving your opinion on the matter, and also on the difference between axioms and definitions. (Letter 8, p. 779)

Unfortunately, from our perspective as readers, three hundred years later, Spinoza's response is similarly difficult. He replies at length

> as to the questions raised in your group (which is sensibly organized), I see that your difficulties result from your failure to distinguish between the kinds of definition. There is the definition that serves to explicate a thing whose essence alone is in question and the subject of doubt and there is the definition which is put forward simply for examination. The former, since it has a determinate object, must be a true definition, while this need not be so in the latter case. For example, if someone were to ask me for a description of Solomon's temple,[4] I ought to give him a true description, unless I propose to talk nonsense

with him. But if I have in my own mind formed the design of a
temple that I want to build, and from its description I conclude
that I will have to purchase such-and-such a site and so many
thousands of stones and other materials, will any sane person
tell me that I have reached a wrong conclusion because my
definition may be incorrect? Or will anyone demand that I prove
my definition? Such a person would simply be telling me that
I had not conceived that which in fact I had conceived, or he
would be requiring me to prove that I had conceived that which
I had conceived, which is utter nonsense. Therefore a definition
either explicates a thing as it exists outside the intellect- and
it should be a true definition, differing from a proposition or
axiom only in that the former is concerned only with the
essences of things or the essences of the affections of things,
whereas the latter has a wider scope, extending also to eternal
truths- or it explicates a thing as it is conceived by us, or can be
conceived. And in that case it also differ from an axiom and
proposition in requiring merely that it be conceived, not
conceived as true, as in the case of an axiom. (Letter 9,
pp. 781–782)

Spinoza's extended response may also be helpful to us because,
through it, we see that there are two kinds of definition. The first
describes the essence of an empirical fact, external to our thinking.
The second follows from a speculative idea in thought. The first must
be true; but not necessarily the second. Beyond this, the axiom and
proposition are broader in scope than definition, with the axiom indicative of what is true as against the proposition which is open to
questioning. Together, definition, axiom and, proposition describe a
grid ranging on the one axis, from (1) true depiction of what is factual, if external to mind to (2) conceptual description of what is
speculative; and on the other axis, from the particular to the general.
For our clinical purposes of inquiry, all categories are open to
questioning.[5]

Immediately, in encountering Spinoza's Axioms, we recognize a
difference in breadth from his Definitions. He affirms broadly, for
example, that "the essence of man does not involve necessary ex-
istence|" (II. Axiom 1, p. 244). Spinoza defines what he means, stating

that from the order of nature it can happen equally that this or that man does exist, or that he does not exist (II. Axiom 1, p. 244).

Implicit in this axiom is the step beyond omnipotent narcissism as well as a necessary reckoning with our individual contingencies. What humans share relates to all of us as a species. For the clinician, this first axiom in Part II presents a stark existential caesura. However inconceivable to each of us that we are not "necessary" within the flux of nature, we are to ourselves and others necessary, both as intergenerationally efficient effect and cause within the limited scope of our lives.

Yet, within this reduced cosmic status, Spinoza affirms some of our gifts. Primary is the dual recognition that we think and also "know that we think" (II. Axiom 2, p. 244).[6] Addressing both process and content, this axiom casts thinking as an active and transitory function of human nature; and explicitly objectifies the subjective registration of our thought processes.

Importantly, relative to psychoanalytic psychology, Spinoza observes that there are "no modes of thinking", by which he means "love, desire, or whatever is designated by the word affects of the mind" that operate independently of an object of thought. Thought does not function "unless there is in the same individual, the idea of the thing loved, desired and the like" (II. Axiom 3, p. 244). For clinical purposes, this addresses two notions. The first is that Spinoza would recognize the psychoanalytic conception of drive and object as a singularity; however, we might fractionate these two, conjoined functionalities. The reader remembers from Part I that our capability for conceptual analysis does not signal the correctness of our imagination. This is the same issue addressed by John Dewey in his holistic challenge to the piecemeal understanding of the reflex arc, the kind of atomism also derided by Lou Andreas-Salomé in her observations (Dewey, 1890; Andreas-Salomé, 1964). For Spinoza, thought-as-fact is depicted as an integration of thinking and that to which thinking is directed, a linkage of thought and object.

The second notion is that our contemporary familiarity with WR Bion's relation between preconception and realization is foreshadowed both by Spinoza and in extension of Spinozan thought, by A.N. Whitehead (1978). Whitehead's concept of "prehensions" comes close to Bion's "preconceptions", but is a function of what

Bion might call the *constant conjunction* of different relationships within Spinoza's mental operations. Their behavioral extension toward object-related action in the external world, Bion's *realization*, is provided with added-value through Whitehead's extension of Spinozan monism from internal process to external action, originally marked by Spinoza through different terms, corresponding to different contexts for similar forms of action—such as will within the internal world and its transformations as appetite and desire within the external world. Whitehead conjoins the act of Bionian realization with the meaningful experience of that act to the actor, which he terms a "superject" (Whitehead, 1978, p. 32). Both Spinoza and Whitehead view this action through the lens of process singularity, however divisible analytically into relations between multiple functions.

Elaborating the registration of emotion, Spinoza observes that "we feel a certain body (our body) to be affected in many ways" (II. Axiom 4, p. 244). The clinical reader is reminded of Paul Federn's conception of ego-feelings, themselves differently inflected embodied registrations of internal states of mind[7] (Federn 1926). While the indeterminacy between the unions of physical and psychic fields involved in thinking, feeling, and of the emotions as the dependent forms of embodied action functioning as mind, at the same time these functions might be thought of as efficient rather than as primary. That is, they are always the transformed product of earlier processes; and in this they are imprecise. Still, within these axioms, there is plenty to reckon with. Thought itself is an internal function, constructive of its outside. Spinoza recognizes that in the immediacy of perception

> We do not feel or perceive any individual things except bodies and modes of thinking. (II. Axiom 5, p. 244)

That is, mind begins with the registration of embodied experience, what Spinoza terms the *affects*. Within the functioning of mind, the individual begins to construe an external world; and through trial and error, that world becomes more greatly reliable. Today, we associate such thinking with the observation of the infant's creation and increasing differentiation of its own external world.

Propositions

The clinical reader recognizes a gap between Spinoza's Part II Axioms and Part II Propositions. Expecting from what we have read, to embark upon *Ethics'* study of mind, we are again confronted with repetition. Spinoza only begins to consider the topic of mind at II Proposition 11, which begins

> that which constitutes the actual being of the human mind is basically nothing else but the idea of an individual actually existing thing. (II. Proposition 11, p. 290)

His scholium, however, addresses the reader's perplexity, announcing that

> at this point our readers will no doubt find themselves in some difficulty and will think of many things that will give them pause. So I ask them to proceed slowly, step by step with me, and to postpone judgment until they have read to the end. (II. Proposition 11, Scholium, pp. 250–251)

To arrive at that end requires traversing: eight definitions with three explications; eleven axioms; forty-nine propositions; sixty-two proofs; nineteen corollaries; seven lemmae; six postulates; and twenty-three scholia.

Looking backward from Proposition 11, two familiar ideas emerge. The first is that by enlarging the scope of our thoughts in concordance with the external world, we arrive at greater possibilities of understanding. This recapitulates the earlier idea, that

> the greater the degree of reality that belongs to the nature of a thing, the greater amount of energy it has for existence (I. Proposition 11, Scholium, p. 223)

through the generative idea that

> the more things a thinking being can think, the more reality or perfection we conceive it to have. (II. Proposition 1, Scholium, p. 245)

As in psychotherapy, the greater the range of allowable thought in alignment with reality, the livelier is the wrestling with an idea toward its greater clarity. But Spinoza's interest here is not immediately therapeutic. Rather, he seeks to link our human capacity to conjure an infinity of ideas with Nature as itself, inclusive of thinking and extension. Yet again, as in Part I, Spinoza differentiates Nature's power from the common anthropocentric conception of earthly authority and power (II. Proposition 3, Scholium, p. 246).

The second familiar theme addresses the complexity of Spinoza's thinking, which he acknowledges as problematic, hopeful that we as readers proceed with him, "step by step". The root of this complexity. is in the consistent pattern of singular expressions containing multiple dimensions. The clinical reader recalls the difficulty of differentiating between Spinoza's geometric categories: definition, axiom, proposition, and the like. Reflecting back to his correspondence with Simon de Vries in attempting to parse a seemingly straightforward concept such as *definition* itself, we find that definition may be both factual and speculative, true or not true, depending on context. Now, too, with Proposition 7, Spinoza generates a series of illustrations beginning with a complicated idea, claiming that

> thinking substance and extended substance are one and the same, comprehended now under this attribute, now under that. (II. Proposition 7, Scholium, p. 247)

Attributing this idea to its reception from Jewish philosophy, as truth that "seems to have been glimpsed by some of the Hebrews", this notion affirms God's singularity as *intellectual cognition, intellectually cognizing subject*, and *intellectually cognized object* (Maimonides, I. 68, p. 163).[8] Spinoza immediately attempts clarification through geometric example, explaining with reference to "a circle existing in Nature and the idea of the existing circle" (II. Proposition 7, Scholium, p. 247). The contemporary clinician is familiar with this general idea, although stated very differently in W.R. Bion's distinction between a preconception and its realization, itself a transformation of A.N. Whitehead's prehension and actual entity (Whitehead, 1978, p. 40). For Spinoza, such Bionian duality is apprehended as a single thing: the concrete form of the circle representative of extension and the idea of the circle representative of thinking. Poetically describing this concept in translation from the Latin, translator Edwin Curley describes such multiplicity "as if through a cloud" (De Spinoza, 1996, II. Proposition 7, Scholium, p. 35). It is this Spinozan combination of the precise with the fleeting or transitory, that caused me to think about *Ethics'* psychological model as reflecting a *cloudy mathematics*. Spinoza recognizes the ubiquity of imprecision in relation to psychology because

> the idea that constitutes the nature of the human mind is likewise shown, when considered solely in itself, not to be clear and distinct, as is also the idea of the human mind and the ideas of affections of the human body insofar as they are related to the human mind, as everyone can easily see. (II. Proposition 28, Scholium, p. 262)

While Spinoza's psychology specifies forms of mental functionality, he is also aware of limitation in observing precise mental dynamics. Still, he is determined to demonstrate what we can appreciate through the logic of mathematics.

Immediately following this proposition, and with the geometric image of the circle still within the reader's thinking, Spinoza proposes that

> the ideas of nonexisting individual things or modes must be comprehended in the infinite idea of God in the same way that formal essences of individual things or modes are contained in the attributes of God. (II. Proposition 8, p. 248)

The modern reader is jarred momentarily back to *Ethics* Part I, with the wresting of Nature from theology. Under this seemingly regressive pull, a certain disappointment infuses our reading until, reading again, we recognize that Spinoza has just affirmed the idea of mind's limitless unconscious domain. What had felt initially to be a confusion leading to "lesser perfection" shifts upon this recognition into clarifying the infinite range of "greater perfection". Spinoza elaborates again through the geometric illustration of the circle. This image stirs immediate clinical resonance in relation to the mind's wresting of consciousness from unconscious psychic presence.[9]

Spinoza's geometric illustration, complete with diagram, is very clear. The example begins in that (1)

> The nature of a circle is such that the rectangles formed from the segments of its intersecting chords are equal. Hence an infinite number of equal rectangles are contained in a circle, but none of them can be said to exist except insofar as it is comprehended in the idea of the circle.

Spinoza continues, (2) by showing that

> Now of this infinite number of intersecting chords, let two, E and D, exist. Now indeed their ideas also exist not only insofar as they are merely comprehended in the idea of the circle but also insofar as they involve the existence of those rectangles, with the result that they are distinguished from the other ideas of the other rectangles. (II. Proposition 8, Scholium, p. 248)

In effect, Spinoza has just led the reader through a thought experiment, demonstrating the fact of unconscious ideas. First, he points out the unlimited range of thoughts contained within a specific thought; and next, designates two specific members of this unlimited range in relation (1) to the original thought, (2) to one another and (3) to all other unlimited thoughts. Clinically, this is as if interpretation "A" and interpretation "B" are drawn as significant from the flux of patient associations. While relating to the full scope of the patient's thoughts, "A" and "B" are also related to one other; with the additional notion that the presence of "A" and "B" does not limit the scope of interpretive range: indeed, that range remains wide-open, subject to further inquiry, formation, and reformation as inquiry proceeds. This process is implied in WR Bion's clinical algorithm, resulting in discernable, if transitory, interpretive positions throughout clinical process (Miller & Sweet, 2018).

Next, Spinoza again locates the individual living thing, the person, in a historical chain of causality (II. Proposition 9). Further, he returns to the question of the essence of man in relation to God (II. Proposition 10). This time, however, Spinoza's argument pertains to his own unique manner of philosophizing, later noted by Lou Andreas-Salomé. He contrasts his systemic approach, beginning with God and continuing in respect to human psychology with other philosophical schemes, observing others'

> failure to observe the proper order of philosophical inquiry. For the divine nature, which they should have considered before all else- it being prior both in cognition and in Nature- they have taken to be last in the order of cognition, and the things that are called objects of sense they have taken as prior to everything. Hence it has come about that in considering natural phenomena, they have completely disregarded the divine nature. (II. Proposition 10, Scholium, pp. 249–250)

Spinoza concludes this scholium in recognition that

> when thereafter they turned to the contemplation of the divine nature, they could find no place in their thinking for those fictions on which they had built their natural science, since these fictions were of no avail in attaining knowledge of the divine nature. So it is little wonder that they have contradicted themselves on all sides. (II. Proposition 10, Scholium, p. 250)

Introducing the Mind

Having formally affirmed the uniqueness of his inquiry, locating the human, whose mental functioning we seek to understand, within the larger domain of Nature, Spinoza sets out to teach the reader how to think practically about psychology. Toward this end, he generates an elemental working model of mind that proceeds: (1) from the idea of mind itself, animated through self-preservative willing; (2) to perception of self and others; and (3) through our representational capability for generating mental images, to the functionality of imagination. Founded on these considerations, Spinoza will later introduce the concepts of association, cognitive error, symbolic functioning, and the nature of human will.

The reader, together with Spinoza, has already observed that the mind, in its actuality, "is basically nothing else but the idea of an individual actually existing thing" (II. Proposition 11, p. 250). Mind is not brain; but rather, itself a functional concept dependent and responsive to the body which is also its object. Mind is reflexively self-perceptive such that

> whatever happens in the object of the idea constituting the human mind is bound to be perceived by the human mind; i.e., the idea of the thing will necessarily be in the human mind. That is to say, if the object of the idea constituting the human mind is a body, nothing can happen in that body without its being perceived by the mind. (II. Proposition 12, p. 251)

Necessarily, mind is integrated with its bodily object, which, following Spinoza's systemic formulation is itself "a definite mode of extension actually existing and nothing else" (II. Proposition 13, p. 251). In modern language, the functionality of mind conforms to the notion of dependent concomitance, also adopted by Freud (Grossman, 1992). Spinoza observes that this generality extends not only to human function, but also to the functioning of other animate species; and that to understand the union of body and mind "adequately or distinctly", we must first gain "adequate knowledge of the nature of our body" (II. Proposition 13, Scholium, p. 251).

Spinoza recognizes variation between different bodies, minds, and mental ideas, observing that

> we cannot deny too, that ideas differ among themselves as do their objects, and that one is more excellent and contains more reality than another, just as the object of one idea is more excellent than that of another and contains more reality. (II. Proposition 13, Scholium, p. 252)

The reader will recall Spinoza's earlier ideas related to an idea's relative integration with reality, similar to Freud's notion of the Reality Principle (I. Proposition 11, Scholium, p. 235; II. Proposition 1, Scholium, p. 245). In the present example, he contrasts the human mind with other species' mental functioning, noting that such study requires scientific knowledge of the bodies under comparison.[10]

Spinoza now considers the general qualities of bodies including: motion, rest, and speed (II. Proposition 13, Scholium, Axioms 1 and 2, p. 252); how bodies are affected by other bodies (II. Proposition 13, Corollary, Axioms 1 and 2, p. 253); and importantly, how the formal structure of the body is maintained despite change, such that

> if from a body, or an individual thing composed of a number of bodies, certain bodies are separated, and at the same time a like number of other bodies of the same nature take their place, the individual thing will retain its nature as before, without any change in its form. (II. Propodition 13, Lemma 4, p. 254)

Not only does the clinical reader think of the physical constancy of bodily function, but also of constancies both in forms of societal action and in individual character formation. Spinoza approaches bodily complexity from what today we would term a *systems perspective*, noting that

> we can now see how a composite individual can be affected in many ways and yet preserve its nature. Now previously we have conceived an individual thing composed solely of bodies distinguished from one another only by motion-and-rest and speed of movement; that is, an individual thing composed of the simplest bodies. If we now conceive another individual thing composed of several individual things of different natures, we shall find that this can be affected in many other ways while still preserving its nature. For since each one of its parts is composed of several bodies, each single part can therefore (preceding Lemma) without any change in its nature, move with varying degrees of speed and consequently communicate its own motion to other parts with varying degrees of speed. Now if we go on to conceive a third kind of individual things composed of this second kind, we shall find that it can be affected in many other ways without any change in form. (II. Proposition 13, Scholium 2, pp. 254–255)

In this way, Spinoza conceives not only individual and social functioning, but also Nature itself as a singular system,

> one individual whose parts- that is, all the constituent bodies-vary in infinite ways without any change in the individual as a whole. (II. Proposition 13, Scholium 2, pp. 254–255)

Having established not only individual, but also social and systemic functioning of multiple bodies, both evolving through change while maintaining certain formal constancies, Spinoza turns to the question of how the mind apprehends this changing world through determination by its own body. He writes

> if the human body is affected in a way that involves the nature of some external body, the human mind will regard that same external body as actually existing, or as present to itself, until the human body undergoes a further modification which excludes the existence or presence of the said body. (II. Proposition 17, p. 256)

Spinoza, without qualifying, moves from the physical domain of perception, of registration by the mind of bodily affection, to apperception, the field of interpretation based upon perceptual data. Such interpretation risks distortion, when the memory of experience no longer conforms to the ongoing existence of its remembered object.

Spinoza's illustration is important for contemporary clinicians. While it aims toward the mind's capacity for memory as well as the principle of doubt which he will expand later, it locates squarely an enduring difficulty in interpersonal relations, labeled the *psychologist's fallacy* relative to William James' pairing of researcher and subject in the 19th century psychological laboratory, substituting the observer's viewpoint for the perspective of the person observed (James, 1981, p. 195).

Spinoza's illustration concerns two characters he calls Peter and Paul. He begins by recognition that Peter's idea of self emerges from the immanent immediacy of Peter's present existence, Peter's here-and-now, without reference to Peter's enduring physical existence. Peter, for Peter, is simply, who and how it is (II. Proposition 17,

Scholium, p. 257). Differing from this idea is Paul's idea of Peter. This latter idea forms from Paul's apprehension of Peter's physical body. Paul's is a view of Peter external to Peter's subjectivity.

Spinoza bases his observation on this psychological difference in perception: Peter's sense of Peter emerges from the affectations of Peter's body upon Peter's mind; Paul's sense of Peter emerges from the external fact of the physical Peter as that object obtrudes upon Paul's body. While conceptions of Peter follow a similar course from body to mind, both in Peter and Paul, Paul's apprehension of Peter is what later theorists would call experience-distant, in that it is extrinsic to Paul, maintained in memory by what Spinoza postulates as *images*. Commenting upon Paul's experience of Peter, Spinoza observes that

> to retain the usual terminology, we will assign the word 'images' to those affections of the human body the ideas of which set forth external bodies as if they were present to us, although they do not represent shapes. And when the mind regards bodies in this way, we say that it 'imagines'. (II. Proposition 17, Scholium, p. 257)

Images, of course, are the product of *imagining*, which together with *perceiving*, will conjoin with *feeling*, *willing*, or *endeavoring*, and *reasoning*, in Spinoza's early modern variation upon medieval, Aristotelian agencies of mind.[11]

Before leaving the example of Peter and Paul, Spinoza comments importantly upon cognitive error, instructing the reader that

> at this point, to begin my analysis of error, I should like you to note that the imaginations of the mind, looked at in themselves, contain no error; i.e., the mind does not err from the fact that it imagines, but only insofar as it is considered to lack the idea which excludes the existence of those things which it imagines to be present to itself. For if the mind, in imagining nonexistent things to be present to it, knew at the same time that those images did not exist in fact, it would surely impute this power of imagining not to the defect but to the strength of its own nature, especially if this faculty of imagining were to depend solely on its own nature. (II. Proposition 17, Scholium, p. 257)

Just as in clinical *free association*, where no error exists in the associative elements themselves, but rather from within the conjoining of elements, imaginative error for Spinoza exists only in its fixity or foreclosure. A frequently noted clinical example is within the operation of *transference*, where imagination construes present reality along the lines of imagined resonance with personal history. The working-through of transference entails, at least in part, acceptance of doubt, which for Spinoza, questions the "existence of those things which it imagines to be present to itself" (II. Proposition 17, Scholium, p. 257).

Error and Clarity

Ethics Part II continues, aligned with two significant points. The first is the observation of projective identification unquestioningly believed as fact, noted in the Appendix to Part I; and the second is location of the basic error or confusion, unchecked by doubt, of human reliance from within our imaginative capabilities, what therapists term our *fantasies*.

Developing this theme, Spinoza introduces the idea of *association* in memory, observing in Proposition 18 that

> if the human body has once been affected by two or more bodies at the same time, when the mind afterward imagines one of them, it will straightaway remember the others too. (II. Proposition 18, p. 257)

Memory, for Spinoza, is the containing of imagination, explained as

> simply the linking which occurs in the mind parallel to the order and linking of the affections of the human body. I say, firstly, that it is only the linking of those ideas that involve the nature of things outside the human body, not of those ideas that explicate the nature of the said things. For they are in fact ideas of the affections of the human body which involve the nature both of the human body and of external bodies. (II. Proposition 18, Scholium, p. 258)

Spinoza's second explanatory purpose is to differentiate human memory as psychological process from "the linking of ideas in accordance with the order of the intellect", which returns the reader's attention to the intrinsic resonance within Spinoza's thinking, between the capability within each of us to "perceive things through their first causes", itself a linkage that transforms the medieval striving to apprehend divine intelligence into intrinsic, human resonance with Nature's processes.

Our contemporary reader is momentarily befuddled by Spinoza's assumption of acquaintance with Aristotelian and Neo-Platonic conceptions of the *Active Intellect*.[12] Luckily, hardly registering our modern oblivion to what had been a pressing medieval philosophical issue, the reader is immediately rewarded with Spinoza's clear explanation of subjectivity within associative memory with the example,

> from thinking of the word "Pomum" [apple] a Roman will straightaway fall to thinking of the fruit, which has no likeness to that articulated sound nor anything in common with it other than that the man's body has often been affected by them both; that is, the man has often heard the word "pomum" while seeing the fruit. So everyone will pass on from one thought to another according as habit arranged the images in his body. (II. Proposition 18, Scholium, p. 258)

Spinozan association within memory here links sound to the visualized image either of a word as a symbol, or the actual image of the object symbolized. Continuing his generalized description of associational memory, Spinoza provides another example, linking the apprehension of a visually presented symbol with linkages to procedural knowledge, gained through differing fields of experience, as

> a soldier, for example, seeing the tracks of a horse in the sand will straightaway pass on from thinking of the horse, to thinking of the rider, and then thinking of war, and so on. But a peasant, from thinking of a horse, will pass on to thinking of a plough, and of a field, and so on. So every person will pass on from thinking of one thing to thinking of another according as he is in

the habit of joining together and linking the images of things in various ways. (II. Proposition 18, Scholium, p. 258)

The clinical reader, like our earlier commentators in psychoanalysis (Smith, 1925), will recognize such associational thought as the foundation upon which the psychoanalytic technique of free association depends. Given our sudden enthusiasm (or relief in finding something we recognize) in this scholium, concern for our befuddlement only several lines earlier, seems to vanish. Yet, like the soldier who puts thoughts of ploughing from his mind while contemplating battle, or the peasant who puts thoughts of strife from his mind while contemplating the field, each in sorting out the meaning of hoof-prints on a beach, the philosophical reader interested in Spinoza's transformations of medieval theology into modern, scientific thought would mine this scholium from a different perspective than the psychologist, perhaps subordinating the articulation of psychological associational process to philosophy, without focus upon Spinoza's generative model of psychological functioning.

The reader is reminded of Harry Wolfson's comments about the congealing of thought similar to the grouping of magnetized iron filings, wherein each of us also apprehends differently, the multiple thoughts which Spinoza richly provides in his scholia. It is from such experience that Deleuze recognizes the multiplicity of ideas, the doublings, which underlie as multiple themes, the more manifest considerations in *Ethics'* Propositions. It is through consideration of these multiple levels of thought that Lou Andreas-Salomé recognizes how Spinoza meets us everywhere in our psychoanalytic inquiries (Andreas-Salomé, 1964).

Spinoza further explains the mind's easy susceptibility to distortion with the claim that

the human mind has no knowledge of the body, nor does it know it to exist, except through ideas of the affections by which the body is affected. (II. Proposition 19, p. 258)

The affections, what we call *emotions*, comprise the mind's distorting mirror through which the body, upon which the emotions depend, becomes known to us. Not only does something become known to us

(II. Proposition 21, Scholium, p. 259), but also, the "ideas of these affections" are perceived by us (II. Proposition 22, p. 259). However, both the affections and the ideas of the affections, "insofar as they are related only to the human mind, are not clear and distinct, but confused" (II. Proposition 28, p. 261). Though we can specify mind as the object of our inquiry, and recognize more broadly several functional aspects of mind such as variations upon the Aristotelian idea of the Soul's nutritive, vegetative, sentient, imaginative, and rational functionalities, precision still inheres in the realm of *cloudy mathematics* because

> the idea that constitutes the nature of the human mind is likewise shown, when considered solely in itself, not to be clear and distinct, as is also the idea of the human mind and the ideas of affections of the human body insofar as they are related to the human mind, as everyone can easily see. (II. Proposition 28, Scholium, p. 262)

Spinoza underlines this cloudiness as a proposition, writing that

> the idea of the idea of any affection of the human body does not involve adequate knowledge of the human mind. (II. Proposition 29, p. 262)

Neither does the mind perceive the body through clear and adequate knowledge, nor does the body's apprehension of mind require accuracy. Spinoza clarifies, writing that

> I say expressly that the mind does not have an adequate knowledge, but only a confused and fragmentary knowledge, of itself, its own body, and external bodies whenever it perceives things from the common order of nature, that is, whenever it is determined externally- namely by the fortuitous run of circumstance- to regard this or that, and not when it is determined internally, through its regarding several things at the same time, to understand their agreement, their differences, and their opposition. For whenever it is conditioned internally

in this or another way, then it sees things clearly and distinctly, as I shall later show. (II. Proposition 29, Scholium, p. 262)

What Spinoza will later demonstrate is that the activity of thinking, akin to Bion's understanding of the process, refines thought toward its utility in action (Bion, 1962; Miller, 2016). For the moment, Spinoza focuses on circumstance, or what other philosophers have called "luck", in the conjoining of multiple things having agreement, difference, and opposition. Such is James' later "blooming, buzzing confusion" (James, 1981, p. 462), as well as the neurotic condition of conflictual feelings and ideas. It will be to this situation that Spinoza extends the rational principle of doubt.

Doubt operates upon

the privation of knowledge which inadequate ideas, that is, fragmentary and confused ideas, involve. (II. Proposition 35, p. 264)

Expanding upon this proposition, Spinoza stakes out a position later repeated by Erich Fromm (1962a) that

men are deceived in thinking themselves free, a belief that consists only in this, that they are conscious of their actions and ignorant of the causes by which they are determined. Therefore, the idea of their freedom is simply the ignorance of the cause of their actions. As to their saying that human actions depend on the will, these are mere words without any corresponding idea. For none of them knows what the will is and how it moves the body, and those who boast otherwise and make up stories of dwelling places and habituations of the soul provoke either ridicule or disgust. (II. Proposition 35, Scholium, p. 264)

Again, Spinoza brings an example based in mathematics; but in mathematic reasoning tested empirically, by science. The reader recalls that in addition to his philosophical work, Spinoza was also a grinder of optical lenses. The following example is based on his empirical experience in this regard, when we gaze at the sun, we see it as some two hundred feet distant from us. The error does not consist in simply seeing the sun in this way but in the fact that while we do so we are not aware of the true distance and the cause of our seeing it so. For although we may later become aware that the sun is more than six hundred times the diameter of the earth distant from us, we shall nevertheless continue to see it as close at hand. For it is not our ignorance of its true distance that causes us to see the sun to be so near; it is that the affections of our body involve the essence of the sun only to the extent that the body is affected by it. (II. Proposition 35, Scholium, p. 264)

That is, our perception is constrained by our embodied capabilities, which must be understood and questioned, if we are to understand beyond the constraints of naïve experience. So too, the causes determining our beliefs, necessitating doubt that exposes the *privation of knowledge*.

Common Notions of Error

So far, *Ethics* Part II has introduced the idea of mind, and also addressed certain confusions and clarities in mind's reflexive awareness. Spinoza maintains that the generation of imaginative thought itself contains no error. Rather, it is when such thought, unexamined, becomes the basis for action, that error may occur; as thought may not agree with what later clinicians will term the *Reality Principle*. Spinoza writes,

> inadequate and confused ideas follow by the same necessity as adequate, or clear and distinct, ideas. (II. Proposition 36, p. 264)

How are we to differentiate between them? Spinoza establishes criteria, distinguishing between those

> common to all, which ones are clear and distinct only to those not laboring under prejudices and which ones are ill-founded. (II. Proposition 40, Scholium 1, p. 266)

He begins this early differentiation between clear and normally *neurotic*[13] functioning, by separating terms that are clear and distinct from those that are confused; and dismisses terms including "entity", "thing", "something" that are *transcendent*, by which he means images, formed simultaneously that are "utterly confused" (II. Proposition 40, Scholium 1, p. 266). This is so because the body

> being limited, is capable of forming simultaneously in itself only a certain number of distinct images. If this number be exceeded, these images begin to be confused with one another (II. Proposition 40, Scholium 1, p. 266)

The psychologist is reminded of George Miller's classic cognitive research on our human capacity to manage multiple ideas, with arrival at an estimate of our capability to juggle simultaneous thoughts without becoming overwhelmed at *7 plus or minus 2* discrepant notions (Miller, 1956). Beyond this quantity, our thoughts, as Spinoza recognizes and clinicians frequently observe, do become confused.

Spinoza now considers common terms or universals, composed of so many images simultaneously that the "mind is unable to imagine the unimportant differences of individuals" (II. Proposition 40, Scholium 1, p. 267). However, he notes too, that while such terms are held commonly

> it should be noted that not all men form these notions in the same way; in the case of each person the notions vary according as that thing varies whereby the body has more frequently been affected, and which the mind more readily imagines or calls to mind. For example, those who have more often regarded with admiration the stature of men will understand by the word "man: an animal of upright stature, while those who are wont to regard a different aspect will form a different common image of man, such as that man is a laughing animal, a featherless biped, or a rational animal. (II. Proposition 40, Scholium 1, p. 267)

That is, some common notions are more commonly agreed upon through consensus than others. Spinoza addresses here, the subjective individual conviction that contemporary clinicians understand as parataxic distortion (Moore, 1923; Sullivan, 1953).

More extensively, he recognizes that even consensual validation, the social agreement upon what is deemed common or universal, may vary from one group holding something in common to another such group. Universals, despite their prefix "uni" are themselves, variable and socially constructed from agreed-upon subjectivities within particular groups. WR Bion later reprises this idea in his definition of common sense as

> a term commonly employed to cover experiences in which the speaker feels that his contemporaries, individuals whom he knows, would without hesitation hold the view he has put forward in common with each other. Common sense, the highest common factor of sense, so to speak, would support his view of what the senses convey. Furthermore, he has a feeling of certitude, of confidence, associated with a belief that all his senses are in harmony and support each on the evidence of the rest. (Bion, 1992, pp. 9–10)

Continuing, Spinoza generates a three-fold typology of knowledge (II. Proposition 40, Scholium 2). The first category, "knowledge of the first kind" is based upon opinions and imagination. These originate in two ways. *Knowledge of the first kind*, as in Bion's example of common sense above, is sensory-based, drawn

> from individual objects presented to us through the senses in a fragmentary and confused manner without any intellectual order; and therefore I call perceptions 'knowledge from casual experience'. (II. Proposition 40, Scholium 2, p. 267)

Knowledge of the first kind may also be symbolic. Earlier, Spinoza described the symbolic relation to the word through sound (his example is the Latin word for apple, *pomum*) as well as our subjective understandings of visual signs, with his example of hoofprints on the beach (II. Proposition 18, Scholium, p. 258). He now explains the symbolic relation, linked to associative process in that,

from having heard or read certain words we call things to mind
and we form certain ideas of them similar to those through which
we imagine things. (II. Proposition 40, Scholium 2, p. 267)

Passing from knowledge of the "first kind" to knowledge of the
"second kind", or "reason", Spinoza provides a cursory description,
of common notions having "adequate ideas of the properties of
things" (II. Proposition 40, Scholium 2, p. 267).

Relative to the earlier equivalence of parataxic distortion to
knowledge of the first kind, the contemporary clinician understands
reason in this sense, to occupy the realm of "consensual validation"
to the degree that social and interpersonal consensus is adequate
(Sullivan, 1953). Spinoza will amplify these categories later.[14]

Finally, passing from parataxic distortion and consensual validation, Spinoza refers to "intuition" as the third kind of knowledge.
Through Spinoza's example, the contemporary clinician recognizes
the intuitive form as similar to Bion's *selected fact*, the essence of
a therapeutically relevant idea. Of this, Bion comments

> what does the psycho-analyst do? He observes a mass of
> 'elements'[15] long since known but'- till he gives his interpretation—
> 'scattered and seemingly foreign to each other'. If he can tolerate
> the depressive position, he can give this interpretation; the
> interpretation itself is one of those 'only facts worthy of our
> attention' which, according to Poincare, 'introduce order into this
> complexity and so make it accessible to us'. The patient is in this
> way helped to find, through the analyst's ability to select, one of
> these unifying facts. (Bion, 1992, p. 5)

Illustrating intuition, Spinoza utilizes the ratio as a common mathematical example such that

> this kind of knowledge proceeds from an adequate idea of
> the formal essence of certain attributes of God to an adequate
> knowledge of the essence of things. I shall illustrate all these
> kinds of knowledge by a single example. Three numbers are
> given; it is required to find a fourth which is related to the third
> as the second is to the first. Tradesmen have no hesitation in

multiplying the second by the third and dividing the product by the first, either because they have not yet forgotten the rule they learned without proof from their teachers, or because they have in fact found this correct in the case of very simple numbers, or else from the force of the proof of Proposition 19 of the Second Book of Euclid. But in the case of very simple numbers, none of this is necessary. For example, in the case of the given numbers 1,2,3, everybody can see that the fourth proportional is 6, and all the more clearly because we infer in one single intuition the fourth number from the ratio we see the first number bears to the second. (II. Proposition 40, Scholium 2, p. 268)

Very elegantly, Spinoza provides us with an example of practical intuitive wisdom, referencing Euclid for the first time in *Ethics*. Despite the ancient authority of Euclid's geometric demonstrative method, corresponding to the overall structure of *Ethics* (however doubled through the supercommentary of the cumulative scholia), Spinoza reduces mathematics here, to illustrative analogy, by an example drawn from everyday life through which "adequate knowledge" is discerned intuitively.

Spinoza's ratio example fits his definition of "true idea" in that

nobody who has a true idea is unaware that a true idea involves absolute certainty. To have a true idea means only to know a thing perfectly, that is, to the utmost degree. Indeed, nobody can doubt this, unless he thinks that an idea is some dumb thing like a picture on a tablet, and not a mode of thinking, to wit, the very act of understanding. And who, pray, can know that he is certain of something unless he is first certain of it? (II. Proposition 43, Scholium, p. 269)

The truth or falsity of ideas relates to Spinoza's hierarchy of knowledge. Knowledge of the *first kind*, our parataxic understandings and symbolic misconceptions, are "the only cause of falsity" (II. Proposition 41, p. 268). Knowledge of the *second kind* and *third kind*, "teaches us to distinguish true from false" (II. Proposition 42, p. 268).

Spinoza's standard in reason's discernment of true from false ideas, is the test of necessity: a clear boundary between what an idea is; and what it is not (II. Proposition 43; II. Proposition 44). However, the clinician recognizes that much challenge inheres within the fuzzy realm of in-between, which Spinoza recognizes resides within the imagination. Perhaps the most crystalline explanation of the human transition from what is to what is not, is presented by Freud in *Mourning and Melancholia* (1915). While death transforms what is alive to the absence of physical aliveness, the mourner's grieving unites the realms of feeling, memory, and imagination; and only after long oscillation between what had been and its absence in present reality, does the Spinozan "wavering of the imagination" (II. Proposition 44, Scholium, p. 270) settle in relation both to past and present time. Such oscillation is fundamental too, to the Bionian algorithm, based on the Kleinian shift between P/S and D (Miller & Sweet, 2018), with Bion taking as elements of mind,

> (... the elements common to all scientific disciplines, the elements that are also the feature of the paranoid-schizoid position and are synthesized in the depressive position) that have to be transformed into 'ideas' so that they then become part of an ideational system. (Bion, 1992, p. 4)

Returning to the link between the human mind and apprehension of God, Spinoza writes

> that men do not have as clear a knowledge of God as they do of common notions arises from the fact that they are unable to imagine God as they do bodies, and that they have connected the word "God" with the images of things which they commonly see; and this they can scarcely avoid, being affected continually by external bodies. Indeed, most errors result solely from the incorrect application of words to things. (II. Proposition 47, Scholium, p. 271)

The reader remembers *Ethics'* psychological starting point in projective identification, together with Spinoza's argument against the anthropocentric idea of God. Here, such human distortion is again addressed; but having treated the processes of association and memory as well as knowledge of the first kind in its fragmentary certainty of truth while lacking both necessary data and the necessity of reflexive doubt, Spinoza returns to the common distortions of religious belief. Importantly, he addresses the problem of communicative language. Elaborating, he notes

> likewise, when men make mistakes in arithmetic. They have different figures in mind from those on paper. So if you look only to their minds, they indeed are not mistaken; but they seem to be wrong because we think that they have in mind the figures on the page. If this were not the case, we would not think them to be wrong, just as I did not think that person to be wrong whom I recently heard shouting that his hall had flown into his neighbor's hen, for I could see clearly what he had in mind. Most controversies arise from this, that med do not correctly express what is in their mind, or they misunderstand another's mind. For, in reality, while they are hotly contradicting one another, they are either in agreement or have different things in mind, so that the apparent errors and absurdities of their opponents are not really so. (II. Proposition 47, Scholium, pp. 271–272)

Rational intuition, then, also demands the listener's equanimity in thinking-through the meaning of the speaker's words, as in Spinoza's humorus aside about his neighbor's hen. However, the distortions and confusions in communicative language join the imperfect understandings and distortions of the mind in the field of human error.

Not unexpectedly, after his return to erroneous conceptions of God, Spinoza returns next to erroneous concepts of free will, writing

> in the mind there is no absolute, or free, will. The mind is determined to this or that volition by a cause, which is likewise determined by another cause, and this again by another, and so ad infinitum. (II. Proposition 48, p. 272)

But, now having considered mind, and having introduced the reader to the distinction between first and proximate cause, the aggregate work of mind can almost be pictured by the reader as responding first to this cause and next to that, each generative of different volitional orientations, whether conflictual or harmonious. Spinoza's scholium is quite clear

> in the same way it is proved that in the mind there is no absolute faculty of understanding, desiring loving, etc. Hence it follows that these and similar faculties are either fictitious or nothing more than metaphysical entities or universals which we are wont to form from particulars. So intellect and will bear the same relation to this or that idea, this or that volition, as stoniness to this or that stone, or man to Peter and Paul. (II. Proposition 48, Scholium, p. 272)

The functional domains of mind are themselves formed from particular causes, originating in the body. The relation of intellect to will resembles the relation of intellect to extension in Spinoza's earlier contemplation of God; and so mirrors an essential natural relationship within its human operation. Thinking and willing are in every idea, every relationship. Spinoza continues, clarifying that

> it should be noted that by will I mean the faculty of affirming and denying, and not desire. I mean, I repeat, the faculty whereby the mind affirms or denies what is true or what is false, not the desire whereby the mind seeks things or shuns them. But now that we have proved that these faculties are universal notions which are not distinct from the particulars from which we form them, we must inquire whether volitions themselves are anything more than ideas of things. We must inquire, I say, whether there is in the mind any other affirmation and denial apart from that which the idea, insofar as it is an idea, involves ... for by ideas I do not mean images such as are formed at the back of the eye- or if you like, in the middle of the brain- but conceptions of thought. (II. Proposition 48, Scholium, p. 272)[16]

What is commonly termed "free will" is relegated by Spinoza to an idea within the idea of mind, of willing as the action of affirmation or denial relative to particular objects of intellect. Very clearly, Spinoza differentiates such willing from the action of desiring, transforming Aristotle's ancient categories of the Soul's appetitive action into the intrapsychic acts of willing, together with their interpersonal extension into the world external to the mind, in appetite and desire, more fully described in *Ethics* Part III.

Spinoza's next proposition brings *Ethics* Part II to a close. True to form, he argues that all willing, as affirmation or negation, inheres inseparably within its particular ideas (II. Proposition 49, p. 272). Providing another geometrical example as proof, a corollary declares, "will and intellect are one and the same thing" (II. Proposition 49, Corollary, p. 273). Unfortunately, this singular claim has been frozen erroneously by our psychological commentators on Spinoza. Misunderstood as a simple principle rather than within the transformational dynamism between intellect within will, this reduction by Smith (1925) and Tanner (1907a) trips upon a warning, earlier extended by Spinoza, reducing an idea to "some dumb thing like a picture on a tablet, and not a mode of thinking" (II. Proposition 43, Scholium, p. 269).

Spinoza returns to further clarify his understanding of errors in thinking, writing again that falsity concerns an absence of full knowledge. Drawn from fragmentary and confused ideas, Spinoza construes such falsity only in the privation of knowledge that fragmentary and confused ideas involve. Therefore, a false idea, insofar as it is false (however adamantly it may be maintained) does not involve certainty. So when

> we say that a man acquiesces in what is false and has no doubt thereof, we are not thereby saying that he is certain, but only that he does not doubt, or that he acquiesces in what is false because there is nothing to cause his imagination to waver. (II. Proposition 49, Scholium, p. 273)

Clinically, we encounter such Spinozan falsity in fixed beliefs, where doubt is entirely foreclosed (Miller, 2021). Ferenczi and Rank similarly observe that this form of fixed insistence by the patient requires the therapist's challenge, in order to generate doubt. Centered on the problem of difficulty arising in the "step by step" process of therapy. They comment all these "resistances", varying greatly in importance, which affect the course of the libido transference in the way we have described, are analyzed step by step during the analysis. Mostly the narcissistic resistances, proceeding from the ego, and the ideal formation appear at first; these are particularly difficult to overcome, because the patient, with the full weight of his whole actual personality, opposes the automatic unwinding of the libido attempted by his unconscious. Frequently the overcoming of these ego resistances only succeed after wounding the narcissism of the patient. (Ferenczi & Rank, 1924, p. 9)

Spinoza clarifies too, the distinction between an idea as conception of mind, and the verbalized images of our imagination. He writes,

again, it is essential to distinguish between ideas and the words we use to signify things. For since these three- images, words, and ideas- have been utterly confused by many, or else they fail to distinguish between them through lack of accuracy, or finally, through lack of caution, our doctrine of the will, which it is essential to know both for theory and for the wise ordering of life, has never entered their minds. For those who think that ideas consist in images formed in us from the contact of external bodies are convinced that those ideas of things whereof we can form no like image are not ideas, but mere fictions fashioned arbitrarily at will. (II. Proposition 49, Scholium, p. 273)

Spinoza continues,

so they look on ideas as dumb pictures on a tablet, and misled by this preconception they fail to see that an idea, insofar as it is an idea, involves affirmation or negation. Again, those who confuse words with idea, or with the affirmation which an idea involves, think that when they affirm or deny something merely by words contrary to what they feel, they are able to will contrary to what they feel. Now one can easily dispel these misconceptions if one attends to the nature of thought, which is quite removed from the concept of extension. Then one will clearly understand that an idea, being a mode of thinking, consists neither in the image of a thing nor in words. For the essence of words and images is constituted solely by corporeal motions far removed from the concept of thought. (II. Proposition 49, Scholium, p. 274)

Of course, this scholium stands Spinoza's earlier proof and corollary on their head: while will and intellect may be the "same thing" in their joint emergence from a "particular volition and idea", because the nature of intellect "is quite removed from the concept of extension", of the action of affirming or denying, the nature of will and intellect, while operating conjointly, are not exactly the same, except in their inseparability.

Spinoza's Shift in Voice

Ethics Part II, continuously engaging the reader's attention, proceeds along two conjoined paths. The first, which the reader absorbs, responsive to Spinoza's guidance in the perplexities of human psychology, is methodological, or "step by step" (II. Proposition 11, Scholium, p. 251), just as is the process of psychoanalytic inquiry (Ferenczi & Rank, 1924, p. 9). As in psychotherapy, this involves the iteration and reiteration of statements, subtly changing form as Spinoza works to what he (and Freud) term his "doctrine" concerning will; for it will be the variations of willing, the affirming or denying of ideas partaking of the mind's perceptive, imaginative, feeling, endeavoring, and reasoning functionalities, which will figure as the primary efficient or proximate cause within Spinoza's psychological model.

En route to introducing the doctrine of willing, Spinoza comments on the necessity to maintain an open, questioning perspective on the imaginative or fantasy contents of one's mind. Through illustrative thought experiments ranging from (1) the text-based to the (2) mathematic/geometrical to (3) current 17th scientific findings in optics, and to (4) observations of daily life, the distortions and confusions of mind always contrast in their cloudiness to specific causal bodily determinants. In this sense, Spinoza's model is a strong precursor to John Dewey's holistic recognition of the neural reflex arc in that the multiple processes underlying psychological functionality operate as proximate or efficient cause, sufficient to intuit the relationship of cause-and-effect, but indistinct in empirical determination of underlying causality (Dewey, 1890).

Spinoza's causal model of psychological functioning, based in the doctrine of will, is good enough in demonstrating determinism within human action. His formulations are uniformly cast in monistic fusions such as thought and extension or thinking/thinker/and object-of-thought. While separation of these categories is possible as an intellectual exercise, they are functionally reckoned with in their multidimensional wholeness.

As Spinoza leads us through his ideas, we are exposed to an early model of systemic thinking, a precursor of General Systems Theory (Levinson, 1979), wherein general laws oversee continuous change, while stabilities of form are maintained.[17] Unconscious, unformulated, and parataxic levels of mental activity operate together, both in harmony and in conflict, within ideas that vary from (1) vacillation to (2) adequacy to (3) fragmentation and distortion in their lack of information corresponding with Freud's *Reality Principle*.

Finally, in *Ethics* Part II, together with the centrality of willing, Spinoza articulates three levels of knowledge: (1) hearsay, opinion, and symbolic distortion; (2) consensual reasoning; and (3) intuition. Throughout, the improvement of intellect and extension into action is maintained through successive approximations increasingly aligned with physical reality.

At the same time, and in parallel with the structural literary importance of his Part I Appendix argument, Spinoza concludes Part II in a very different voice than that heard in its' prior forty-eight propositions. Spinoza's narrational tone shifts from the explanatory to the aspirational.

It is this aspirational voice that influences the early embrace of Spinoza within psychoanalysis. Spinoza's psychological model provides a pathway, for example, through which M. Hamblin Smith discerns a parallel with psychoanalysis in establishing "how a complete adaptation to reality can best be obtained" (Smith, 1925, p. 257). Indeed, the rationale for the reckoning by early psychoanalytic commentators with *Ethics* Parts I and II, is to arrive at the final three chapters, beginning with Spinoza's observations of psychodynamics in Part III and continuing to the application of ethical behaviors in Parts IV and V, leading to the fantasy of human transformation through Spinozan *blessedness* (II. Proposition 49, Scholium, point (1), p. 276). *Smith writes, toward this end, that*

> Spinoza also points out how determinism confers advantages upon social as well as upon individual life, inasmuch as it teaches us not to despise, hate or ridicule any one, to be angry with and envy no one (II49). Further, it teaches us that each one should be satisfied with what he has, and should be ready to help his neighbor, from the guidance of reason. Can more than this be claimed for psychoanalysis? (Smith, 1925, p. 262)

Frederick Weiss is so ardent about the conclusion of *Ethics* that he claims, through a parapraxis in his reading, that Spinoza's "first chapter of his *Ethics*, (is) entitled 'On Human Bondage'" (Weiss, 1952, p. 41), when in fact, this is the first section of Part IV—driving Spinoza's aspirational teleology of humanity's ethical choices. Such aspirational desire is limited in the absolute sense by physical determinism, but presided over by reason and the mobilization of human striving both to affirm and deny, as against the Spinozan observation paraphrased by Erich Fromm, that

> man believes himself to be free because he knows his desire, but he is not aware of the causes for his desires (Fromm, 1964a, p.71).

Spinoza provides solid ground for proceeding along this aspirational path in application of his psychological model. Absent recognition of change in his literary expression, the step-wise progression of *Ethics* from Parts I to V would also suggest this interpretation. But by now, the reader will have recognized Spinoza as a master of doubling, of expressing multiplicity within apparent singularity. Indeed, this corresponds to the basic parallelism between thought and extension! From this perspective, the aspirational quality of Spinoza's thinking, reflective too of his early orientation within *Treatise on the Emendation of the Intellect* is the extension of the thought represented in his psychological model.

Our literary clues are twofold. First, Spinoza's animated reflection concludes Part II, just as earlier animated reflection concluded

Part I. Next, is Spinoza's agenda itself. He explains that, "my final task is to show what practical advantages accrue from knowledge of this doctrine", reminding the reader that *Ethics* is firmly rooted in the tradition of practical philosophy (II. Proposition 49, Scholium, p. 276).

Here, the tone shifts from exploration to intoxication. Spinoza provides four distinctive benefits of his doctrine. First, it

> teaches that we act only by God's will, and that we share in the divine nature, and all the more as our actions become more perfect and as we understand God more and more. Therefore, this doctrine, apart from giving us complete tranquility of mind, has the further advantage of teaching us wherein lies our greatest happiness or blessedness, namely, in the knowledge of God alone, as a result of which we are induced only to such actions as are urged on us by love and piety. Hence, we clearly understand how far astray from the true estimation of virtue are those who, failing to understand that virtue itself and the service of God are happiness itself and utmost freedom, expect God to bestow on them the highest rewards in return for their virtue and meritorious actions as if in return for the basest slavery. (II. Proposition 49, Scholium, p. 276)

Next, this doctrine

> teaches us what attitude we should adopt regarding fortune, or the things that are not in our power, that is, the things that do not follow from our nature; namely, to expect and to endure with patience both faces of fortune. For all things follow from God's eternal decree by the same necessity as it follows from the essence of a triangle that its three angles are equal to two right angles. (II. Proposition 49, Scholium, p. 276)

The third doctrinal point is recapitulated by M. Hamblin Smith, and promised by Spinoza to be demonstrated in Part IV. The doctrine of willing

> assists us in our social relations, in that it teaches us to hate no one, despise no one, ridicule no one, be angry with no one, envy

no one. Then again, it teaches that each should be content with what he has and should help his neighbor, not from womanish pity, or favor, or superstition, but from the guidance of reason as occasion and circumstance require. (II. Proposition 49, Scholium, pp. 276–277)

Spinoza concludes Part II with his fourth doctrinal point, itself setting up the reasoning he will pursue later in Parts IV and V. He writes,

finally (277), this doctrine is also of no small advantage to the commonwealth, in that it teaches the manner in which citizens should be governed and led; namely, not so as to be slaves, but so as to do freely what is best.

The conclusion of Part II provides the programmatic extension of Spinoza's psychological model of mind, leading directly to *Ethics'* Parts IV and V. Read in unbroken, linear fashion, *Ethics* proceeds through its elaboration of Spinoza's psychological observations to its conclusion, mirrored in the late 20th century, by the humanistic turn in American psychoanalysis.

However, our reading of Spinoza, following his own lead, is mindful of a continuous doubling, represented often by the explanatory essays Spinoza provides in his scholia. From this perspective, what falls-away in the aspirational development of a practical philosophy anticipating psychoanalysis is attention to its psychodynamic hypotheses, capable of being clinically demonstrated and observed. As I illustrate in Chapters Two and Three, such demonstrations have occurred continually throughout the 20th century's integration of Spinoza within psychoanalysis.

Having established his basic model of mind through the developments of *Ethics* Parts I and II, Spinoza's Part III acts as itself a scholium in relation to his broad, humanistic proposition. Part III reflects the nuts-and-bolts of a *clinical* Spinoza, applicable today within a psychoanalysis itself anticipated by Spinozan thinking toward Spinoza's aspirational end of volitional application (Bernard, 1946; Fromm, 1964a; Rathbun, 1934; Smith, 1925; Weiss, 1952), but still requiring clinicians' explicit and conscious practical operationalization.

Notes

1   The reader familiar with American Interpersonal-Relational psychoanalysis recalls that Harry Stack Sullivan begins *The Interpersonal Theory of Psychiatry*
(1953) with similar philosophical categories, Definition (Chapter 2) and
Postulates (Chapter 3). Further on, in Chapter 6, under the concept of
Dynamism, Sullivan explicitly links his thinking to that of Alfred N. Whitehead,
writing, "Let me begin by saying that the present view of the universe, as held by
a great majority of mathematicians, physicists, and other scientists, makes the
discoverable world a dynamism. This is implied in the fundamental postulate
that the ultimate reality in the universe is energy, that all material objects are
manifestations of energy, and that all activity represents the dynamic or kinetic
aspect of energy. A doctrine in which force and the conception of energy—which
underlies the conception of force—is the ultimate conception or postulate would
naturally be a conception of dynamism, a dynamism of the universe. Whitehead,
among the philosophers, has conceived the universe as an organism, and certainly there is no difficulty in seeing living organisms as particular dynamisms"
(Sullivan, 1953, p. 102). Sullivan was probably unmindful that Whitehead's
construal of organic philosophy is "closely allied to Spinoza's scheme of
thought" in transforming the terms and language of Spinoza while seeking systemic "coherence" in "the discovery that the process, or concrescences, of any
one actual entity involves the other actual entities among its components",
congruent with Spinoza's dynamic speculations (Whitehead, 1978, p. 7).

2   Explaining Divine Science, Samuel Ibn Tibbon, Maimonides' translator, observes, "it is a science which discusses that which has no nature, that is, things
that are intelligible and separate from matter, like the Lord". That is, having "no
action in the sensible world". Ibn Tibbon writes, "the root of all books in this
science is Aristotle's book entitled *Metaphysics*".

By contrast, Ibn Tibbon defines nature or natural science from four perspectives (not unlike Spinoza's nuanced illustrations): (1) "the principle of any
change, persistence or abiding"; (2) "the physicians call 'nature' the temperament
and natural heat and the disposition of the organs"; (3) the term "is used for any
disposition by which some species is perfected, whether it be action or passion";
(4) "any power that exists in a thing always, without changing, is called 'nature'"
(Harrison, 2007, pp. 162–163, footnote 109).

3   Spinoza's *conception* is differentiated from the body's passive perceptual receptivity, which registration Spinoza locates within the workings of mind.
Relative to Bion's ideas of preconception and realization, Spinoza understands
conjunction only between the various functionalities of mind, within the active
willing, striving, endeavoring, of *conatus*. Spinozan *conception* is further developed by Whitehead, with internal conjunctions categorized as "prehensions",
and their external extensions categorized as "actual things", similar to Bionian
realization. Such extension of thought is amplified by Whitehead. Motivated by
the appetite of Spinozan desire (attributed by Whitehead to Leibniz), the creative

outcome of extension is for Whitehead, a "superject", achieved in part, through creative action from which satisfaction is a new dimension of experience (Whitehead, 1978, p. 32).

4   While this particular example may strike us as odd, it was directly relevant in Spinoza's time, given competitive and lively interfaith interests (Fisher, 2020; Kaplan, 1989, p. 275). Benjamin Fisher observes that

> Adam Boreel, the Messianic Dutch Collegiant, provided the funding necessary for Rabbi Jacob Judah Leon's construction of a model of Solomon's Temple that was highly popular among Jews and Christians in Holland, and that was exhibited in England and German territories into the eighteenth century. Boreel, who in fact lived with Menasseh ben Israel for several months and learned Portuguese in order to communicate with him better, also collaborated with Menasseh and Leon to produce an edition of the Mishnah with Hebrew vowel points. The fascination and commitment of Messianic Christians to symbols of Jewish messianism may have also played a significant role in stimulating Morteira's belief that certain Christians were approaching the acceptance of Jewish doctrines. (Fisher, 2020, p. 202)

Spinoza's acceptance among Dutch Collegiants after expulsion from the Jewish community, also depended, in part, on the usefulness of his Hebrew skills, eventually deployed together with mathematical analysis in the *Theological-Political Tractacte*'s disconfirmation of the Hebrew bible's absolute truth in relation to Jewish claims of Chosenness.

5   As thought-experiment, I applied this grid in relation to recent supervisory experience. A therapist, characteristically tentative about genuine engagement with her patient, had finally made significant contact. However, in the following session, her patient challenged her with the threat of termination. The therapist, anxious about the maintenance of her practice, entirely missed the Spinozan moment. Her earlier intervention had been effective, triggering the patient's Spinozan "resistance" in defense against the momentary distress of uncertainty, so possible diminution of power: the patient's new form of resistance had signaled progress. From the viewpoint of this Part II definitional grid: (1) rather than hearing the patient's threat as speculative rather than factual (the first axis), (2) the therapist also distorted the particular nature of a significant therapist-patient interaction, into a generalized panic triggered by the therapist's own career anxieties (the second axis). That is, she heard the patient's threat as a generalized flight from psychotherapy rather than a specific commentary upon an experience in clinical process.

6   Such duality is later extended by Whitehead in his concept of the *superject*, pairing the material fact of our externalized actions with the creative experience entailed through our actions (Whitehead, 1978, p. 32).

7   Such analytically discernable ego-feelings, registered mentally in relation to separable real-world objects and their creative construction—for example, in

transference—link directly to the imbuing of meaning through Spinozan extension of desire into the external world, recognizable in the experiential "creation" of Whitehead's *superject*. Through processes of internalization (Ferenczi, 1909; Schafer, 1968), in what Whitehead terms an "incoming of appetition" (Whitehead, 1978, p. 212), these become subject to new, uniquely subjectivized layers of mental process—Whitehead's "private ideal, gradually shaped in the process itself" (Whitehead, 1978, p. 212), through conjunctive integration between multiple levels of Spinozan conception.

8   Maimonides writes that, "In fact our saying that He is the intellectual cognition as well as the intellectually cognizing subject and the intellectually cognized object will appear to him as if we had said whiteness, that which has become white, and that which whitens are one and the same thing" (Maimonides, I .68, p. 163.)Maimonides continues with a fierce pugnacity, antedating if also providing a model for Spinoza's: "How many ignoramuses there are who hasten to refute us by means of this and similar examples, and how many pretending to knowledge there are who have great difficulties with regard to this and who hold that the minds cannot attain the knowledge that it is correct that this matter should be necessarily true. Yet this notion is a matter of demonstration and is quite clear, as the theologizing philosophers have demonstrated" (I.68, p. 163). The reader will immediately recognize Maimonides' prescriptive demand for formal philosophical demonstration, satisfied by Spinoza's geometric demonstration in *Ethics*.

9   Parallel to this action is the observation of Maurits Katan, who, in a series of papers between 1949 and 1954, presents the idea of wresting non-psychotic functioning from its underlying psychotic substructure, in an analogy paralleling Dutch reclamation of land from the sea. I have written about this idea as convergent in bringing together the thinking of such psychoanalytic thinkers as Waelder, Bion, Klein, Fairbairn, and Hartmann (Miller & Sweet, 2018, pp. 51–65).

10   Spinoza's insistence on conatus as (1) primary self-preservative striving, (2) unconscious motivation, (3) observable appetite, as well as (4) conscious desire or wish, is derived, in part from Gersonides' transformation of animal biology, itself an idea received from Averroes and Galen. This chain of thinking, from Galen, Averroes, Gersonides, through Spinoza, differentiates the human mind's functional capabilities from animal instinct (now understood with greater complexity inclusive of animals' means-end protosymbolic capability (Tolman, 1932). Conatus, willing or striving, itself represents Spinoza's transformative advance upon animal instinct within the human species (Green, 2015, p. 92).

11   Aristotle posited the following mental agencies: (1) vegetative; (2) sentient (including the five senses); (3) imaginative; (4) appetitive (the growth principle); and (5) reason. By contrast and through receptive, transformative interpretations of Aristotelian concepts, Spinoza's categories: (1) lack the vegetative, which now resides in the body; (2) transforms the sentient into the perceptive, while adding the subjective registration of pleasure and pain as (3) feeling; (4) maintains the

imaginative and the capacity for (5) reason. The fundamental shift seems motivational, along the lines of the Aristotelian growth principle; and is a transformation of Spinoza's own Maimonidean reception (Gorfinkle, 1912). Spinoza next differentiates (1) the motivational engine of conatus from (2) its unconscious action, (3) its conscious action as appetite, and (4) consciousness of appetite as desire.

12 Tamar Rudavsky explains the Active Intellect as "a term that refers back to Aristotle's actual intellect as described in *De Anima* 3.5. The term was transmitted to Jewish and scholastic writers through Islamic philosophers and it came to represent not only a part of the human soul but the domain of Divine intellectual cognition as well" (Rudavsky, 2018, footnote 6, p. 209).

13 I am aware that when I chose the much later term *neurotic*, it is intrinsically tied to the biological concept of neuronal or nerve causation. As such, the whole sense of this word is intrinsically anti-Spinozan. My use, however, is more casual, following Spinoza's *second kind of knowledge*, in mobilization of the term as it is used in common contrast between so-called *normal* and so-called *neurotic* individuals. It is Spinoza's position, as it is Freud's and Sullivan's, that normal and neurotic processes are similar in their dynamic forms.

14 As the reader keenly appreciates, consensual agreement may itself contain distortion. Spinoza's banner example of social agreement about the anthropocentric construction of God resulting from the projective identification, through which Spinoza introduces his psychological model, itself entails such distortion of fact.

15 It is notable that this 1959 description of therapeutic significance by Bion parallels Wolfson's (1934) description, cited above, on the manner in which readers' thoughts consolidate while in the course of reading *Ethics* (Wolfson, 1934, p. 5).

16 The stoic philosopher, Epictetus, construes a similar psychic function, a "faculty of choice and refusal, of desire and aversion, or in a word, the faculty which makes use of external impressions" (Epictetus, 1995, Bk. I.1.12, p. 11). Spinoza's *conatus* necessarily conjoins affirmation/denial with desire.

17 Kurt Lewin, earlier, wrote that psychological explanation must entail: "1. The general laws of the particular events; 2) the momentary constitution of the whole situation" and that in order to analyze the situation, one must characterize the situation, that is, the psychological environment and the psychological person, through concepts that are logically, clearly, and completely enough defined to allow logical derivations and which can be used as constants in place of the variable values of the equations which characterize the general laws (Lewin, 1933, p. 319).

Chapter 8

A General Understanding of Clinical Method

This is the first of two chapters focused upon Spinoza's presentation of a clinical psychological model in *Ethics*, Part III. It is divided into four subsections, corresponding to central themes in Spinoza's presentation: A Confluence of Perspectives; A Pleasing Conflict of Lines and Angles; Spinoza's Dynamics: Conceiving an Unconscious Matrix; and Clinical Observations Conjoining Willing, Pleasure, and Pain.

A Confluence of Perspectives

Reading *Ethics* closely, we begin with Spinoza's general understanding of the mind's functional activity, with affective experience mediating between body and environment. Part III occupies the center of *Ethics'* five-part sequence. The clinical reader has already observed that *Ethics* unfolds along two dimensions as Spinoza generates ideas, axioms, and propositions, concerning the place of human psychology in the natural order. His repetitive appeal is to the mathematic logic of planes, lines, and geometries, narratively illustrative of his theoretical claims. Against this cool rational clarity, Spinoza observes what humans do in our uninterrogated acts of projection and assertions of power, demonizing what we don't understand. Observing specific instances of seemingly irrational behavior, not unlike Freud in *Psychical (or Mental) Treatment* (1890), Spinoza asks

> how one should reckon a man who hangs himself, or how one should reckon babies, fools, and madmen. (II. Proposition 49, Scholium, p. 276)

DOI: 10.4324/9781003246404-12

Instead of rationally pursuing this question, we cloak our ignorance in arrogantly claimed false certainty and abusive power. Perhaps Spinoza's most vitriolic condemnation of this situation is reflected in the epigram written for the Dutch translation from Latin of his *Short Treatise on God, Man and His Well-Being*, a precursor to *Ethics*. Justified for his audience through appeal to Christian love, with reference to the "spirit of tenderness and tolerance, after the example of the Lord Christ, our best Teacher" (Spinoza, 2002, *Short Treatise*, p. 33), Spinoza offers this vernacular translation

> for the use of the Lovers of Truth and Virtue: so that they who spout so much about it and put their dirt and filth into the hands of simpletons as though it were ambergris, may just have their mouths stopped, and cease to profane what they do not understand: *God, themselves, and how to help people to have regard for each other's well-being*, and how to heal those whose mind is sick. (p. 33, italics are Spinoza's)

Writing in the Preface to *Ethics* Part III, Spinoza reiterates his consistent position (similarly articulated in the conclusion of Part II as well as in the explanatory form of projective identification presented in Part I), targeting through his philosophy those who would

> therefore bemoan, ridicule, despise, or as is most frequently the case, abuse. He who can criticize the weakness of the human mind more eloquently or more shrilly is regarded as almost divinely inspired. (III. Preface, p. 277)

Spinoza's aspirations for sharpening peoples' regard of our mutual well-being and for healing psychological suffering,[1] rise to the level of inflamed prophecy. Only through action based in *acquisition*[2] of clear and distinct self-understanding will such goals become achievable. This is the passionate Spinoza whose rationality and humanism captivate the psychological thinking of Lou Andreas Salome, Karen Horney, M. Hamblin Smith, Constance Rathbun, Walter Bernard, Amy Tanner, Frederick Weiss, and Erich Fromm. Mediating between aspiration and behavioral observation with its cause-and-effect relations is method. Writing in the *Treatise on the Emendation of the Intellect*, Spinoza explains that

> method must necessarily be discourse about reasoning or intellection. That is, method is not reasoning itself which leads to the understanding of the causes of things, and far less is it the understanding of the causes of things. It is the understanding of what is a true idea, distinguishing it from other kinds of perception and examining its nature, so that we may thereby come to know our power of understanding and may so train the mind that it will understand according to that standard all that needs to be understood, laying down definite rules as aids, and also ensuring that the mind does not waste its energy on useless pursuits. (Spinoza, 2002, *TEI*, p. 11)

Like Levenson's concept of a methodological algorithm characterizing each therapist's subjective engagement within therapeutic experience (Levenson, 1983), Spinozan method presides over both the act of reasoning and upon the understanding of causation. Similarly, Kurt Lewin observes that

> the goal of *analysis* is to *characterize the facts* so that one can *strictly derive the behavior*, or any other kind of psychological event, in a logical way, or (to say the same from another point of view) to be able to *predict* actual occurrences. The theoretical and practical goal of analysis is reached when such derivation is possible and then the task is completed. (Lewin, 1933, pp. 318–319; italics are Lewin's)

The engagement of such method, situated in the psychotherapeutic two-group, is described by Sullivan in *The Psychiatric Interview* (Sullivan, 1954).

Ethics Part III begins with the conjoining of these three Spinozan streams: passionate aspiration; pursuit of clear understanding; and methodological demonstration. This arrival parallels what will become characteristic of psychoanalysis during its period of humanistic development. Addressing the nature of psychoanalysis from this perspective, John Reid observes that psychoanalysis is three different things. It is a technical procedure for investigating unconscious mental processes and for treating psychoneuroses; it is a systematic body of fact and theory concerning the relations of conscious and unconscious mental processes; and it is, finally, a philosophy of life, in the sense that it is a way of looking at, of thinking about and of appraising some of basic habits, attitudes, and beliefs. (Reid, 1955, p. 115)

Ethics, in Spinoza's weaving of aspiration, observation, and method, anticipates this integrative understanding of psychoanalysis: (1) with aspiration as the looking, thinking and appraising of what we do toward greater perfection of thought and action including the healing of individual and interpersonal relations; (2) with *Ethics* Parts I and II generative of Spinoza's systematic presentation of theory and fact; and (3) with Part III, the strong clinical statement not only of what we do, but also how we characterize and address what we do, toward what Spinoza years before termed, the *emendation of the intellect.*

A Pleasing Conflict of Lines and Angles

The Preface to Part III argues that 17th-century conventional wisdom has got it wrong in the conviction that man

disturbs rather than follows Nature's order, and has absolute power over his actions, and is determined by no source other than himself. (III. Preface, p. 277)

Following from this cardinal error is its assertion that

the cause of human weakness and frailty not to the power of Nature in general, but to some defect in human nature. (III. Preface, p. 277)

By contrast, Spinoza, like the later Freud, who began his career arguing that both the hysteric and the *gebildete mensch* functioned according to similar psychological patterns, discerns that the continuum from human defect to human excellence occurs under Nature's common laws. From this recognition, Spinoza's programmatic position is clear: psychological suffering is not to be demeaned as weakness; nor is it to be addressed abusively, but rather, it is to be healed.[3]

Operating from the perspective that however unknown, psychic suffering follows Nature's laws, Spinoza condemns those who derive their social status and praise from hurting others. Just as Spinoza's concluding argument in Part I demonstrates the common construction of God in the form of projective identification, the introduction to Part III suggests that human ignorance regarding the cause of emotional pain is defended against through intolerance and persecution.

Alternatively, Spinoza pursues understanding of human affects or emotion, a field of inquiry inaugurating the modern study of Psychology. Against the arrogant claim that mind controls both body and Nature, Spinoza observes that,

> as far as I know, no one has defined the nature and strength of the emotions, and the power of the mind in controlling them. (III. Preface, p. 277)

Having observed the regularity of psychological laws within a framework of thinking and extension, unifying living things from their beginnings in Nature's first cause, then extended in a chain of efficient causation, Spinoza's *Ethics* Part III introduces dynamic psychology. It is dynamic in two senses. The first is in detailing the changing forms of human thought and extension from one state to another. In so doing, the second is Spinoza's arrival at a general model, bridging intrapsychic and interpersonal relations, in a psychology unifying both human motivational strivings and the objects of strivings' desires. Spinoza distinguishes his own program from Descartes, noting competitively that

> I know, indeed, that the renowned Descartes, though he too believed that the mind has absolute power over its actions, does explain human emotions through their first causes, and has also zealously striven to show how the mind can have absolute control over the emotions. But in my opinion he has shown nothing else but the brilliance of his own genius. (III. Preface, p. 277)

Instead, operating on the cause-and-effect relationships of proximate causation, and opposed to wrong-headed contemporary thought regarding psychopathology, he affirms the logic of his method, writing

> I should attempt to treat of the faults and follies of mankind in the geometric manner, and that I should propose to bring logical reasoning to bear on what they proclaim is opposed to reason and is vain, absurd, and horrifying. (III. Preface, p. 278)

Strongly arguing for a position which still endures in today's human sciences, he notes that

> in Nature, nothing happens which can be attributed to its defectiveness, for Nature is always the same; that is, the laws and rules of Nature according to which all things happen and change from one form to another are everywhere and always the same. So our approach to the understanding of the nature of things of every kind should likewise be one and the same; namely, through the universal laws and rules of Nature. (III. Preface, p. 278)

Through this argument, Spinoza turns his registrations of hatred and abuse themselves, into the object of scientific inquiry, brilliantly writing that

> the emotions of hatred, anger, envy, etc., considered in themselves, follow from the same necessity and force of Nature as all other particular things. So these emotions are assignable to definite causes through which they can be understood, and have definite properties, equally deserving of our investigation as the properties of any other thing, whose mere contemplation affords us pleasure. (III. Preface, p. 278)

Famously, Spinoza now proposes to utilize the same method followed in Parts I and II, first in discussion of Nature/God and next in general discussion of mind such that

> our approach to the understanding of the nature of things[4] of every kind should likewise be one and the same; namely,

through the universal laws and rules of Nature. Therefore, the emotions of hatred, anger, envy etc., considered in themselves, follow from the same necessity and force of Nature as all other particular things. So, these emotions are assignable to definite causes through which they can be understood, and have definite properties, equally deserving of our investigation as the properties of any other thing, whose mere contemplation affords us pleasure. I shall then, treat of the nature and strength of the emotions, and the mind's power over them, by the same method as I have used in treating of God and the mind, and I shall consider human actions and appetites just as if it were an investigation into lines, planes, or bodies. (III. Preface, p. 278)

Remembering readers' anxious experience of Part II Proposition 11, at which point Spinoza therapeutically recommended suspending judgment until after proceeding with his thinking, *step by step* (II. Proposition 11, Scholium, p. 241), the clinical reader cautiously scans Spinoza's Part III *Definitions.*[5] Spinoza reiterates and expands three important ideas. The first addresses *adequate cause*, which Spinoza terms a "cause whose effect can be clearly and distinctly perceived" (III. Definition 2, p. 278). Such adequacy is faced by *inadequate* or *partial* cause, the effect of which cannot be understood "through the said cause alone" (III Definition 2, p. 278). The reader recognizes that most causality is located within this second type: at best, polyvalent interactions emergent through intuitive inquiry to approximate adequacy in relation both to the clinician's and patient's understanding.

Next, Spinoza differentiates between active and passive experience. He calls active that which occurs either in us or external to us, that which is clear and distinct, so *adequate*, from "our nature alone". Passivity follows from internal or external experience "of which we are only the partial cause" (III Definition 2, p. 278; also, II. Proposition 3, p. 282). Passivity, under this definition, is the dominant mode of human interpersonal registration. However it may emerge actively into adequate cause, our registrations generally interact with the inadequate or partial causalities associated within unconscious experience.

Thirdly, Spinoza characterizes emotion or affect arithmetically, moderating the body's energic activity through addition and subtraction as

> the affections of the body by which the body's power of activity is increased or diminished, assisted or checked, together with the ideas of these affections. (III Definition 2, p. 278)

The reader notes that the causal reliance of mind upon body, in registration of what Freud will later call the body's *demand for work*, is supplemented by the self-reflective possibility of our recognizing the "ideas of these affections" (III Definition 3, p. 278). Emotions, therefore, (1) represent the increase, decrease, or maintenance of psychological vitality and (2) are themselves knowable through individual reflection as combinations of mental function. Spinoza reminds us that steady states exist despite the changing conjunctions of mind in that

> the human body can undergo many changes and nevertheless retain impressions or traces of objects and consequently the same images of things. (III. Postulate 2, p. 279)

Much as in the progressively integrative experience of psychotherapy, the reader of *Ethics* Part III experiences an increasing cohesion of thought beyond Parts I and II. Not only have newly assembled ideas been encountered earlier, but also the memory of these ideas in new contexts, provides a subjective sense of greater coherence than earlier, when first encountered.

Like Wolfson's image of iron filings, at first, "indistinguishable and shapeless" and "clinging to the propositions as bits of scrap-iron cling to a magnet" (Wolfson, 1934, p. 5), our continuous, iterative reading allows: (1) the grouping and solidifying of ideas; (2) the differentiation of ideas; (3) their crystallization along the lines of general principles such as the conjoining of thought and extension; together with (4) the resultant similarity to our therapeutic interests. These include Spinoza's: parallelism of thinking and acting; recognition of mind's determination by body, although with inadequate knowledge by mind both of its own contents and those of its embodied object's affections; and of the generalized *willing, striving,* or *going on being* within each momentary thought, affirming or denying perceptual experience.

Still, the system as a whole is too complex to be simply held. Remembered partly, restlessly highlighting shifting elements in changing focus, it does not cohere as a thing; but as a topography of contrasting dynamisms: the overarching premises of thought-and-extension; recognition of the singularity of thinker, thought, and thought's object; and the modest model of proximate, adequate, causality. The difficulty in this conflictual scheme, extended in the form of lines and angles as thought and extension ramify in different attributes, is in discerning the local pathways of our therapeutic, clinical interests.

Luckily, our tenacity is quickly rewarded in Spinoza's claim that

> nobody as yet knows the structure of the body so accurately as to explain all its functions, not to mention that in the animal world we find much that far surpasses human sagacity, and that sleepwalkers do many things in their sleep that they would not dare when awake- clear evidence that the body, solely from the laws of its own nature, can do many things at which its mind is amazed. (III. Proposition 2, Scholium, p. 280)

Pivoting from sleepwalking, Spinoza introduces a series of observations that immediately remind the clinical reader of Freud's observations both in "Psychic (Mental) Treatment" (1890) and in *The Psychopathology of Everyday Life* (1901). Like Freud in recognition of unconscious determination, Spinoza recognizes that in regarding the structure of the body,

> when men say this or that action of the body arises from the mind which has command over the body, they do not know what they are saying, and are merely admitting, under a plausible cover of words, that they are ignorant of the true cause of that action and are not concerned to discover it. (III. Proposition 2, Scholium, p. 280)

Like Freud, Spinoza begins empirically, multiplying his recognitions of what we do not understand. He begins with consideration that the human condition would indeed be far happier if it were equally in the power of men to keep silent as to talk. (III. Proposition 2, Scholium, p. 281)

He elaborates, writing that

experience teaches us with abundant examples that nothing is less within men's power than to hold their tongues or control their appetites. From this derives the commonly held view that we act freely only in cases where our desires are moderate, because our appetites can then be easily held in check by the remembrance of another thing that frequently comes to mind; but when we seek something with a strong emotion that cannot be allayed by the remembrance of some other thing, we cannot check our desires.[6] (III. Proposition 2, Scholium, p. 281)

Expanding on the consequences of immoderate talk, Spinoza provides multiple examples resulting from unconscious determination, "when we are at the mercy of conflicting emotions" (ibid, p. 281). These include: (1) a baby's thought that "it freely seeks milk"; (2) an angry child's belief "that it freely seeks revenge"; (3) a timid man's notion that "he freely seeks flight"; and (4) a drunken man's belief

that it is from the free decision of the mind that he says what he later, when sober, wishes he had not said.[7] (III. Proposition 2, Scholium, p. 281)

Continuing with reference to "the delirious man, the gossiping woman, the child and many more", Spinoza uses these observations to show that we are unconscious of the causes of our mental decisions. Rather, the decisions we believe to be freely made are "nothing more than the appetites themselves", the externalization of the mind's purposive willing. He writes that

each man's actions are shaped by his emotion; and those who furthermore are a prey to conflicting emotions know not what they want, while those who are free from emotion are driven on to this or that course by a slight impulse. (III. Proposition 2, Scholium, p. 281)

Elaborating, Spinoza writes that decision, operating as thought, simultaneously parallels the physical state of the body, operating as appetite. Further, in order to act as a consequence of mental decision, as in the example of uttering a word, it is necessary that first, "memory comes into play" (III. Proposition 2, Scholium, p. 281).

Associating from the relation of memory to action, Spinoza observes that mind is not free to remember or to forget anything; but rather, that both memory and forgetting are motivated. He concludes this scholium with some thoughts on dreaming, later the province of Freudian thought. He observes that

> when we dream that we are speaking, we think that we do so from free mental decision; yet we are not speaking, or if we are, it is the result of spontaneous movement of the body. Again, we dream that we are keeping something secret, and that we are doing so by the same mental decision that comes into play in our waking hours when we keep silent about what we know. Finally, we dream that from a mental decision we act as we dare not act when awake. So I would very much like to know whether in the mind there are two sorts of decisions, dreamland decisions and free decisions. If we don't want to carry madness so far, we must necessarily grant that the mental decision that is believed to be free is not distinct from imagination and memory, and is nothing but the affirmation which an idea, insofar as it is an idea, necessarily involves (II. Proposition 49). So these mental decisions arise in the mind from the same necessity as the ideas of things existing in actuality, and those who believe that they speak, or keep silent, or do anything from free mental decision are dreaming with their eyes open". (III. Proposition 2, Scholium, p. 282)

Dreaming with their eyes open is an idea of fundamental unconscious error that connects ancient philosophic wisdom from Ecclesiastes to Lucretius, through modern construction of the psychoanalytic encounter, itself modeled on the dream (Stern, 2013b). What joins such distortion is obliviousness to clear and distinct approximations to reality.

Arrayed against distorted thought is Spinoza's bold dynamic conception, anchored in the principle of organic self-preservation. Echoing the terminology of then contemporary theorists Hobbes and Descartes, Spinoza's notion of *conatus* is announced in several steps. Initially, Spinoza introduces the general principle in nature that "each thing, insofar as it is in itself, endeavors to persist in its own being" (III. Proposition 6, p. 283). This concept is next broadened as

> the conatus with which each thing endeavors to persist in its own being is nothing but the actual essence of the thing itself. (III. Proposition 7, p. 283)

That is, for Spinoza, the essence of each human is in the passionate struggling which characterizes the persistence and tenacity of each. Following from Spinoza's transformation of the 14th-century Provencal Jewish philosopher, Gersonides, such striving (*hishtadlut* in Hebrew) is the human correlate through the activity of mind, to the instinctual actions of infra-human species (Green, 2015, p. 34; Harvey, 2012, p. 283).

Under a causal scheme akin to the later dependent concomitance of Hughlings Jackson, Spinoza mobilizes the transformed, ancient motivational concept of conatus, or organic self-preservation as definitional of human essence, to build upon two forms of primary emotion. The first is the summative registration of pleasure and pain, in ranging from temporary to more enduring compromise formations. The second, more sophisticated, anticipates DW Winnicott's idea of our creative discovery of the world upon which we act[8] (Winnicott, 1953). For Spinoza, this arises from generalized internal will, extended outward to appetite and awareness of appetite's object, with these two latter forms of extension fundamental to desire. Next, in a manner anticipating Ferenczi's (1909) articulation of introjection relative to projection, desire as externalized emotion (itself the transformation of will first into appetite and next into conscious awareness), is again internalized, together with its discernable effects, in the registration of feedback upon our mental perceptions.

The transit of our extended mental faculties, mediated by pleasure and pain, into the external world, causes us to mark objects as "loved" or "hated"; and further, the operation of our self-generated desire creates a kind of dynamic supercharge (akin to the later Freudian cathexis), such that we strive to preserve the things we love, and also endeavor to remove or destroy the things we hate.

Spinozan Dynamics: Conceiving an Unconscious Matrix

Introducing *conatus* as the essential nature of mind in human self-preservative striving or endeavoring, Spinoza provides a general overview, observing that

> the mind, both insofar as it has clear and distinct ideas and insofar as it has confused ideas, endeavors to persist in its own being over an indefinite period of time, and is conscious of this conatus. (III. Proposition 9, p. 284)

Whether ideas are aligned with reality or whether they are a function of fantasy, as elemental qualities of mind they are both functional in their endeavor: (1) to persist across time and also, (2) in implicit recognition of this persistent striving. Spinoza's explanatory scholium proposes the clinically useful recognition that

> when this conatus is related to the mind alone, it is called Will [*voluntas*]; when it is related to mind and body together, it is called Appetite[*appetitus*], which is therefore nothing else but man's essence, from the nature of which there necessarily follow those things that tend to his preservation, and which man is thus determined to perform. Further, there is no difference between appetite and Desire [*cupiditas*] except that desire is usually related to men insofar as they are conscious of their appetite. Therefore, it can be defined as follows: desire is "appetite accompanied by the consciousness thereof". (III. Proposition 9, Scholium, p. 284)

Just as the mind's ideas (including the idea of mind itself) are potentially knowable to the thinker, so too does the extension of intrapsychic Will into appetitive enactment become consciously acknowledged as Desire. This same dynamic details the interaction between the private, internal world essential to humans, and the external world, accessible to others' apprehensions (readers will remember the example of Peter and Paul in II. Proposition 17, Scholium, p. 257). In so doing, Spinoza describes the continuous action between mind and environment, observable in clinical psychoanalysis. Unnoted explicitly by 20th-century commentators on Spinozan links with psychoanalysis, Spinoza generates a hypothetical feedback loop of human *thought* and *extension*. While complete as a general construct of process, Spinoza's model of psychological action is the forerunner of such generalized mathematical models as: (1) Levenson's concept of an algorithmic procedural model (1983); (2) the vectors and lifespaces of Kurt Lewin's field theory (Brown, 1936; Lewin, 1933, 1936; Stern, 2013a, 2013b); and (3) the clinical algorithm detailing minute shifts between hypothesized internal psychic positions, advanced by Bion (Bion, 1962; Miller & Sweet, 2018). Each of these constructs, anchored in a generalized, testable hypothesis, conforms to what I have termed *cloudy mathematics*, following the multiple levels of Spinoza's thought (II. Proposition 7, Scholium) in that each model prescribes an adequate general idea; but that the interpreted specifics of the psychological situation are necessarily partial—and often the focus of therapeutic resistance—rendering the outcome imprecise, much as with the demonstrative illustrations of Spinoza's *Ethics.*

Spinoza concludes this scholium with the binding of the unbounded free will imagined by his philosophical adversaries. Similar in form to the late 19th-century James-Lange theory of emotion, Spinoza writes,

> it is clear from the above considerations that we do not endeavor, will, seek after or desire because we judge a thing to be good. On the contrary, we judge a thing to be good because we endeavor, will, seek after and desire it. (III. Proposition 9, Scholium, p. 284)

Recapitulating Part III Definition 3, Spinoza proposes that

> whatsoever increases or diminishes, assists or checks, the power of activity of our body, the idea of the said thing increases or diminishes, assists or checks the power of thought of our mind. (III. Proposition 11, p. 284).

Expanding upon this definitional commentary on mind, Spinoza's scholium achieves the explanatory level of a supercommentary, detailing the continuous mental activity of advance and regression,[9]

> we see then that the mind can undergo considerable changes, and can pass now to a state of greater perfection, now to one of less perfection, and it is these passive transitions that explicate for us the emotions of Pleasure and Pain. So in what follows I shall understand by pleasure, "the passive transition of the mind to a state of greater perfection", and by pain "the passive transition of the mind to a state of less perfection". (III. Proposition 11, Scholium, p. 285)

Spinoza's correlate of the psychoanalytic *Pleasure Principle* operates along the same continuum as affects themselves: through increase and decrease. Where the relation of affect to mind concerns "the power of thought of our mind (III. Proposition 11, p. 284), the relation of pleasure and pain corresponds to the adequacy of thinking itself".[10]

It is at this point that Spinoza illustrates his understanding through reference to empirically observable behaviors. Just as earlier, he had differentiated the intrapsychic action of willing from its external projection as appetite and conscious desire; he now differentiates between different titrations of pleasure and pain along a continuum from the extreme of titillation to the extreme of anguish. Between these extremes lie cheerfulness and melancholy. What distinguishes the extreme from the more moderate position is the degree to which different parts of the body and mind are affected by pleasurable or painful stimulation (III. Proposition 11, Scholium, p. 285). The reader notes Spinoza's precision, on the one hand, in differentiating observable states of mind; and on the other hand, the vagueness of discerning the complication of different "parts" of the embodied mind, with titillation and anguish suggestive of an unequal registration of pleasure and pain by the body; and with cheerfulness and melancholy suggestive of an equal mental registration.

Reiterating his doctrine, Spinoza again emphasizes three kinds of primary emotional registrations: pleasure, pain, and willing (III. Proposition 9, Scholium, p. 284; III. Proposition 11, Scholium, p. 285).

Emphasizing the mind's orientation toward increasing the "body's power of activity" (III. Proposition 12, p. 285), Spinoza reflects that

> when the mind thinks of those things that diminish or check the body's power of activity, it endeavors, as far as it can, to call to mind those things that exclude the existence of the former. (III. Proposition 13, p. 286)

From within the Spinozan model, the mind operates in intrinsic defense against its diminution of power. Clinically, we can appreciate that on the side of symptomatic obstinacy, this suggests a basic orientation toward mobilizing those behaviors that have been proven, however unrecognized, to work. Spinoza's doctrine goes farther, suggesting the mobilization through our intrinsic willing, of thoughts that negate ideas that themselves, threaten the mind's conception of its own power. While not derived from a theory of repression, the result of such observation is of a mind armored against perceived diminution of power. What we recognize as defensive operations are therefore implicit correlates of this conception.

Pivoting from this idea that "the mind is averse to thinking of things that diminish or check its power and the body's power" (III. Proposition 13, Corollary, p. 286), Spinoza's scholium turns to external aids and threats to the maintenance of such power. His definition of Love and Hate extends directly from the respective internal registration of pleasure and pain, such that

> Love is merely "pleasure accompanied by the idea of an external cause" and Hatred is merely "pain accompanied by the idea of an external cause" (III. Proposition 13, Scholium, p 286). Love and hate, like pleasure and pain, are registered in relation to the mind's maintenance of its own self-preservative endeavoring. Conceptually, just as the internally experienced Will is externalized into Appetite and Desire, the internally experienced pleasure and pain are externalized into respective Love and Hate. (III. Proposition 13, Scholium, p. 286).

Naturally, Spinoza observes that

we see that he who loves necessarily endeavors to have present
and to preserve the thing that he loves; on the other hand, he who
hates endeavors to remove and destroy the thing that he hates.
(III. Proposition 13, Scholium, p. 286)

But from this clear observation, the reader can discern a familiar
clinical problem: in encountering the fixed attitude of the patient
in maintaining either love or hate for another, the clinician will
necessarily encounter resistance in attempting to inquire into such
position, as it will threaten a developed mental pattern in affirming
the mind's own power. Indeed, the clinical emergence of a paranoid
state of mind would seem probable, given such external disturbance,
until it can both be demonstrated and considered plausible, that
the fixed attitude is itself partial, distorted, or self-deceptive. If
so, then the paranoid state might shift into confusion or anxiety,
given the rebalancing of environmental (or intrapsychic) registration
of pleasure and pain.

Clinical Observations Conjoining Willing, Pleasure, and Pain

While we have read that the central Spinozan idea of conatus is what
DW Winnicott would term a generalized *going on being* in affirming
self-preservative aliveness (Abrams, 1996, pp. 67–78; Winnicott
1960), Spinoza's recognition of what humans find pleasurable and
painful is equally generalized. Emotions seem to operate by the
mind's recognition of patterned pleasure and pain. Spinoza writes,

if the mind has once been affected by two emotions at the same
time, when it is later affected by the one it will also be affected by
the other. (III. Proposition 14, p. 286)

That is, the conflictual nature of emotional pleasure and pain resides
not only in cognitive memory, but in what Federn (1926) will term
embodied *ego feelings*, themselves occupying a gradient from clarity
to confusion. Additionally, Spinoza observes that "anything can indirectly be the cause of Pleasure Pain or Desire" (III. Proposition 15,
p. 286). Because the mind is often uncertain or even oblivious in

knowing itself (II. Proposition 23, p. 260; II. Proposition 24, p. 260; II. Proposition 27, p. 261) our ideas about emotion "are not clear and distinct, but confused" (II. Proposition 28, p. 261). From this, our emotional attributions are often cloudily indistinct such that

> we understand how it can come about that we love or hate some things without any cause known to us, but merely from Sympathy and Antipathy, as they are called. We should also classify in this category those objects that affect us with pleasure or pain from the mere fact that they have some resemblance to objects that are wont to affect us with the same emotions. (III. Proposition 15, Scholium, p. 287)

Spinoza further observes that

> From the mere fact that we imagine a thing to have something similar to an object that is wont to affect the mind with pleasure or pain, we shall love it or hate it, although the point of similarity is not the efficient cause of these emotions. (III. Proposition 16, p. 287)

With this, Spinoza mobilizes the concept of association, the subjective, cognitive examples of which, he illustrated in Part II, citing the meaning of the Latin *pomum*, and the meanings to different individuals of horse-tracks on a beach (II. Proposition 18, Scholium, p. 258). Here, the emotional linkage to pleasure and pain is similarly evoked through imagination or fantasy; this too, as with other associative processes, is dependent upon memory. Spinoza extends his thoughts about emotional association, writing that

> if we imagine that a thing which is wont to affect us with an emotion of pain, has something similar to another thing which is wont to affect us with an equally great emotion of pleasure, we shall hate it and love it at the same time. (III. Proposition 17, p. 287)

We are familiar with this condition, later termed *ambivalence* by Eugen Bleuler. Spinoza terms it, the *vacillation* of mind, observing that the vacillation of two conflicting emotions corresponds to the sphere of feeing just as the doubt he describes in the scholium to IIPr 44 is related to the function of imagination (III. Proposition 17, Scholium, p. 288). Complicating matters,

> since one and the same thing can be affected in many ways, it can likewise affect one and the same part of the body in different ways. From this we can readily conceive that one and the same object can be the cause of many conflicting emotions. (III. Proporsition 17, Scholium, p. 288)

Further complicating the variations of emotion is our relation to time, based on imagination. Spinoza proposes that

> from the image of things past or future man is affected by the same emotion of pleasure or pain as from the image of a thing present. (III. Proposition 18, p. 288)

He elaborates through two scholia, beginning with clarification that

> I call a thing past or future insofar as we have been, or shall be affected by it; for example, insofar as we have seen or shall see it, it has refreshed or will refresh us, it has injured or will injure us, etc. For insofar as we imagine it this way, to that extent we affirm its existence. (III. Proposition 18, Scholium 1, p. 288)

Unlike the disaffirmed action of free will, with the mind reigning over the actions of the body, the unconscious mental action of imagination affects the body. Spinoza observes that

> the body is not affected by any emotion that excludes the existence of the thing, and so (II. Proposition 17) the body is affected by the image of a thing in the same way as if the thing itself were present. However, since it is generally the case that those who have had much experience vacillate when they are regarding a thing as future or past and are generally in doubt as to its outcome (II. Pr 44 schol), the result is that emotions that arise from similar images of things are not so constant, but are

generally disturbed by images of things until men become more assured of the outcome. (III. Proposition 18, Scholium, p. 288)

Pausing from the continuous press of *Ethics'* propositions and scholia, the clinical reader observes that without explicit notation, Spinoza has accomplished a very contemporary approach to human understanding. Like W.R. Bion, centuries later, Spinoza has presented a grid of clinically observable processes as scaffolding for the understanding of the mind's unconscious matrix. It operates across multiple dimensions, beginning with the three fundamental elements of willing, pleasure, and pain. The vicissitudes of willing, integrated with registrations of pleasure and pain, are extended externally from the internal world, into appetite and desire. The efficacy of such actions is recognized by the body, with the mind's registrations of such variable mixtures of pain and pleasure as those detailed by Spinoza in the second scholium of III.Proposition 18, reflecting such complex mental states as: hope, fear, confidence, despair, joy, and disappointment. These are not simply emotional states of arrival, but rather, function unitarily in describing the reciprocal internal registration or internalization, of the effects of willing's externalization. That is, beginning with willing, pleasure, and pain, from thought to externalization in action, we recognize consequential effect. We are interested in this effect, registering it perceptually, with the new resonances of our feeling and imaginative functions, operating together with the continuing function of willing, overseen (or not) by the rational function.

Spinoza describes a 17th-century feedback loop, including: (1) willing or conatus; (2) pleasure; (3) pain; (4) extension and its effects; (5) internalization; (6) new registrations across the functional mental domains of perception, feeling, imagination, willing, and reason. Necessarily, this action unfolds across time. Not only must it occur formally in diachronic time, but its registration also involves immediate and sometimes discernable synchronic arrivals, both temporary and enduring. Spinoza explains, for example, that

hope is "inconstant pleasure, arising from the image of a thing future or past, of whose outcome we are in doubt". Fear is "inconstant pain, likewise arising from the image of a thing in doubt". Now if the element of doubt be removed from these emotions, hope becomes confidence and fear becomes despair, that is "pleasure or pain arising from a thing which we have feared or hoped". Joy is "pleasure arising from the image of a past thing of whose outcome we had been in doubt". Finally, disappointment is "the pain opposite to joy". (III. Proposition 18, Scholium 2, pp. 288–289)

Added to this grid or matrix, therefore, is the element of time, as it is interpreted via the efficacy of action undertaken from the conjoining of willing, pleasure, and pain. Spinoza's recognition is effectively characterized by Bion's Kleinian expression of (1) the patient's movement observed by the analyst in extension from a particular position at one discrete moment in time; (2) to a revised iteration of that position, en route to (3) a later position, at another moment of clinical process (Miller & Sweet, 2018).

While Bion's process-markers are expressed as Paranoid, Schizoid, and Depressive positions, at time periods (n) through (n + 1, n + 2, n + 3, etc), the Paranoid, Schizoid, and Depressive states of mind, correspond approximately to Spinoza's transitory terms of hope, fear, confidence, despair, joy and disappointment. Spinoza's unconscious process matrix, like Bion's, is complicated further by the associative processes of affective resonance and image, together with memory, complicated by the relative endurance of mental objects, however absent in present time.

Generated in clear and descriptive language, accenting differently observable expressions of mental activity, Spinoza presents a holistic and unitary system; and with this, the clinical possibility of translating behavior, both in motivation and outcome, to patients in exploration or articulation of momentary and more extensive thoughts and feelings.

Notes

1 Readers will remember from the *Tractate on the Emendation of the Intellect* that Spinoza's first ethical work begins from the foundation of his own personal experience,

After experience had taught me the hollowness and futility of everything that is ordinarily encountered in daily life, and I realized that all the things which were the source and object of my anxiety held nothing of food or evil in themselves save insofar as the mind was influenced by them, I resolved at length to enquire there existed a true good, one which was capable of communicating itself and could alone affect the mind to the exclusion of all else, whether, in fact, there was something whose discovery and acquisition would afford me a continuous and supreme joy to all eternity. (Spinoza, 2002, p. 3)

2 The idea of *acquired* knowledge suggests Spinoza's linkage with Aristotelian thought, as transformed by Maimonides in *Eight Chapters*, Chapter Two, who describes three kinds of intellectual virtue. The first is experiential, "the knowledge of the direct and indirect causes of things based on a previous realization of the existence of those things". The next is composed both of (1) the inborn capacity for registering first impressions; and (2) the "acquired intellect", is itself a transformation of Averroes' commentaries on Aristotle, of knowledge gained in grasping the nature of things. The third is immediate perception (Gorfinkle, 1912, pp. 49–50).

3 Spinoza's intended therapeutic utilization of *Ethics* follows Maimonides' applied practical philosophy. *Eight Chapters* is itself positioned by Maimonides as "a treatise on the soul, its characteristics and powers, and their employment toward the goal of moral perfection" (Gorfinkle, 1912, p. 11). Toward this end, Maimonides, like the later Spinoza, affirms that "he who tries to cure the soul, wishing to improve the moral qualities, must have a knowledge of the soul in its totality and its parts, must know how to prevent it from becoming diseased, and how to maintain its health" (Gorfinkle, 1912, p. 38).

4 The reader notes implicit reference to Lucreius' work, *De rerum natura*, also cited by Freud in the *Interpretation of Dreams*.

5 In fairness to Spinoza's stepwise care, our two English-language translations give us two divergent perspectives on Spinoza's methodological description for his readers. Translating *Ethics* IV. P18, Schol, Curley depicts this method, almost apologetically, as "our cumbersome geometric order" (De Spinoza, p. 125). By contrast, Shirley translates the same concept as "our detailed geometrical order" (Spinoza, 2002, p. 330). The reader is invited to construct whichever Spinoza she desires, apologetic or rigid. However, the degree of suggested self-revelation in these words will have implication for the clinician's freedom of expression in relation to patients, as we apply Spinoza in the clinical setting.

6 That moderation is the key to our free activity follows from Aristotelian consideration of virtuous action developed as the mean between two extremes. Textual examples of such thinking, known to Spinoza, include Maimonides' *Eight Chapters*, itself a transformation of al-Farabi's earlier Aristotelian transformations (Gorfinkle, 1912).

7 In an earlier work, I recognized Freud's similar descriptive style in his 1890 essay on psychotherapy (Freud, 1890, p. 284), in that "Freud reminds his medically informed audience of the reciprocal intertwining within medical practice of body and mind. Moving from consideration of symptomatic plasticity, as well as the magical valence of words, Freud presents the reader in rapid order with multiple and disparate considerations including a carnival seer who reads facial expressions, the behavior of children, considerations of religious martyrs, and the tenacity of wounded soldiers engaged in combat" (Miller & Sweet, 2018, p. 8).

8 Alfred North Whitehead makes explicit this creative domain of human motivation, construing it as "another rendering of the Aristotelian 'matter'" (Whitehead, 1978, p. 31). Linked together in the striving of conatus, the twinned action of *creativity* and *going on being* provide a solid Spinozan link with the metapsychological assumptions of our contemporary psychoanalytic vernacular (Miller, 2015), derived directly from the contributions of D.W. Winnicott (Winnicott, 1953; Winnicott, 1960).

9 Whereas the reception history of Spinoza's sources approximate supercommentaries upon commentaries, such as Maimonides' reliance upon al-Faradi preceded by al-Faradi's commentary upon Aristotle, or Spinoza's own assimilation and transformation of Hasdai Crescas, Maimonides, Gersonides etc, his particular mobilization of the demonstrative form allows Spinoza himself to comment upon the commentary that he has already established. This is reflected in Deleuze's recognition that the "broken" chain of scholia represent a line of thinking different from the "unbroken" chain of propositions, axioms, etc (Deleuze, 1988, p. 29). Considering present readers' immersion in psychoanalytic thought, we might recognize a similar pattern in the writings both of Freud and post-Freudians. Later thinkers—including Freud, while elaborating or deviating from earlier work—often begin from considerations conceived by earlier generations of psychoanalysts, in the unacknowledged hermeneutic form of supercommentary.

10 It is helpful here, to discern both Spinoza's reception of Maimonides' transformed Aristotelian psyche, as well as Spinoza's own transformation of the Maimonidean model. For the purpose of psychological remediation, Maimonides departs from the Neoplatonic division of soul into physical, vital, and psychical functions (Gorfinkle, 1912, p. 37, ft 4). Instead, following Aristotle, he advocates a five-part system including: (1) nutritive; (2) perceptive; (3) imaginative; (4) appetitive; and (5) rational functions (Gorfinkle, 1912, pp. 37–43). Spinoza's innovation is in relegating the nutritive function to the body itself, while expanding the perceptive function into another function, the range of subjective feeling. However, notably, Spinoza employs Maimonides' differentiation between capabilities within the appetitive function, to elevate affirmation and denial as the cardinal action of conatus, linked through

subjective registration of pleasure and pain. Further, Spinoza differentiates between internal and external fields of individual thought and extension, thereby facilitating his own dynamic algorithm. Spinoza's final section of Part III, *Definition of the Emotions*, corresponds to Maimonides' listing of psychological behaviors in *Eight Chapters*, with the difference that Spinoza's derivations are through a dynamic matrix whereas Maimonides' correspond to the classic Aristotelian balance between extremes of too much and too little in relation to virtue and vice.

Chapter 9

Conclusion, Part III

This chapter concludes discussion of Part III, the locus of our *clinical Spinoza*. Not only does Spinoza generate a matrix of clinical process familiar to contemporary, 21st-century psychoanalysis, but also, the thorny process of apprehending *Ethics* generates the same kind of confusion and panic as in the negotiation of challenging contemporary papers in clinical psychoanalysis (Miller, 2016).

Spinoza's Clinical Field

In powerful literary form, suggestive of Spinoza's conjoining of thought and extension, *Ethics* proceeds from Part III to Parts IV and V, integrating the two Spinozan currents of passionate humanistic aspiration and of cool psychological demonstration. Central to this brilliant fusion is Spinoza's consolidation of clinical considerations presented in the *Definition of the Emotions* that follows Part III. Proposition 59. Inclusive of 48 explications, this section generates a glossary of human emotions, with the particulars of each discerned from combination of the three elements of conatus, pleasure and pain, essential to human being (III. Definitions of the Emotions, 1, 2, & 3, p. 311).

The particularities in *Definition of the Emotions* culminate in a *General Definition of Emotions*. The reader, having discerned the importance of earlier chapter conclusions in Parts I and II, recognizes in these *Definitions*, a formal literary difference. Unlike Spinoza's generally lively prose narratives, *Definition of the Emotions* reads ploddingly, like a listing today, of informational bullet points. This compositional form

DOI: 10.4324/9781003246404-13

conjures memory for the reader, of listed human temperaments, presented through the lens of medieval compilation. But unlike the Aristotelian considerations of virtue and vice in Maimonides' *Eight Chapters*, Spinoza does not generate a simple mathematics of mean behavioral forms derived from extreme behavioral binaries.[1] Instead, he lists conclusions derived from the matrix of unconscious and conscious process observations, generated earlier in Part III. These include fifty-seven observations of behavioral forms including: cheerfulness; titillation; melancholy; anguish; wonder; contempt; veneration; scorn; love; hatred; inclination; aversion; devotion; derision; hope; fear; confidence; despair; joy; disappointment; pity; compassion; approbation; indignation; over-esteem; disparagement; envy; compassion; self-contentment; humility; repentance; pride; self-abasement; honor; shame; bashfulness; impudence; longing; emulation; gratitude; benevolence; anger; revenge; cruelty; mercy; boldness; cowardice; consternation; timorousness; stupefaction; hesitation; courtesy; ambition; dissipation; drunkenness; avarice; and lust (III. *Definition of the Emotions*, pp. 311–319).

Generalized, these particulars are enlisted by Spinoza to arrive at the universal observation concluding *Ethics* Part III, that

> the emotion called a passive experience is a confused idea whereby the mind affirms a greater or less force of existence of its body, or part of its body, than was previously the case, and by the occurrence of which the mind is determined to think of one thing rather than another. (III. *General Definition of Emotions*, p. 319)

This translates to us, simply, as: (1) human psychological receptivity, based in inadequate and partial comprehension; of (2) the mind's confused and distorted registrations, responsive to the body's underlying physical nature; that (3) determine, in action, through the conjoint operation of mind's multiple functions, effect upon a particular object of thought. This is Spinoza's summary statement concerning the psychological nature of unconscious experience, potentially knowable to the individual in the same sense as Freud's later affirmation that *where id was ego shall be* (Freud, 1923).

As a central component within the five-part sequence of *Ethics*, the findings in Part III are enlisted by Spinoza as conclusive proof against the common assumption of free-will in mind's purported

suzerainty over body. Alternatively, he proves the body's determination of mind in precipitating behavior. Spinoza's purpose for such
demonstration is linked to the applications of our limited, if considerable, range of ethical choices, given the pull of our emotions he
later terms "human bondage" under

> man's lack of power to control and check the emotions. For a
> man at the mercy of his emotions is not his own master, but is
> subject to fortune, in whose power he so lies that he is often
> compelled, although he sees the better course, to pursue the
> worse. (IV. Preface, p. 320)

From this perspective, Parts IV and V extend the clinical psychology
developed in Part III to the aspirational *blessedness* promised in the
Appendix to Part II, where Spinoza claims that

> this doctrine, apart from giving us complete tranquility of mind,
> has the further advantage of teaching us wherein lies our greatest
> happiness or blessedness. (II. Appendix, p. 276)

Yet, however Spinoza's doctrine is implemented by the individual
toward "such actions as are urged on us by love and piety" (II.
Appendix, p. 276), his underlying model of clinical psychology
whispers a doubling in the turmoil and confusion generated by the
confluence of willing, perceiving, imagining, and feeling; and tamed
only by assiduous attention to the pursuit of rational thinking, recommended through Parts IV and V, and broadly congruent with the
therapeutic tasks of psychoanalysis (Andreas-Salomé, 1964; Bernard,
1946; Fromm, 1964a, 1964b; Rathbun, 1934; Reid, 1955; Smith,
1925, 1926; Weiss, 1952).
    Disclosed through our reading of *Ethics* informed by clinical psy-
choanalytic practice, Spinoza's matrix illuminates an affective
pathway through which inadequate, distorted, confused, and partial
registrations are processed en route from human physiology to
human action. Our recognition of this clinical Spinoza affirms Lou
Andreas Salome's observation a century ago, that Spinoza's thought
meets us everywhere on the path of psychoanalytic development.
With this affirmation, our present task of discerning the *clinical*

Spinoza, departs from Spinoza's original agenda; and operates as a supercommentary upon the development of a contemporary psychoanalysis, itself emergent in part from received Spinozan thought. Recognition of Spinoza's psychological model is informed by the clinical reader's familiarity with today's psychoanalytic *vernacular expression* (Miller, 2016), especially in reference to Winnicott's *going on being* and the cloudy mathematics of Bion's algorithmic recognitions, extending to the post-Lewinian mathematics of the clinical field (Stern, 2013a, 2013b). All of these are connected, in therapeutic process, by the analyst's own negotiation of the analytic process, once described by Sullivan as expertise in the conduct of the psychiatric interview, a

> situation of primarily *vocal* communication in a *two-group*, more or less *voluntarily integrated*, on a progressively unfolding *expert-client* basis for the purpose of elucidating *characteristic patterns of living* of the subject person, the patient or client, which patterns he experiences as particularly troublesome or especially valuable, and in the revealing of which he expects to derive *benefit*. (Sullivan, 1954, p. 4)

Demonstrating a Clinical Matrix of Mind

We have seen above, that by *Ethics* III. Proposition 18, Spinoza presents a grid of observable process considerations, establishing a framework for understanding the unconscious matrix of mind. Its central affective qualities are: (1) the self-preservative idea of willing in the affirming or denying of ideas; together with the (2) changing balances between mind's registrations of pleasure and pain, and (3) imagination. This integration is fundamental to the externalization of private thought into (a) unreflective appetite and (b) conscious desire. Because pleasure and pain are subjectively complex, such that "anything can indirectly" become their efficient cause (III. Proposition 15, p. 286), what may be painful for one individual may be registered as pleasurable by another. Further, our resonances with subjectively felt pleasures and pains are compounded: through the activities of memory and association; by perceptual similarity to other objects evoking feeling (III. Proposition 16); and by our imagination twinned with feeling, such that similar things affect us in similar ways (III. Proposition 17). From such complications, Spinoza details the mind's *vacillation,* today's *ambivalence,* as an intrinsically confusing conflictual condition within the mind's emotional registration. Just as doubt challenges the certainty of imagination, so does vacillation challenge the certainty of feeling.

However, vacillation and doubt are themselves, difficult conditions to endure. The mind is also challenged by reliance upon inadequate *knowledge of the first kind,* fragmented and confused opinion (II. Proposition 40, Scholium 2, p. 267), which nevertheless, relieves the tensions of mind's intrinsic "privation of knowledge" (II. Proposition 35, p. 265). Such essential resistance to clear and distinct thinking is heightened by mind's aversion to generating thoughts which "diminish or check the body's power of activity, its endeavors" (III. Proposition 13, p. 286). However unnamed explicitly, but intrinsic to Spinoza's dynamics of mind, are the unpleasant and even unbearable, states of anxiety recognizable in clinical psychoanalytic practice.

Spinoza's descriptions operate across five generalized functional aspects of mind. These correspond, roughly, through transformed medieval reception, to Aristotelian categories. Spinoza's scheme includes: (1) perception, or the mind's registration of external and internal events upon the body; (2) imagination, our fantasy, as the mind's ongoing play with its registrations of perception and feeling; (3) feeling, the locus of the pleasure and pain fundamental to the Spinozan system; (4) integrated toward action, with imagination's containment of memory and associational functioning, through conatus or Willing, our lively striving in going on being; and (5) presided over, in the sorting out of the mind's registrations in relation to reality, by Reason. Together with these functionalities, Spinoza describes two psychological fields integrating the fusion of object and desire: the intrapsychic world and the external world of interpersonal relations. Complicating matters, mental functioning achieves temporary consolidations and internal relations on the temporal continuum of past, present, and future.

From the perspective of this conceptual model, the behavioral positions consolidated at the conclusion of Part III function as evidential markers demonstrative of Spinoza's clinical matrix. This demonstration, beginning with Scholium 2 at III. Proposition 18 and continuing through III. Proposition 59, works backward from positions of observable behavioral effects to linkage with the plausible dynamics of efficient cause. Because Spinoza's intention is to demonstrate the unconscious determination of human action rather than to endorse a clinical model, the reader only discovers the elements of his thinking as illustrative fragments, mobilized toward a different purpose. However, having recognized Spinoza's clinical matrix, the reader's attempt to trace it clearly through III. Proposition 59 leads approximately, after the fashion of *cloudy mathematics*, from sometimes-glimpses of Spinoza's imposed mathematical thinking upon human behavior, to Spinoza's own associations and repetitions, generated by the force of his own thinking harnessed in the service of describing commonly observed human behaviors.

The first examples of mind's determined acts in *Ethics* Part III concern the observation of hope and fear[2] (III. Proposition 18, Scholium 2, p. 288). Spinoza notes that each end-state is characterized by a dominant quality of feeling: hope by pleasure; fear by pain. Yet, in neither state is such feeling constant. Instead, its inconstancy creates the condition of vacillation. Affective inconstancy interacts with imagination in at least two ways. The first is in the pairing of pleasure or pain with the "image of a thing", the object of thought, imagined either as past or future. The second is in the imagination of doubtful outcome. The reader notes that in addition to suggesting simultaneous and multiple levels of imagination's functioning, Spinoza also generates through the mind's toleration of hope or fear, the containment of uncertainty. This binding of its own generated anxiety is a necessary, if unnoted, aspect of Spinoza's model of mind.

Fascinating from the reader's clinical perspective, is that consistent with his model of mind, even Spinoza's literary presentation of these two affectively inconstant states presses for resolution, accenting the mind's challenge in tolerating uncertainty. To this end, Spinoza demonstrates that the uncertainty of hope and fear pivot on the centrality of doubt. As writer, he quickly resolves such doubt by consideration next of "confidence" and "despair" (III. Proposition 18, Scholium 2, p. 288). These are the respective successor states to "hope" and "fear" in that the former condition (hope or fear) describes affective experience at time (n) and the latter (confidence or despair) describes transformed affective experience at time (n + 1). Spinoza writes that

> if the element of doubt be removed from these emotions, hope becomes confidence and fear becomes despair, that is "pleasure or pain arising from a thing which we have feared or have hoped". (III. Proposition 18, Scholium 2, p. 289)

Additionally, Spinoza details a third affective state founded upon this progression from time (n) to time (n + 1). That English-language translators of Spinoza's Latin disagree on its linguistic markers, parallels the variety in different clinicians' verbal articulations of what seems momentary significant in interpretation of therapeutic process. Here, one translator pairs the polarity of joy and disappointment as successor states to hope and fear, following certain removal of doubt (Spinoza, 2002, p. 289) where another translator calls such joy, "gladness", and disappointment, "remorse" (De Spinoza, 1996, p. 81). Fundamental to each is that both joy/gladness and disappointment/remorse are representative again, of predominating states of pleasure or pain, after hope or fear have traversed uncertainty. The contrast between terms used by different translators of Spinoza, like interpretations differing between therapists, also suggests a form of *cloudy mathematics* in that a general central idea, not quite precise or articulated in exactly the same way, is extended to the reader, who understands the generality across multiple possibilities of expression.

Spinoza mobilizes his conceptual elements in an emotional journey within the realm of pleasure and pain, across time from (n) to (n + 1) to (n + 2). Throughout, feelings of pleasure and pain are paralleled by fantasy or imagination in an always-present construal of past or future, relative to the possibility of successful or failed attainment of desire. The temporal arc from time (n) to time (n + 2) describes the process under which the anxious uncertainty which has been central as inconstant pleasure or pain shifts to relatively constant certainty. Because mental functioning is conjoined and simultaneous, one cannot clearly differentiate the locus of inconstancy; so must assume that registration of inconstant pleasure or pain resonates not only throughout the function of willing, but also through feeling and imagining.

Eventually, the predominant affirmation of willing is mobilized, at least in imagination, toward its external extension as desire; and empirically discernable external facts are themselves internalized, affecting further change in internal feeling states. Spinoza's model lacks explicit description of the internalization this requires. The clinical reader must appreciate Spinoza's model as an incomplete scaffolding, revealing gaps that are answered through the later development of philosophy and psychoanalysis. For example, the projective Spinozan extension of fused affect/cognition requires the individual's reciprocal reception of feeling-toned registrations engendered in action: what Whitehead terms a *superject* (Whitehead, 1978, p. 32). Sandor Ferenczi's early observation of the introjection that functions reciprocally with projective mechanisms (Ferenczi, 1909), satisfies this theoretical and practical need.

The schematic nature of Spinoza's elements, conjointly in simultaneous functioning and following the parallelism of thought and extension explored in *Ethics* Part I, models a muscular and testable general model of observable process. In so doing, Spinoza generates an early modern therapeutic algorithm, Levenson's "systematic series of steps for achieving an outcome" (Levenson, 1983, p. 9).[3] Like Maimonides' apertures of the filigreed apple, itself derived imaginatively as commentary upon Scriptural verse in harmony with Greek philosophy, the general form of Spinoza's matrix reveals through its gaps, the gold both of particular experience and of future conceptual elaboration.

Returning to the trajectory of hope and fear, Spinoza illustrates the simple resolution of this dynamic first, through confidence or despair; and onward, toward joy and disappointment, through restless emotional change. Because the resolution of doubt functions as a pivot point resolving anxiety, the clinical reader necessarily asks, what happens when doubt is denied through the very agency of willing? Such a situation is mirrored by Freud in comparison of normal and pathological mourning in *Mourning and Melancholia* (1917). The certainty of death facilitates the process of normal mourning in its oscillation from the doubtful question, "how could this be?" to the grim certainty that, this is how it is. Vacillation, however generative of anxiety, contrasts with the pathological denial of doubting itself, in the unresolved mourning that illustrates Freud's melancholia. Such oscillations also underlie the Kleinian shuttle between the fixity of the paranoid/schizoid position and the resolution of the depressive position (Klein, 1946; Miller & Sweet, 2018). Spinoza's dynamic applied model engages such vacillation in doubt,[4] challenging the mind's intrinsic resistance to limitation of its power (III. Proposition 13, p. 268).

Having considered Freud's thoughts on mourning relative to Spinoza's thoughts on doubt, the clinical reader is not entirely unprepared to encounter Spinoza's next propositions. Like the reader's activity as thought-partner with Spinoza in developing the implications of clinical thinking, Spinoza now considers the field of interpersonal relations through the individual's identifications with others. With this consideration, the reader also begins to discern Spinoza's thickening of terms, beginning with Love and Hate, extending to Hope and Fear, and now, internalized to attitudes of Sympathy and Antipathy (III. Proposition 15, Scholium, p. 287). Consistently, Spinoza's generation of terms descriptive of psychological action seems to be the natural outcome of his essay-like scholia, elaborating successive propositions. The concluding *Definitions of the Emotions* is arrayed as a glossary of terms reflective of psychological positions, under a compression that distorts their complex, determinative dynamics. However, the generative complexity of Spinoza's clinical matrix can be glimpsed through the apertures of familiar words, amassed as proof of mind's mediating activity between the body and behavior, that unreflectively, is commonly and mistakenly taken to originate in *free will*.

Spinoza next focuses on a series of propositions centered on the vicissitudes of externalized pleasure and pain in loving and hating others. Unnamed, but clearly present, is the individual's internalization and interpretation—through perception, feeling, imagining, and willing—of extended behavior's consequences. Implicit is what later thinkers will term *mitleid* (Goetschel, 2004, Ch 7), a German term for the fellow-feeling of suffering that Ferenczi would recognize clinically as *mutuality* (1933).

Proposition 18 reflects a familiar *one-person* intrapsychic psychology (Miller, 2017), demonstrated clinically in *transference*. Spinoza generalizes that from the image of things past or future man is affected by the same emotion of pleasure or pain as from the image of a thing present. (III. Proposition 18, p. 288)

With Proposition 19, Spinoza focuses upon the mind's imagination of an external, loved object. He writes,

he who imagines that what he loves is being destroyed will feel pain. If, however, he imagines that it is being preserved, he will feel pleasure. (III. Proposition 19, p. 289)

Continuing with Propositions 20 and 21, the reader recognizes a unique presentational quality emerging from within this propositional cluster: (1) that the object of these observations is the extension of intrapsychic activity into the interpersonal field; and (2), that this series follows a logic, operating through reversals in mental registrations of pleasure and pain, taking the form of mathematical equations.

For the purpose of convenience, let us suppose: (1) that the symbol $(+)$ refers to pleasure; (2) that the symbol $(-)$ refers to pain; and (3) that the symbols (f) and (i) refer respectively, to feeling and imagining functions of mind. Proposition 19 would translate: He who imagines that the loved object $(+)$ is being destroyed $(-)$ feels pain $(-)$. If the loved object $(+)$ is preserved $(+)$, he will feel pleasure $(+)$. Symbolically, this reduces to two equations: 1) $[(+)(i)](-) = [(f) (-)]$; and 2) $[(+)(i)](+) = [(f)(+)]$.

By contrast, Proposition 20 imagines a hated object $(-)$ destroyed $(-)$, as generating a feeling of pleasure $(+)$: $[(-)(f)](-) = [(f)(+)]$.

Proposition 21 generalizes these mathematically derived behavioral observations in narrative form, stating

He who imagines that what he loves is affected with pleasure or pain will likewise be affected with pleasure or pain, the intensity of which will vary with the intensity of the emotion in the object loved. (III. Proposition 21, p. 289)

According to Spinoza, the emotional mathematics reflected in Proposition 21 explain a discrete end-state, Pity, or "pain arising from another's hurt" (III. Proposition 22, Scholium, p. 290). Now, Spinoza explicitly extends his one-person, intrapsychic psychology, oriented to a singular external object, to the larger social world of multiple individuals in interaction such that

> If we imagine that someone is affecting with pleasure the object of our love, we shall be affected with love toward him. If on the other hand we think he is affecting with pain the object of our love, we shall likewise be affected with hatred toward him. (III. Proposition 22, p. 290)

The reader notes that symbolically, this is similar to what we have already recognized in that: $[(i)(+)](+) = [(f)(+)]$; and $[(i)(+)](-) = [(f)(-)]$. What changes is imagination's horizon. Its viewpoint has expanded from (1) the mind's imagined relationship to an individual external object to (2) the mind's imagined relationship both to an individual external object and to a third party, operating independently in relation to the loved or hated object. Spinoza has described a shift from the vectors of one Lewinian lifespace to those of another (Brown, 1936; Lewin, 1936). Still focused upon the internal dynamics of the individual, Spinoza extends the operation of mind to perceive and to be affected by the interactions of others in the external world. Further, he employs this observation to generate the behavioral positions of Approval and Indignation (III. Proposition 22, p. 290).

The logic of mathematic thinking is the route by which Spinoza generalizes his mental calculus, aligning the dynamics of mind with observations of common behaviors. Sensing that outcomes may be unpleasant rather than aspirationally blessed, he notes grimly that pleasures emergent from pain caused to hated objects, "can scarcely be unalloyed and devoid of conflict of feeling" (III. Proposition 23, Scholium, p. 291). Leaping across four propositions, Spinoza promises to demonstrate in Proposition 27 that

> Insofar as he imagines a thing similar to himself to be affected with an emotion of pain, to that extent he is bound to feel pain, and contrariwise, if he imagines it to be affected with pleasure. (III. Proposition 23, Scholium, p. 291)

Spinoza extends his consideration of how humans take pleasure in others' pain, citing Envy and "similar emotions" which

> can therefore be defined as 'hatred insofar as it is considered to dispose a man to rejoice in another's hurt and to feel pain at another's good. (III. Proposition 24, Scholium, p. 291)

Spinoza underlines the discomfort and anxiety in taking pleasure form another's suffering. Proposition 27, with its scholium generative of the positions Pity and Emulation, insists

> From the fact that we imagine a thing like ourselves, toward which we have felt no emotion, to be affected by an emotion, we are therefore affected by a similar emotion. (III. Proposition 27, p. 292)

He does not construe the possibility that imagination itself might either fail or refuse to credit another human being to be a "thing like ourselves". This invalidation of the Other's humanity, as in our contemporary expression, "he is dead to me", effectively reduces another to no-thing (Miller, 2018a). Such action links to the narcissistic phenomena that we term omnipotence, idealization, and denigration, about which Spinoza writes,

> Thus we see that it easily happens that a man may have too high an opinion of himself and of the object loved, and on the other hand too mean an opinion of the object of his hatred. This way of thinking, when it concerns the man who has too high an opinion of himself is called *Pride* [*superbia*], and is a kind of madness, in that a man dreams with his eyes open that he can do all those things that his imagination encompasses, which he therefore regards as real, exulting in them, as long as he is incapable of thinking of those things that exclude their existence and limit his power of activity. Therefore, pride is "pleasure arising from the fact that a man has too high an opinion of himself".[5] Again, "pleasure that arises from the fact that a man has too high an opinion of another" is called "Over-esteem [*existimatio*]". Finally, "pleasure arising from

the fact that a man has too mean an opinion of another" is called Disparagement [*despectus*]. (III. Proposition 26, Scholium, pp. 291–292)

Pride, as a character trait, develops out of self-affirmation, a taking of oneself as the mind's object. Spinoza considers two forms of self-affirmation in Propositions III.25 and III.26. The former affirms whatever causes the individual and her loved object pleasure. The latter negates what causes pain to self and other. The reader recognizes that within Spinoza's matrix, these are narrowing operations upon conatus itself, in its affirming/negating capacities. The second, similarly affects willing, but in conjunction with imagination, endeavoring

To affirm of that which we hate whatever we imagine affects it with pain and on the other hand to deny what we imagine affects it with pleasure. (III. Proposition 26, p. 291)

It is from this proposition, that Spinoza discerns narcissistic omnipotence, idealization, and denigration. His writing suggests that in concert with imagination, such development may reflect actual impingement upon our range of willed affirmations and denials. The reader might conjecture that the effects of traumatic experience and self-affirmation might cause such limitation, a characterological development distorting the operation of how we endeavor in our going on being as a limiting of the relationship of willing and endeavoring, based in experiences of pleasure and pain, and underlying the nature of prejudice, in striving to affirm the imagination of pain in what we hate, denying it of pleasure. Perhaps this is the Spinozan answer to "he is dead to me": that we come to negate and disaffirm that which we imagine will cause us pain. Together with this, imagination is such that from the perspective of the individual's own omnipotence, the Other poses no threat.

Indeed, two scholia suggest a conjoining of mental patterns, limiting thought. The first, at III. Proposition 13, reminds us that when mind

thinks of those things that diminish or check the body's power of activity, it endeavors, as far as it can, to call to mind those things that exclude the existence of the former. (III. Proposition 13, p. 286)

The second, at III. Proposition 18, concerns memory and the affirmation or denial of a thing's existence, a confluence of imagination and willing in its capacity to affirm or to deny. Spinoza writes that under such negation, "the body is not affected by any emotion that excludes the existence of the thing" (III. Proposition 18, Scholium 1, p. 288). From these, there is strong suggestion in *Ethics*, of the human capacity to negate the humanity of others, under perceived threat to the Self's wellbeing.

Doubling, Folding, and Spinoza's Filigree Apple

Spinoza's organization of Part III is founded upon his organization of Parts I and II; as is the conclusion to Part III. The glossary presented in the concluding *Definition of the Emotions* is itself the building block of affective conjunctions upon which the functioning of Reason shall be demonstrated in Parts IV and V, toward the betterment of individual and society. But a subtle reasoning also underlies the construction of Part III. It begins with a general model of psychological functioning, founded on conjunctions of pleasure, pain, and the going on being Spinoza calls willing or conatus. *Ethics* Part III concludes with the terse consolidation already described, of behavioral positions that are specific demonstrations of Spinoza's general model. In-between is a long middle-portion, roughly one-third of Part III, in length.

This section is electric in its generation of clinical observables. But in its impatient dynamic demonstrations, it causes the reader confusion, with propositions and scholia becoming difficult to remember in their consecutive emergence. Thinking about this momentary turn in the quality of Spinoza's writing, I was reminded of Gilles Deleuze's observation concerning Gottfried Leibniz, a younger contemporary of Spinoza. Like Maimonides' filigreed apple, like the doubling of meaning between scholia and propositions, Deleuze considers another image that conceals one level of ideas under another. He terms this a *fold*; and locates such reciprocal relations of the disclosed and undisclosed as characteristic of the baroque era (Deleuze, 1993).

I recognized a similar quality, first in the mathematical reversals noted above, characterizing Spinoza's sequencing of Part III propositions; and then, through my own association, to Bach's complex *Goldberg Variations*.

My associative references to Bach and to Deleuze's fold signaled experience of my own anxiety. Midway through *Ethics* Part III, anxious about losing the thread of a once-glimpsed clinical matrix, I understood that the *clinical Spinoza* I had sought was my goal alone, to be differentiated from Spinoza's. This recognition allowed me a certain pause, a caesura separating me from my experience of reading Spinoza.

Beginning in doubt, my viewpoint shifted to appreciation of difference, freeing my own curiosity about what Spinoza as philosopher was now doing, whether related or not to my conscious objective.

With this thought, I recognized that very consistently, Spinoza had demonstrated, as he had set out to do in the Preface to Part III, the nature of certain things: including Love, Hate, Pride, and Envy. In so doing, he had suggested that the forms of what society takes to be amoral, such as taking pleasure at another's pain, are as normal under general psychological laws as taking pleasure at another's joy. But such generalized summarizing was also a sop to my own continued state of vacillation.

As reader, I now allowed myself to associate *freely*, recognizing both from Spinoza and Freud that such freedom is only ostensible. I hoped that this truly determined path of association might generate something of significance, which in its import, paradoxically, would help to free me from confusion.

My first productive association was to the cartoon image of proliferating, scrubbing brooms, in the classic Disney animation, *Fantasia* (Disney, 1940). Momentarily, I identified with that overwhelmed Mickey Mouse, tripping on his oversized costume, and harassed by the sorcerer's magical hat, falling over his eyes.

And then I reflected (employing reason) and considered my confusion (feeling and imagination) and my desire, too: to link Spinoza's anticipations of psychoanalysis to psychoanalysis as I understand it now, in 2021. And with this, necessarily, the markers by which I had once discerned psychoanalysis: including its *vernacular expression* as an evolving historical process in the realm of applied, practical ideas;

as well as the daily clinical utility to me, of Bion's extraordinary clinical algorithm (Miller, 2016; Miller & Sweet, 2018).

These were particularities of my own experience; but I also thought about them as indices of a momentary associational process, itself tethered to making my way again, toward an understanding of Spinoza's writing. It was then that I remembered Spinoza's *pomum,* his Latinate apple, which, like another image of a horse's tracks on sand, epitomized both the consensual and subjective nature of the associational process. I laughed, realizing that Spinoza's Latin apple and the filigreed apple in Maimonides' *Guide of the Perplexed,* may be the same piece of fruit. Originating in the Hebrew of Scripture, expressed in Maimonides' Arabic, translated into Hebrew by the Provencal Samuel Ibn Tibbon, residing in Spinoza's library, and expressed by Spinoza in Latin, the apple's filigree symbolizes a particular kind of knowledge: we recognize that the surface presentation of things affords glimpses of what lies beneath.

The filigreed apple's clever design reflects a doubling, with the surface indicative to those who attend to such things, of underlying process. Certainly, this was the case in the harmonization of Sophia, of Wisdom or Philosophy and Hebrew text, that is at the root of Jewish philosophy. But this thought became burdensome too, as it led me away from Part III and my confusion. Like my experience of Spinoza at this moment, I was generating interesting ideas that just didn't join up.

I returned to my momentary identification with Mickey Mouse as *Sorcerer's Apprentice.* My own grandiose ideas were getting the better of me, threatening the thread of my hypothesized clinical Spinoza; and then I remembered Proposition 19,

> He who imagines that what he loves is being destroyed will feel pain. If, however, he imagines that it is being preserved, he will feel pleasure. (III. Proposition 19, p. 289)

Recognizing my discomfort within this proposition, I also recognized my internalization of a Spinozan generality, mobilizing it toward understanding my own associative process: my beloved object of thought was now under threat. Suddenly, the vast chasm between the general and the specific seemed to loom up; and I remembered *cloudy mathematics*, the idea of general precision linked to imprecise human experience. This was my own transformation of a single translator's interpretation of Spinoza's allusion to his transformation of Maimonides. Hardly scientific: but then, a pathway not dissimilar from Bion's (1959) mobilization of Poincare's philosophy in discerning what he took to be a *significant fact* (Bion, 1992, p. 5). Discerning both the general and the particular in the same moment, as through a cloud, I recognized the convergence of Spinoza's intuitive "third kind" of knowledge with Bion's intuitive, selected fact.

Certainly, the ideas were plentiful, but my associative process was incomplete. Where had I felt and imagined in this way before? Where and when had the confusion felt so paralyzing? I remembered. It had been in my attempt to synthesize the contemporary clinician's integration of psychoanalytic theory, based in the ten most popular papers in the digital psychoanalytic library, the PEP archive. I reckoned then that each of us, each clinician, must subjectively wrangle our understanding and clinical wisdom from along the same rocky path. So, I consulted my own work and found narratives of confessed dread. Reading Bion (1962) and

> failing to understand the first paragraph, the reader seeks an alternative path. He attempts to locate the main point, the fact around which Bion's allusions to mathematics and philosophy cohere. Breathing deeply, slowly, patiently, he reads again; and the patience pays off in a dispelling of dreadful uncertainty, at least for the moment. (Miller, 2016, p. 56)

Finding a parallel between reading and the psychoanalytic theory of thinking, together perhaps with the bearing of uncertainty necessary in the therapist's experience in continuous inquiry into the unknown, I recognized in the present psychoanalytic vernacular, a marked deviation from the early psychoanalytic desire for scientific certainty. Rather, both in our received writing and in clinical practice, supervised by elders and peers, psychoanalysis had evolved into a practice of facing uncertainty, symbolized by Bion's O (Reiner, 2021).

Reading myself further, I recognized congruence with my Spinozan experience, pausing, the reader is overcome with strong conflicting emotion. The work of thinking is exhausting. And involuntarily, the thought, "Perhaps I'll abandon this effort", momentarily forms in the mind. Perhaps the project of reading the PEP's two strongest interpreters of psychoanalysis is misguided? How can this 1962 paper be one of the five most important definitional works in contemporary psychoanalysis, whether in the reading habits of 2014–2015 clinicians or in its citations within the psychoanalytic literature? And then the reader masters his emotion, remembering two things flooding in upon one another suddenly and forcefully. The first, and more recently experienced within this reading project, concerns Winnicott's 1949 differentiation between the job of psychotherapy and the emotional constellation generated within the clinician in the doing of the job. The next is Bion's own shift in writing style, meant to convey the clinical experience of conducting and enduring psychotherapy (Bion, 1962; Bion-Talamo, 2015, p. 3; Miller, 2015). That is, like the comparisons to philosophy and mathematics, whether pure or applied, of the 1962 paper, even Bion's communicative form of expression, his writing, is meant to convey an experiential process knowable primarily by those who have undergone it and so recognize its emotional demands. (Miller, 2016, pp. 57–58)

I continued, recognizing the deep emotional congruence I had experienced, between this present, iterative, reading of Spinoza, and my psychoanalytic reading in that

the painful experience induced in the reader by the paper's reading is therefore motivated on all sides: both in the desire of the writer to convey and in the desire of the reader to learn. It is the reader's elective choice in performing the job of reading to endure, to tolerate what the writer's writing generates emotionally for the reader in his struggle at apprehension. Apprehension, of course, conjoins the idea of dreadful anxiety with understanding. And with this recognition, the penny drops. Bion, in however jagged and difficult a presentational manner, is setting the bar for clinical practice; and clinical practice in facing elements of psychosis. Absent of the hope for clarity, much less certainty, he deepens the Winnicottian premise of tolerating confusion by insistence on the clinician's capacity for toughness, for bearing the pain and anxiety necessary for the work of psychotherapy. (Miller, 2016, p. 58)

I had adduced through direct experience, the proof of my proposition, that Spinoza's theory anticipates not only the early development of psychoanalysis, but also the post-modern variations within psychoanalytic expression and practice, current today. This proof, differing from the philosophic and mathematical forms either of Spinoza or Bion, had been experiential, emotionally resonant. I had discerned it years ago in defining clinical psychoanalysis itself, and now again, in reading what analytic thinkers take as Spinoza's psychoanalytic anticipations, if of a psychoanalysis at a far later developmental stage.

With this understanding, my reading progression from III. Proposition 26 forward to III. Proposition 59, clarified. For my own purpose, I could discern the baroque variations of Spinoza's folded elements: conatus, feeling, perception, imagination, and reasoning, both internally and externally, and in relation to fields of intrapsychic and interpersonal relations and conjoinings. Central to Spinoza was the linkage between human traits of character and personality, as well as common attitudes, and their psychic determination. On the way, Spinoza would generate complicating elements in the conjoining of his clinical model, later elaborated in psychoanalysis and clinical psychology. These include: our hard-wired desire for obtaining pleasure and for eliminating unpleasure (III. Proposition 28); conforming our behaviors to what other people do (III. Proposition 29); self-regard (III. Proposition 25; III. Proposition 30) and competitive desire such that

If we think that someone loves, desires, or hates something that we love, desire or hate, that very fact will cause us to love, desire, or hate the thing more steadfastly. But if we think he dislikes what we love, or vice versa, then our feelings will fluctuate. (III. Proposition 31, p. 294)

This last consideration, concerning another's negative assessment of what we hold dear, is an early recognition of what today is called *cognitive dissonance*. Spinoza embroiders this idea with a poetic quote from Ovid, and from it discerns that our willing to "bring it about that everyone should approve of one's loves and hates" (III. Proposition 31, Scholium, p. 295). From this, he continues to narrate the human difficulty in allowing difference in human subjectivity in

> that it is in everyone's nature to strive to bring it about that others should adopt his attitude to life; and while all strive equally to this end they equally hinder one another, and in all seeking the praise or love of all, they provoke mutual dislike. ((III. Proposition 31, Scholium, p. 295)

Here, as proposition and scholium, is the underbelly of Oedipal challenge and differentiation between generations, as between individuals. Immediately following this recognition is another iteration of destructive envy in that

> if we think that someone enjoys something that only one person can possess, we shall endeavor to bring it about that he should not possess that thing. (III. Proposition 32, p. 295)

Spinoza here discerns a similar root for compassion, greed, envy, and ambition, rooted in childhood development, in that

> men pity the unfortunate and envy the fortunate, in the latter case with a hatred proportionate to their love of what they think another posseses. (III. Proposition 32, Scholium, p. 295).

Next, Spinoza turns to the desire for reciprocal love (III. Proposition 33, p. 295; III. Proposition 34, p. 296) as well as the interpersonal situation when the love object prefers a third party with the same or greater feeling (III. Proposition 35, p. 297).

Spinoza calls the resultant hatred, extended toward the third party, and heightened by envy, Jealousy or "vacillation arising from simultaneous love and hatred accompanied by the idea of a rival who is envied" (III. Proposition 35, Scholium, p. 296). Here, the individual begins with love for another, the extension of pleasure outward as desire to an external object. But he registers the love object's greater love for yet another, precipitating a transformation of the individual's initial love at time (n) to pain in the disappointment of rejection (n + 1). Absent rational mediation, this pain is transformed into anger, projected externally as hatred (n + 2). Yet in this irrational transformation, not only does the formerly loved object become hated, but also (1) her own lover is envied; and (2) through the distorting prism of affective process, imagined within a complicated internal drama of rivalry, as if the "winning" of the singular loved object were at stake!

Spinoza's clinical matrix is helpful in clarifying not only the discrete transformations in emotional experience from the internal world to the external world and back, but also in the sharp affective reversals resultant from perceived failure and rejection. The intermediating states that result, such as the hurt and anger projected outward as hatred, also force a deformation of imagination, here illustrated as the fantasy of rivalry.

Proposition 36 elaborates the pain of nostalgic longing in that

> he who recalls a thing which once afforded him pleasure desires to possess the same thing in the same circumstances as when he first took pleasure therein. (III. Proposition 36, p. 297)

Spinoza comments too, on the vicissitudes of hatred from disappointed love, extending his mathematical calculus in the idea of proportional love and hate, in that

> if anyone has begun to hate the object of his love to the extent that his love is completely extinguished, he will, other things being equal, bear greater hatred toward it than if he had never loved it, and his hatred will be proportionate to the strength of his former love. (III. Proposition 38, p. 298)

But hatred is tempered by fear of pain. While the desire of the spurned individual is to inflict pain on another, it is quelled through imagining that the injured party will inflict greater injury (III. Proposition 39, p. 298).

Suddenly, the reader recognizes that (1) between illustrating his clinical matrix and (2) establishing a glossary of familiar behavioral positions through lawful and regular psychological processes, Spinoza seems (3) to generate a self-help pamphlet in rationally based, consensual understanding of familiar psychological dynamics, as if by a wise therapist steeped in years of experiential knowledge. His perspective is focused through the lens of what an individual experiences subjectively as "good" or "bad", dependent on our desire, such that

> by "good" I understand here every kind of pleasure and furthermore whatever is conducive thereto, and especially whatever satisfies a longing of any sort. By "bad" I understand every kind of pain, and especially that which frustrates a longing. (III. Proposition 39, Scholium, p. 298)

For example, he generalizes that

> he who imagines he is hated by someone to whom he believes he has given no cause for hatred will hate him in return. (III. Proposition 40, p. 299)

Observed through his clinical matrix, Spinoza describes what today we might call the "paranoid position" of a person without special feelings of pleasure or pain for another, who imagines that he is the object of someone else's hatred. Without describing the pressure of such belief in affecting one's clear mobilization of rationality or even summoning imagination's contents, the hated individual cannot think of why he should be hated. But immediately, as if in defense, he mobilizes his reciprocal hatred.

Spinoza continues to detail situations involving the extension to one or more others, the fruits of one's pleasures and pains, in Love and Hate. Together with these situations, he details the intermediary dynamics with further shape the individual's relation to self and others (III. Proposition 41–III. Proposition 49). At III. Proposition 46, he describes hatred of others based on membership in social groups with which the individual is not identified, striking even today, in Spinoza's clear articulation of prejudice. He writes

If anyone is affected with pleasure or pain by someone of a class or nation different from his own and the pleasure or pain is accompanied by the idea of that person as its cause, under the general category of that class or nation, he will love or hate not only him but all of that same class or nation. (III. Proposition 46, p. 302)

Extending this theme, he considers the repetitive reenactment of trauma, in recalling the image of a thing, long past but still subject to imagination, with its painful recall satisfied time and again through recollection that the direct pain no longer exists. Instead, there is a new kind of derivative pleasure-pain feeling when

the image of the said thing is activated, since it involves the existence of the thing it determines one to regard the thing with the same pain as when one was wont to regard it when it did exist. But since one has associated with the image of the said thing other images which exclude its existence, this determination to pain is immediately checked, and one feels a renewed pleasure, and this is so whenever the series of events is repeated. (III. Proposition 47, Scholium, p. 302)

He continues, specifically focusing on the repetitions of traumatic memory, as a repetitive cycle of fear and relief, in that

it is the same cause that makes men feel pleasure whenever they recall some past ill and makes them enjoy talking about perils from which they have been saved. For when they imagine some peril they regard it as though it were still to come and are determined to fear it, a determination which is again checked by the idea of their escape which they associated with the idea of this peril when they did in fact escape it. This idea makes them feel safe once more, and so their pleasure is renewed. (III. Proposition 47, Scholium, p. 302)

Finally, the propositions of Part III, draw to a close with a sequence of generalities that repeat earlier recognitions on the subjectivity of psychological experience. These include: that anything can be a cause of hope or fear (III. Proposition 50); that different men can be affected differently by the same object and that the same man can be affected differently by the same object in different ways and times (III. Proposition 51); that we pay more attention to objects that seem directly relevant to our situation than to those that don't (III. Proposition 52). Also, that the mind's self-regard of its own activity causes the feeling of pleasure (III. Proposition 53); that "the mind endeavors to think only of the things that affirm its power of activity" (III. Proposition 54, p. 306); and that "when the mind thinks of its own impotence, by that very fact it feels pain" (III. Proposition 55, p. 306).

Spinoza's Part III propositions end in a succession of four generalizing propositions, but the reader may be so exhausted by the preceding proofs and scholia, that he nods only, in quiet assent.[6] Luckily, they are iterative, repeating and combining what has already been proposed:

1. There are as many kinds of pleasure, pain, desire, and consequently of every emotion that is compounded of these (such as vacillation) or of every emotion that is derived from these (love, hatred, hope, fear, etc.) as there are kinds of objects by which we are affected (III. Proposition 56, p. 307).
2. Any emotion of one individual differs from the emotion of another to the extent that the essence of one individual differs from the essence of the other (III. Proposition 57, p. 308).
3. Besides the pleasure and desire that are passive emotions, there are other emotions of pleasure and desire that are related to us insofar as we are active (III. Proposition 58, p. 309).
4. Among all the emotions that are related to the mind insofar as it is active, three are none that are not related to pleasure and desire (III. Proposition 59, p. 310).

Here then, is the finale of the clinical matrix: composed of pleasure, pain, and desire in all its possibilities of union. The unique individuality of each individual transformed into the unique complications of each of us, reflective of who we are, not only in the general sense of shared humanity, but along the lines of experiential transformation in the domains of perception, feeling, imagination, and desire, what today might be reflected in the analyst's "perceptive identification" (Bollas, 2006). That much in the domain of pain and pleasure is passive, fragmented, and inadequately recognized; while too, there are complete conscious recognitions. And yet, again, every kind of emotional experience begins in the matrix of pleasure, pain, and the striving that is *going on being*.

Notes

1 While confusing when glimpsed through the presentational order of *Ethics*, Spinoza's accomplishment in *Definition of the Emotions* represents an early modern dynamic turn from interpreting behavior through extension of the arithmetic mean, understood by medieval philosophy as resulting in human behavioral characteristics. Read in parallel with Maimonides *Eight Chapters*, Spinoza's fifty-seven behavioral derivations rival Maimonides' earlier fifteen (Gorfinkle, 1912, pp. 55–56) including: abstemiousness; passion; insensibility to pleasure; liberality; sordidness; extravagance; courage; recklessness; cowardice; dignity; haughtiness; loutishness; and humility, followed by the pair of characteristics under which J. Tigner propels *Ethics* into *clinical* Spinoza, via consideration of the similarities between arrogance and self-abasement, earlier presented both by Maimonides and Spinoza (Tigner, 1985).

2 It may be that Spinoza's own thinking about hope and fear was inspired by his reading of Seneca, who similarly tackles this binary in his own *Letters on Ethics* (2015). Writing in Letter 5, line 8 (p. 32), Seneca observes that for both hope and fear, "the principle cause of both is that we do not adapt ourselves to the present, but direct our thoughts toward things far in the future"; and, earlier, that "just as the prisoner and the guard are bound to each other by the same chain, so these two that are so different nonetheless go along together; where hope goes, fear follows" (Letter 5, line 7; p. 32).

3 While, as Wolfson has observed, there is no record of discrete literary sources used by Spinoza, relative to the Maimonidean tradition, close reading of Samuel Ibn Tibbon's Commentary on Ecclesiastes, Paragraph 34 (Robinson, 2007, p. 176) suggests a similar step-wise conjunctive process, over time. At time (n), the writer comments upon his self-willed repression conjoining longing to write with his announcement of intuited truth. He writes, "My longing remained in my heart as if a burning fire were shut up in my bones". The physicalized ego feeling is a product of unexpressed desire. At a later time (n2), the philosopher expresses his weariness "to hold in what, it seemed to me, I had understood of its meanings and words". Both at time n and at time (n2), the writer is aware of the tension between his internal psychic process and public opinion. Finally, at time (n3), affective propulsion rather than a process of reasoning causes him to make public the formerly repressed, "Thus I could no longer refrain from writing what was revealed to me". Just as earlier, the writer had surveyed the psychosocial landscape,

mindful of public censure, he offers two levels of interpretive justification. The first is his productive joining of a continuing literary-philosophical tradition. The second is his own use of writing as a marker to place his thoughts.

4   The engagement of doubt by Spinoza, a questioning of the foreclosed affirmation of mind that is itself an intrinsic aspect of conatus in functional assertions of affirmation or denial, transforms the earlier Aristotelian challenge to behavior through therapeutic prescription of antagonistic behavioral binary positions, meant to break habitual forms determined by repetitive practice, as illustrated by Maimonides *in Eight Chapters,* through experience of that which is "too" much or little, by its opposite (Gorfinkle, 1912, p. 54).

5   The reader discerns a bright line from III. Proposition 26, Scholium, in Spinoza's description of pride as "a kind of madness in that a man dreams with his eyes open" in grandiose fantasy, to Weiss' (1952) observations of *neurotic pride with omnipotence strivings* (Weiss, 1952, p. 40) which are themselves examined relative to Spinoza, yet again, by Joyce Tigner (1985).

6   I would understand only later, through comparative reading with Maimonides' *Eight Chapters,* that my confusions and anxieties in negotiating *Ethics* III may have arisen because Spinoza's interest had been in generating a psychological model radically differentiated from Maimonides' Aristotelianism. Rather than anticipating the impossible—discerning the interests of a psychologist three hundred and fifty years after his writing—Spinoza challenges the certain, a philosophical model generated five hundred years earlier.

Part IV

Chapter 10

Clinical Spinoza

Ethics offers contemporary psychoanalysis two critical gifts. The first is a dynamic precursor system to modern psychology, cohesive and coherent in underlying the conceptual development of psychoanalysis. The second is in the difference between Spinoza's viewpoints and our received psychoanalytic traditions. Psychoanalysis itself has achieved in its long clinical development, what Aristotelian philosophers term a *greater perfection,* toward unconscious alignment with Spinozan thought in our contemporary vernacular expressions; and with this, the observation that Spinoza functions still as a critical commentator and supervisor upon what may be clinically useful.

The present chapter is the first of two, focusing upon our contemporary clinical Spinoza, derived from *Ethics* I, II, and III.

This chapter is divided into four subsections: Glimpsing Spinoza; Clearly Discerning a Clinical Spinoza; Spinoza's Demonstrated Method of Inquiry; and Earlier Applications.

Glimpsing Spinoza

By the mid-20th century, the intuition of Lou Andreas-Salomé had been proven correct. Spinozan thought had risen to meet psychoanalysis on its path of development. But in so doing, the uniqueness of Spinozan presentation had been overshadowed by psychoanalytic progression. Neatly conjoining Freud and Spinoza at midcentury, John Reid would comment that

DOI: 10.4324/9781003246404-15

Freud, like the great Spinoza, by his counsel and example, teaches us that it is better to understand men, than to praise or blame them, and that, if we understand ourselves better, we shall not require so much praise from other men nor be so disturbed by their blame. (Reid, 1955, p. 122)

Reid would frame psychoanalysis as

at least three different things. It is a technical procedure for investigating unconscious mental processes and for treating psychoneuroses; it is a systematic body of fact and theory concerning the relations of conscious and unconscious mental processes; and, it is finally, a philosophy of life, in the sense that it is a way of looking at, of thinking about, and appraising some of our basic habits, attitudes, and beliefs. (Reid, 1955, p. 115)

It is toward Reid's third current of psychoanalytic thought, that he poetically recapitulates *Ethics* within a framework of value. Included in Reid's description are the markers of Spinoza's basic clinical model: (1) the extension of pleasure and pain in subjective liking and disliking; (2) the necessary functional foundations of perception and feeling, conjoined with imagination; and (3) direct experience and judgment of the world, both from internal and external resonance. Additionally, Reid's ideas of *liking* and *disliking* are recognizable as transformations of conatus into internalized desire. Reid observes this aesthetic union as

a relation between any given content of experience and a motor-affective attitude of liking (when the value is positive) or of disliking (when the value is negative). This content may be sensory or imaginal, and the perception, in which it is ingredient, may be veridical or illusory; the content may be relatively simple, like the look of a homogeneous patch of color or the feel of a smooth piece of velvet, or it may be relatively complex like the façade of Notre Dame cathedral or the slow movement of Bach's Ninth Symphony, as these latter enter into our direct esthetic experience. (Reid, 1955, pp. 115–116)

However consistent the aspirations of Freudian and Spinozan thinking, Spinoza is enlisted only within Reid's third definitional consideration of psychoanalysis, as value enfolded within its

> philosophy of life, in the sense that it is a way of looking at, of thinking about, and appraising some of our basic habits, attitudes, and beliefs. (Reid, 1955, p. 115)

Reid's is a representative position. By midcentury, psychoanalytic reference to Spinoza had come almost to a standstill, with Spinoza mostly relegated to an anticipatory historical figure of psychoanalytic humanism (Fromm, 1964a; Weiss, 1952).[1] Detached both from clinical method and the discernable facts of clinical practice, Spinoza balanced precariously upon disappearance from within the psychoanalytic canon. Representing a philosophical tradition differentiating between theory and practical application, Spinoza had intended that his psychology be used. His aspirational hope, refined by the humanistic development in American psychoanalysis (Fromm, 1964a, 1964b; Weiss, 1952) was toward individual and social melioration. Significantly, it is from within this tradition, that the first clear and modern, clinical application of Spinoza's *Ethics*, was published, thirty years after Reid's essay and twenty after Fromm's historical location of Spinoza within psychoanalytic development (Tigner, 1985).

Joyce Tigner's research is anchored in Spinoza's glossary of observed behaviors, *Definition of the Emotions*, concluding *Ethics* Part III. She extends earlier recognition by Frederick Weiss, of the *emotional bondage* of our affective experiences, understood as aspects of human freedom rather than as overdetermined by our bodies and minds. Centered on *Ethics* Part IV, Weiss cites Spinoza in that

> "Extreme pride as well as dejection indicate an extreme ignorance of the self ... and although abasement is the opposite to pride, he that abases himself is most akin to the proud ... both the proud and the dejected suffer from a weakness of the soul and fall easy prey to drives and therefore to others ..."

It is this "weakness of the soul"—translated into analytical language, this weakness of the real self—which leads man to the surrender of his autonomy, to submission to heteronomous values. (Weiss, 1952, p. 41)

Pursuing Weiss' binary between pride and self-abasement from within the Spinozan tradition of the Horney school, Tigner begins

in parts III and IV of the *Ethics*, Baruch Spinoza (1) discussed in detail the passive emotions of pride and self-abasement. He states in Part III that the two are opposites (1, Definition of the Emotions, 29, explication III). But later, in Part IV, he said that the two are closely related (I Scholium, Proposition 57, IV). The exact relationship of the two is unclear because Spinoza claimed that both are manifest by ignorance of self, impotence, and envy, and that both the prideful and the self-abasing are most subject to emotions, talk of the faults of others, and praise themselves or their characteristics. One is left wondering how two emotions can be closely related, sharing many of the same characteristics, and yet be opposites. (Tigner, 1985, p. 208)

Engaging *Ethics* Part III in excavating the common root of seemingly opposite behavioral observations, passively or inadequately known or understood, Tigner opens our contemporary gateway to a clinical reading of Spinoza. Like her predecessors, from Frederick Weiss' (1952) statement to Karen Horney's medical school commentary on Spinoza, almost half a century earlier, Tigner appreciates Spinoza in his anticipation of modern psychoanalytic practice. Her particular focus is in resolving confusion from within Spinoza's writing, relative to a parallel thread within Horney's conceptions, between *neurotic pride* and *self hate*.

In the same moment that Tigner opens our eyes to the contemporary utility of Spinoza in clinical application, she accomplishes at least two other things. First, she draws to a close almost a century of psychoanalytic efforts to demonstrate Spinoza's anticipation of what would become psychoanalytic psychotherapy. Next, departing from her predecessors, she focuses on the obscurity of Spinoza's text to discern clinical clarity.

As we have seen above, even Spinoza's contemporaries, schooled in similar philosophic ideas, had difficulties with the meanings of his concepts. But what is groundbreaking about Tigner's wrestling with difference, is that through extension, it suggests that the same critical lens might be applied to the difference between Spinozan conceptions and the psychoanalytic! Having developed from Spinozan thought, psychoanalysis might again be receptive to Spinozan commentary.

Clearly Discerning a Clinical Spinoza

Clinical Spinoza is founded on the overdetermined, ongoing psychological conjunctions of thought and extension in action. Emergence of its diverse, lawful forms is congruent with Spinoza's systematic presentation of the natural order in *Ethics*. This begins from Spinoza's innovative philosophical monism, with the attributes of thought and extension bridging the dualistic philosophical caesura between the materiality of bodies, and the immateriality of such ideas as soul or divinely inspired intelligences (Wolfson, 1934, p. 333).

Operatively, the center of Spinoza's human psychology is analogous to the modern Winnicottian concept of *going on being* (Winnicott, 1960), an internal subjectivity, the creative "centre of gravity, arising from our first unitary relations between baby and mother" (Abrams, 1996, p. 68). Spinoza terms this actively striving, self-preservative life force, conatus, or willing. This is an existential endeavoring shared by each of us, Spinoza's elaboration of what Sullivan terms the *one genus postulate* in that we are all "more human than otherwise" (Sullivan, 1953, pp. 32–33). However, in its unique psychological privacy, the striving conatus extends beyond Sullivan's early interpersonal theory in its elaboration as Wolstein's *psychic center of self* (Wolstein, 1987).

Significantly, human conatus is *psychological*. It is a phenomenon within a chain of cause and effect linked to but functionally separate from the body as predecessor condition. A psychoanalysis freed of the Freudian drive metapsychology through which it developed, reverses psychoanalysis' dualistic departures from Spinoza's anticipatory psychology. Indeed, from its early days, psychoanalysis has tolerated both explanatory schemes, with some psychoanalysts preferring Spinoza's psychological conatus to Freud's libido (Andreas-Salomé, 1964; Fromm, 1964b; Smith, 1925, 1926).

Conatus is an essential human quality, the functionality that causes us to be, and in the absence of which, we cease to be. Extended externally, our consciousness of conatus is what Spinoza terms *desire*. The permutations of this desire, both in its basic form of extension from the internal action of willing and in its more sophisticated form, re-internalized as experience and again formative at a new level in further mental conjunctions of perception, willing, imagining and feeling—a precursor to what analysts will term *hypercathexis*—operate together with felt registrations of pleasure and pain. Conatus, pleasure, and pain, all three transformations of the body's physical processes, anticipate what 19th-century scientist Hughlings Jackson and Sigmund Freud, recognize as dependent concomitance (Grossman, 1992, p. 37).

Together with the extension of intrapsychic process externally, where their transformations effect consolidation of the reality principle, these three elements are also prominent in early psychoanalytic theory. Paul Federn observes that

> Freud has concluded that unconscious processes follow only the principle of pain-pleasure. This principle refers to the reactions which every stimulus initiates in the psyche, regardless of whether the stimulus is due to external or internal psychic elements. (Federn, 1915, p. 2)

Federn's restatement of Freud is solidly Spinozan. He also employs the language of Spinoza's conatus, in the psyche's "endeavoring" and "striving", both toward ridding ourselves of pain and increasing our pleasure. Unattributed conceptually to Spinoza by Federn, but similarly observable through its effects, psychic striving, together with registrations of pleasure and pain, extend outward to empirically observable externalities through which

> we obtain our knowledge of such unconscious processes only after their effects enter into consciousness, and unconscious processes as such can only be studied by analyzing their conscious manifestations. (Federn, 1915, p. 1)

As noted in earlier chapters, while Spinoza's psychology provides a durable scaffolding for clinical thought, it is not theoretically comprehensive from the viewpoint of 21st-century clinical psycho-analysis. Purpose built not for the generation of clinically applied method, but as an individual approach aligning human conduct with rational, ethical conduct, *Ethics'* 17th century clinical psychology is developed in parallel with Spinoza's formal geometrical demonstration. Just as the functioning unit of mind is paralleled by the idea of mind, Spinoza's aspirational desire to demonstrate methodically the rational road to *blessedness* is paralleled by his dynamic model of human psychological action.

Read from our clinical perspective three hundred fifty years after its composition, *Ethics* reflects practical lacunae. Notably, while explicit in the detail described in Part III, from within the algorithmic idea I have termed Spinoza's *clinical matrix*, Spinoza's system lacks an explicit mechanism of internalization, allowing the actions and effects of Love, extended externally from internal pleasure, and Hate, extended externally from internal pain, to become functionally present within mind's intrapsychic world, now experientially transformed through environmental extension. Certainly, this movement from experience in the external world, interiorized again within intrapsychic activity, is fundamental to psychoanalysis. Federn observes

> the fact that an idea which is painful springs from the unconscious and is retained in the conscious does not contradict the workings of the principle of pain-pleasure, because in the unconscious the idea is originally pleasurable, and it is the censorship of consciousness that has attached a painful affect to it. It must be repeated that there are in the psyche different layers, which are to a certain extent independent of each other and opposite to each other. Therefore an element that may be painful in the deeper layers is often pleasurable in the higher ones. (Federn, 1915, p. 2)

It is exactly this layered conception of psychic function, operative both in original conjunctive formation and through internalization, with memory and its associations of past, present, and future, again conjoined affectively together with transformations between intrapsychic process and external extension that is encompassed by Spinoza's clinical matrix.

But Spinoza's scholia omit discussion of two crucial clinical concerns. The first is his aspirational bias, potentially detracting in its optimism, from the fact of lawful patterned behavior, whether recognized as partial, inadequate, distorted, or valid. A good example is Spinoza's clinical starting point in the Appendix to Part I, the anthropocentric projection of human anxiety onto a construct of a super-human, godlike king whose imagined pleasures and displeasures are understood to determine human conduct and morality. In his aspirational haste to challenge this idolatrous concept of God, Spinoza does not remind the reader that such patterning, in the service of whatever affective constellation, is itself as lawful and natural as any of those he elaborates in Part III. Just as Freud pessimistically understood, psychopathology and normality form a continuum of determined behavior, potential to us all. Minus the aspirational current so strongly prominent in *Ethics*, Spinoza leaves us simply with the lawful observables of clinical psychological process, neither good nor bad in themselves, simply more human than otherwise.

The second difficulty is that while external extension is prominently featured beyond the intrapsychic, Spinoza only implies the succeeding action of internalization. Having begun *Ethics'* consideration of clinical processes with illustration of projective identification, the clinical reader recognizes that Ferenczi's (1909) work on introjection as the counterpart of projection, supplies good conceptual fit within this basic Spinozan scaffolding; and allows psychoanalytic development itself to elaborate Spinoza's psychological model. Similarly, the philosophically inclined clinician recognizes this internalizing dynamism within Whitehead's organic process thinking, as experience of the completed act or *superject*, resonates with the individual's internal psychic activity (Sullivan, 1953; Whitehead, 1978).

Such thinking reverses the direction of earlier Spinozan integration, especially in its Anglophone development, which take pains to conform Spinozan thought in anticipation of mainstream psychoanalytic thought. In so doing, real differences between Spinoza and Freud are felicitously clouded, with only hints of meaningful disagreement. Instead, following Lou Andreas-Salomé's observation that Spinoza meets us on our developmental path, the present discernment of a *clinical Spinoza* suggests that *Ethics* itself might be seen as a rigorously clarifying commentary upon psychoanalysis in its contemporary, vernacular expression (Miller, 2016).

As in Aristotelian thought, *Ethics* recognizes that our species-wide, shared essence is affected individually by so-called *accidents*, experiences unique to each of us, such as in the sequelae of trauma. For Spinoza, these typify the patterns and modifications allowing for appreciation through observation, of our uniquely formed psychologies. Christopher Bollas' idea of perceptive identification (Bollas, 2006) captures this personalized form of essentialism in contemporary psychoanalysis. Similarly, clinical recognition of characteristic patterns of personality, many of which are elaborated by Spinoza in *Ethics* Part III, result from continuously repetitive forms of affective conjunction, shaping the attitudinal shape and style of our uniquely evolving qualities of striving.

Cardinal in the thought and extension characterizing the individual's psychological activity is the mind's striving both to maintain and to increase its power; and its determined opposition to limitation or diminution of its power. This idea itself underlies *Ethics'* implicit theory of clinical resistance. Seeking agreement with what each of us believes, we are reluctant to accept the challenge of others' disagreements, defending strongly against perceived threats of diminished capability, imagined as limitation upon the strivings of conatus. Functionally, however, with the repetitive layering of environmental experience, reinternalized and operating interactively with fresh iterations of perception, feeling, imagination, and desire, the forms of our striving do become constricted, limited by what we take to be necessary from within our experiential learning.

It is upon such foreclosed rigidities of thought that Spinoza extends the technique of skeptical doubt through the test of negation, later to be recognized by Freud as an incremental step toward modifying an individual's strongly held convictions (1925), whether deployed by the reasoning Spinozan self or by another, such as a therapist. That is, the obdurate claim that something "is" is challenged by the skeptical possibility that the same something "is not".[2] Necessarily, though unremarked by Spinoza, the anxiety generated by this rational process of reality testing, is generative of confusion and anxiety. As in clinical process, this requires the mind's capability to contain or to hold the contradictory idea, without attacking or expelling it (Bion, 1959).

Within medieval philosophy, such practices were understood not only within the individual's solitary pursuit of philosophical wisdom, but also as interpersonally enacted within the teacher-student relationship (Fraenkel, 2009b, p. 192; Robinson, 2007, p. 154). Today, we locate parallel interpersonal cultivation in the interactions of the psychotherapeutic field, as reflected in WR Bion's considerations of the mutually affecting relationship in the roles of analyst and patient (Bion, 1992, p. 6).

Spinoza takes great care in providing copious examples both of situational and characterological behaviors, representing the dynamic interaction of the mental functionalities, perception, feeling, imagining, and willing. His purpose in demonstrating both the effects of mental striving and its proximate or efficient causes, which unseen, might be termed his metaphysics or metapsychology, is to cultivate our reasoning functionality toward what in an earlier essay, he'd termed an *emendation of the intellect*. Today, we would term this, *learning from experience*, the foundation of therapeutic change.

Communication through language, as in psychotherapy, is an integral dimension of Spinozan practice. Distorted and confused verbal expression compounds the distortions and confusions, both unconscious and conscious, necessarily generated in thinking itself. Three types of corroborative knowledge affirm our understanding of reality. *Knowledge of the first type*, the most common, is compounded of hearsay and opinion, as well as untested subjective experience. *Knowledge of the second type* is founded in consensual validation, reliable in its utility, though potentially distorted through its social embeddedness. *Knowledge of the third type*, approximating interpretative truth or the *significant fact* referred to by Bion (1992), is intuitive.

Fundamental to Spinoza's system, whether in questioning primitive constructions of imagination, feeling, and willing, or in clarifying the meaning of communicative language, is impoverished understanding, the *privation of knowledge* (II. Proposition 35, p. 265). While acceptance of new data may be as disruptive to psychic equilibrium as the psychological necessity of doubting, it is only by chancing uncertainty, and disequilibrium, that we learn. In this way,

Ethics gestures to the centrality of anxiety, uncertainty, and their containment, as in contemporary psychotherapy, as well as to the demand that the limitations of our understanding be discerned and supplemented toward an expanded *greater perfection.*

While the three elements of pleasure, pain, and desire are fundamental to Spinoza's psychology, these are necessarily conjoined with subjectively generated images, symbols, and associative memory, always in relation to the object of thought. Like Spinoza's basic parallelism of thought and extension, both the idea of mind and the functionality of mind seem precise and imprecise at the same time. Precision lies in the utility of discerning proximate or efficient cause, working backward from empirically recognized behavioral effects. Consolidating the examples provided by Spinoza in *Ethics* Part III, the clinician apprehends what I have termed Spinoza's *cloudy mathematics*, a grid or matrix, specific and flexible enough to understand both general and specific behavioral outcomes. Conceptually, *cloudy mathematics* extends across three domains including: Spinoza's method of inquiry; the mind's internal and external relational fields; and an algorithmic model of psychological process.

However, prior to considering these domains, it is necessary to consider distortion and misprision within our receptive conceptions of psychoanalysis; and through these, by creative association and necessarily subjective transformation, our approximate linkages with ideas. For example, as reader and commentator writing in 2021, I have felt free to associate Spinozan thought with my understanding of 21st-century psychoanalytic practice. I am also aware that this freedom is time-bound, a function of the present moment in psychoanalytic history. As I have noted elsewhere

> today, after well over a century of psychoanalytic practice, we have the luxury of continuously defining psychoanalytic identity through our repetitive return to the reading of conceptual papers that have defined our development. Our age not only innovates, but also develops upon what has come before us. We can pick and choose analysts whose theories intrigue us and by whose lights we hope to illuminate our practice, by targeting specific readings by specific individuals in our continuing studies (Ogden, 2012). (Quoted in Miller, 2016, pp. 15–16)

Having read *Ethics*, my strong sense was that it corresponded not only generally to the early development of psychoanalysis, but also specifically, to our contemporary expression of vernacular psychoanalysis, with D.W. Winnicott and W.R. Bion its most prominent spokespersons (Miller, 2016). Further, I recognized that (1) the difference between Spinoza's model of efficient causation and Freud's positing of a libidinal model, and (2) the difference between Spinoza's idea of the unconscious and Freud's, were significant shifts between earlier and contemporary conceptions of psychoanalysis. In this case, Spinoza's view is more contemporary than Freud's.

Earlier psychoanalytic writers on Spinoza wrote from very different periods in psychoanalytic development. Keen to establish Spinoza's anticipatory links to formative psychoanalytic transmission, they seem to blur the differences I understand to require sharpening. Constance Rathbun, for example, writes

> While Spinoza never mentions the unconscious as such, there is the possibility that in Spinozistic terminology the unconscious is a collection of the most confused and inadequate of ideas, especially those which correspond to unperceived bodily movement. Thus the problem for psychoanalysis of how the unconscious becomes conscious is for Spinoza the problem of how confused ideas are transformed into clear and distinct ideas. (Rathbun, 1934, p. 3)

Rathbun accurately summarizes the Spinozan unconscious. Its development will correspond in the 19th century to the Jamesian idea of unattended experience (Miller, 1987) and in the 20th century to unformulated experience (Stern, 1987, 1997). Extending past Freud's biological desire repressed under internalized civilizational rules, Rathbun's notion is surprisingly contemporary. Indeed, under Spinoza's concept, the unconscious is continuous in the fragmentation, distortion, and confusion, which is a necessary byproduct of mind's conjunctions. Yet, writing from 1934 and seeking to align Spinoza with the ego psychology nascent in the United States, Rathbun avoids the difference between Spinozan and Freudian views, by harmonizing these radically diverse positions without commenting on significant difference. Subsuming Spinozan considerations of pleasure, pain, conatus, and time within the language and structural forms of psychoanalytic development, her misprision casts Spinoza as an ego psychologist for whom

> the object of these methods is identical; to strengthen the ego, to modify the super-ego, to bring as much of the unconscious material into consciousness as is possible, and so to enable the individual to achieve a satisfactory adjustment to reality through insight into his own character. (Rathbun, 1934, p. 13)

Similarly, while M. Hamblin Smith suggests that conatus may be reasonably understood as a concept "preferable to that of libido", venturing that

> in my judgment, there is much to be said in favor of the psychoanalytic use of conatus, in place of the somewhat unfortunate term libido (1925, p. 265)

he blurs the crispness of his critique. Harmonizing Spinoza and Freud, he clouds their difference noting that

> when we remember, as we always must remember, the extended meaning which Freud attaches to the term 'sex', we shall find that the essentially sexual character of the emotions can be quite well fitted in with Spinoza's definitions. (1925, p. 266)

Almost a century later, the contemporary clinical reader might miss Smith's heretical reading of Freudian libido, adapting instead the softer, more Jungian version rejected by Freud, "of libidinal equivalence to 'psychical interest in general'" (Freud, 1915, p. 80; Miller, 2016, p. 35). Today, this softened libidinal conception is accepted within psychoanalytic understanding via Winnicott's broadening of

> the infant's libidinal pleasure from the pure and often violently experienced emotionality of erotogenic zones to a sexuality rooted in erotogenic zones, but reflective of play, creativity, and quiet self-absorption. In so doing, Winnicott softens or loosens a hard distinction insisted upon by Freud. (Miller, 2016, p. 35)

Here too, Smith, like Rathbun, progresses Freudian concepts through Spinoza to a construction that will become widespread in early 21st-century psychoanalytic transformation. But each does it sub rosa, like the very idea of Spinoza's doubling itself. Their harmonized descriptions require viewing through unwritten scholia to discern disagreement with psychoanalysis as institutionally understood in their times.

In this light, the present reading only makes conscious what my predecessors have chosen to retain as doubled, however present to the reader who understands the contexts from which they write. Today, the psychoanalyst can affirm difference undeterred by the charge of heresy as against orthodoxy (Bergmann, 2017, p. 70). It is not only that Spinoza's unconscious, for which he had no word, extends the scope of the Freudian unconscious. It is not only that Spinoza's conatus parallels psychologically, the sexuality of Freudian libido, but also that these differences are significant; and reflected in contemporary psychoanalytic vernacular expression.

Spinoza's psychology is monistic. It is grounded in efficient cause. Freudian causation is dualistic; and grounded in a metapsychology more deeply biologized than Spinoza's functional transformations of Aristotelian mental domains. Libido, in this sense, is located prior to conatus, imbricated within the biological imperative of *trieb*. While each theorist would agree on the transformational processes of dependent concomitance, and agree also upon the generalized human imperative for self-preservation, Spinoza might shrug his shoulders at Freud's libidinal construction, as unnecessarily generating an infinite regress in the realm of efficient causation. If libido lies behind conatus, then behind libidinal *trieb* lie other embodied physical transformations, the realm of today's neuroscience. Spinoza's early comment on the impossibility of working iron without a hammer, focused upon the fallacy of locating first cause, provides concrete illustration. He writes

> to work iron, a hammer is needed, and to have a hammer, it must be made. For this purpose there is need of another hammer and other tools, and again to get these there is need of other tools and so on to infinity. In this way one might try to prove in vain, that men have no power to work iron. (Spinoza, 2002, *Treatise on the Emendation of the Intellect*, 1660, p. 9)

It is here, obliquely referencing the infinite regress[3] suggested by libido theory that M. Hamblin Smith's audacity as reader peeks out from the caution of his presentation. Mirroring Spinoza's fierce argument as writer, Smith addresses the constant conjunction between mind and body, underlining that

> Spinoza does not look for any explanation of the correspondence of two such dissimilar things as mind and body; he simply says that they are the same thing, and they differ only in being two aspects of the same thing. There is thus no mystery about the parallelism or the mutual interaction of mind and body. The mystery is resolved into an elementary fact. To ask why mind should correspond with matter is like asking why the convexity of a curve should answer to the concavity. Mind and body are distinguishable but not separable. (Smith, 1925, p. 261)

Smith's strong position also echoes Lou Andreas-Salomé's critique of Freud's dualism through observation that Spinoza's monism is "the philosophical step that goes beyond Freud" (Andreas-Salomé, 1964, p. 75).

Spinoza, for whom the curve's convexity needn't answer to its concavity, operates from the premise of efficient cause and effect, characteristic today of psychoanalytic observation, no matter the interpretive intricacy of explanatory verbiage. Pragmatic inquiry must discern whether the relation of effect and cause make sense to the patient; and how.

Smith's understated endorsement of a psychoanalytic conatus replacing the notion of libido is heretical in shaking the metapsychological structure of psychoanalysis. Rathbun's recognition of an unconscious construct far more extensive than Freud's would also seriously challenge the suzerainty of libido; but by the end of the 20th century, the same question would be raised from within mainstream psychoanalysis itself: the necessary apparatus of metapsychology, whether as scientific fact or as a vehicle of clinical psychoanalytic utility (Schafer, 1976, 1999). The Spinozan answer, centered on mind's functionality is reflective of a dynamic and cohesive unconscious system, more compelling than Freudian metapsychology. Practically, as reflected in our contemporary vernacular, Winnicott's gentler notion, *going on being*, a motivational center similar to Spinoza's conatus, would come to inform psychoanalytic vernacular expression.

Spinoza's Demonstrated Method of Inquiry

Close reading of *Ethics* permits us a departure from simply knowing-about Spinoza to knowing Spinoza, at least in the sense of engaging with his thinking as thought partner. From the beginning of my reading, I was reassured by Spinoza scholarship that my very slow integration of his thoughts was a recognizable experience in apprehension, as was the occasional "flash" of illumination (Deleuze, 1988; Wolfson, 1934).

Unlike my early 20th-century psychological predecessors, Spinoza's form of geometric presentation did not detract from my reading; nor, at least in the beginning, was I aware of that form's two-thousand year philosophical heritage[4] (Tanner, 1907a; Smith, 1925). Rather, it challenged. Unprepared for Spinoza's plenitude of explanatory categories, each differing from the other only in extension of thought or minor change of direction, and often redirected through the embroidery of explanatory scholia, I was reminded of other psychoanalytic reading puzzles. From such approach, I understood that, together with patience,

> each of us takes what he knows and strives somehow to link it, joining it with everything else, with autobiography and self-narrative, testing sense-making. (Miller, 2015, p. 11)

From the standpoint of confusion, thrown into conceptual cacophony, I recalled my initial immersion in Bion's *Attention and Interpretation* (1970) where

> departing from unspoken professional consensus regarding the written form of psychoanalytic theory, Bion conveys this classic of psychoanalytic writing through the artful juxtaposition of self-referential, parataxic paragraphs. His numbered clusters of words are dense with information to be parsed or not, by the reader, in onward progress. They are Bion's beta elements, garbage in and

garbage out, yes, no, and maybes, to settle as they may in significance or detritus. What is carried forward, as what is carried forward from psychotherapeutic session to session for the patient, is determined by the reader's experience, illuminating the inchoate. (Miller, 2015, p. 32)

In aiding the reader, Bion comments upon how one must encounter such a muddle, just as the analyst waits for the evolution of analytic process, writing

similarly, the reader must disregard what I say until the O of the experience of reading has evolved to a point where the actual events of reading issue in his interpretation of the experiences. (Bion, 1970, p. 28)

Also, from Freud's cliffhanger 1909 lectures at Clark, I had learned that much is disclosed about clinical engagement through the form by which the analyst describes what he does. Patience, waiting for the other shoe to drop, is essential toward consolidation of understanding. At Clark

Freud concludes these five essays with consideration of the patient's emotional life in relation to the therapist. What begins conceptually in resistance is extended into transference, emergent through material which the patient "can no longer recall to memory" and which is now "re-experienced" in relation to the therapist. Freud terms this relational response the "clinical heart of psychoanalysis"; and construes it within therapy as a "catalytic ferment which temporarily attracts to itself the affects liberated in the process" (p. 50). And so, it is from within transference that the patient (like Freud's reader or audience) develops conviction in the plausibility of method. (Miller & Sweet, 2018, p. 103)

Reading Spinoza, I moved between slow consolidation, associating actively to psychoanalytic understanding and experience, to moments of panic, as I have described above, in attempting to make sense of *Ethics* Part III. I was greatly encouraged by Spinoza's personalized recognition of the reader's difficulty, encouraging a step-by-step understanding until achieving some kind of clarity. Here, too, I recalled the psychoanalytic presentation of ideas, such as Bion's statement that

> I have advised the reader to read straight through this book, not to dwell too long upon difficulties, and in this way to gain a working knowledge of the book itself. But the book will have failed for the reader if it does not become an object of study, and the reading of it an emotional experience itself. My hope is that it will be an experience leading to an increased ability on the part of the analyst to mobilize his own resources of knowledge, clinical observation, theory construction (in the sense of propaedeutic to interpretation) and so to render this work out of date and hasten the day when what is perhaps the most distressing malady a patient and family will have to endure will be classed as 'curable'. (1992, p. 261)

Bion's "secondary but important aim" might similarly be imputed to Spinoza's clinical theory in

> that the form in which I have presented the material will lead to a more rational, and therefore more certainly communicable, method of expression of psycho-analytic theory than obtains at present. (Bion, 1992, p. 261)

Comparing Spinoza with psychoanalytic theorists such as Freud and Bion, I was struck by the writer's conveyance of person, of how the thinker thinks; and of his intentionality to convey his thoughts convincingly. Each generates a subjective, clinically testable commentary on the psyche. As in earlier research, encountering psychoanalytic texts, I was reminded

> of the other's authority, obstinacy, and refusal to yield: the mark of resistance itself as one's tenacious subjectivity. If I wish to continue, I must accept the other's unyielding position. If I wish to continue, I must accommodate this position, noting it within myself, both as a dimension of the other and as a potentially

limiting aspect of our relationship; and then I continue on, learning what can be learned. (Miller, 2015, p. 15)

Together with an implicit clinical theory, glimpsed through the open apertures of Spinoza's aspirational argument for the applicational of rational reflection upon the jumbled mix-ups of feeling, imagination, desire on the one hand and the difficulty of parsing the truth of socially affirmed reality, I discerned a passionate theorist and practitioner, determined to convey a mathematically inspired understanding of how mind works, and how we might address its products toward greater satisfaction: the first modern shop-manual for applied psychology. Necessarily, as within any psychotherapy, however bound by the conventions of method, Spinoza reveals much of himself.

Earlier Applications

Marveling at Spinoza's breadth of thought, Lou Andreas-Salomé observed that if you

think far enough, correctly enough on any point at all and you hit upon him; you meet him waiting for you, standing ready at the side of the road. (Andreas-Salomé, 1964, p. 76)

Reading and rereading *Ethics*, following chains of association, becoming confused, persevering, again reorienting with a crumb of productive thought, kneading that crumb with my own further associations, beginning again, continuing again, I recognized how correct Andreas-Salomé had been; and in relation to clinical psychoanalysis, however mostly without direct attribution. Her Spinoza related to her psychoanalysis, circa 1912; my Spinoza related to my psychoanalysis, circa 2021.

Following footnotes, remembering journal articles, I began to locate indications of Spinozan clinical application. Another later member of Andreas-Salomé's Vienna *Freud School*, Paul Federn, would publish an extraordinarily Spinozan account of pleasure, pain, and desire in transit from the intrapsychic world to the environmental world in which other people, time, and consequences of action would differentiate between the principles of pleasure and reality (Federn, 1915).

A few years earlier, Amy Tanner would detail her own experience of taking on the tasks of oppressed working women, paralleled almost a century later by Barbara Ehrenreich's *Nickel and Dimed* (2001). Tanner's ethnographic technique followed what I would observe as Spinoza's clinical matrix. She detailed the thoughts in her mind, combined with the affective resonance of her body's increasingly challenged demands; and joining feeling, imagination, with her desires—both to report significant and widespread, socially oppressive experience and to discern carefully its psychological effects—drew direct links between resulting actions, states of mind, resistances, and extensions of pain into object-related hatreds and loves—along a clear path almost unimaginable to the reader of her explicitly Spinozan paper, written at the same time (Tanner, 1907a). Like Spinoza's use of scholia, elaborating a psychological world emergent as a parallel counter-text to his formalized demonstration, Tanner achieved through the mobilization of two academic fields of publication (psychology and sociology), a similar Spinozan doubling. "Glimpses at the Mind of a Waitress" (1907b) is Tanner's glimpse at psychological process through Spinoza's filigreed apple, discerned through the skeptical laboratory psychology apertures of "Spinoza and Modern Psychology" (1907a).

The two interlocking fields of Tanner's narrative, the privately internal and the oppressively external, suggest both Spinoza's depictions in *Ethics* Part III of psychological systemic functioning involving three or more individuals, and also the later gestalt *lifespace* of Kurt Lewin, recognized by the 1930s as an intrinsic aspect of psychoanalytic action (Brown, 1936; Lewin, 1936), if integrated more formally and cautiously within our emergent psychoanalytic vernacular only in 21st-century field theories (Stern, 2013a, 2013b). Like Spinoza, Lewin in human psychology and Tolman in wider, mammalian psychology, would illustrate their theories by mathematical example (Tolman, 1932; Lewin, 1933, 1936). Reading *Ethics*, I recognized that such models represent a version of *cloudy mathematics* similar to Spinoza's: to be conceptualized by the observer at the level of general rule; and applied relative to the particularities of the specific psychological situation.

The common contemporary term for this kind of model is *algo-rithm*, itself formed through Latin translation from the Arabic and earlier Greek, much like the trajectory of Spinoza's philosophical background.

Our recognition of Spinoza as the *philosopher of psychoanalysis* begins with the reflections of Lou Andreas-Salomé. Yet, in recognizing our clinical Spinoza, it is important to trace Spinozan moves within the clinical reports of her Spinozan comrade, Viktor Tausk. Reporting in 1917 on the psychology of the war deserter, Tausk differentiates between categories of deserters. Noting that most desertions occur from "non-combatant units in the back areas, from army formations employed on guard or labor duties" (Tausk, 1969, p. 362), Tausk also observes that

> deserters on the run often endure hardships unquestionably more severe than any military duty or danger, in spite of which they return voluntarily to their duty only in very rare cases indeed. I have known deserters who spent months living like wild beasts in the forest, suffering from bitter cold and starvation and constantly exposed to the most wretched of deaths which, however, they preferred to facing their duties with some guard or labor company in the back areas. (Tausk, 1969, p. 362)

This description is extended to a large portion of desertions, of which Tausk writes

> the typical biographies to be extracted from these men lead us quickly to psychological soil of a kind very familiar to us from psychoanalysis. The deserter's misdeed turns out to be a characteristic behavior pattern. All these men have been 'fugitives' since childhood. Some had run away from home innumerable times. Others had never kept a job, or had continually changed it. One was an adventurer who had traveled half the world over and done many different jobs. Those who had been to school had been truants and bad examples to their fellows. They had 'always been like that'. Why? One had a strict father, the other a stepmother. They could not bear it at home. They had stayed away from school because the teacher treated them unfairly.

Father had not allowed them to learn the trade they would have liked, they had to learn something that gave them no pleasure. One had been treated badly by all his maters, another by his masters' wives, yet another by his master's children, or his companions, or fellow-apprentices. "If only I could have taken over my father's business I should have settled down", one of them said to me. As, however, his father had been unwilling to let him do this, he had kept running away from home, and the police had kept bringing him back. (Tausk, 1969, p. 366)

Tausk continues, promising to introduce the reader to "a little psychoanalysis" in order that his interpretive assumptions are found persuasive. He writes further that

what these cases show is that the motivation of desertion in this category originates in childhood and can often be traced to infancy, and that the characteristic experience of these people is the flight from family compulsion. You only have to accept the fact that 'master' and 'teacher' are surrogates for the father, that the master's wife is a surrogate for the mother, and that comrades, fellow-apprentices and classmates are surrogates for siblings, and you will be able to see the complete picture. (Tausk, 1969, p. 367)

What strikes the reader is the similarity of Tausk's psychoanalytic explanation to Spinoza's observation that

hence many men, over-impatient and with false religious zeal, have chosen to live among beasts rather than among men, just as boys or young men, unable patiently to endure the upbraidings of their parents, run away to join the army and prefer the hardships of war and tyrannical discipline to the comfort of home and parental admonition, and suffer burdens to be imposed on them so long as they can spite their parents. (IV. Appendix, xiii, pp. 359–360)

Equally Spinozan, but from a different angle, is Tausk's therapeutic intervention in the case of Ibsen the Druggist (Tausk, 1934).

Tausk's demonstration of Spinozan doubt as a challenge to fixed, resistant thinking, had itself been retold by a later member of Andreas-Salomé's *Freud School*, Robert Waelder (1951). Waelder, like W.R. Bion, had followed Maurits Katan's writings on psychosis; and read Tausk's unattributed Spinozan negation as

> an extra-therapeutic interaction effective in the momentary correction of a paranoid idea. Tausk portrays the links within the mind of his protagonist, Mr. B, between a sculptural representation of the dramatist Ibsen, whose early training had been as a pharmacist, and another druggist with whose wife Mr B is conducting an extramarital relationship. Tausk's presentation is itself a matrix linking: 1) the manifest example of distorted thinking itself; 2) its separate preconceptions as 3) fused elements in compromise formation together with 4) the uncanny apprehension of a formerly recognizable object (the plaster sculpture of Ibsen), now stripped of immediate familiarity in the individual's experience; and 5) an effective intervention aligned with reality, a route Katan might later recognize as expanding the reality-related non-psychotic layer of personality. While illustrating the dynamics of primitive thought, Waelder unwittingly begins to solve the riddle of correcting misconceptions of reality, apparently resistant to clarification. (Miller & Sweet, 2018, pp. 57–58)

My earlier reading of Katan, Waelder, and Tausk, was linked to interest in WR Bion's thinking, reflected in his well-known clinical calculus, suggesting

> a movement over time from a paranoid-schizoid moment to an achieved moment of the depressive position tinctured with paranoid-schizoid experience, itself transitioning over time to a depressive moment manifest in passive or active forms. (Miller & Sweet, 2018, p. 55)

At that time, I had no acquaintance with *Ethics*; and only after reading Andreas-Salomé, did I consider the notion of Tausk as a Spinozan. Still, I was able to see as "remarkable" that in the immediacy of Tausk's own intuition, his awareness of the contextual history of the situation, its characters, and circumstances, and his clear articulation of what Bion would later term the "significant fact" (Bion, 1992; Miller, 2015). Bion's own thinking in arrival at this concept is in consideration of the analyst's containment of the patient's verbal and non-verbal productions, always immediately present within a given session, but continuously emergent in different forms, so articulating different aspects of the patient's personality. These are reflected in the analyst's countertransference, across the timeline of the analysis. The substrate of this action is in the toleration of time: in a session's immediacy; in continuous emergence of narrative; in therapeutic repetitions of action, word, and emotion; in recognition of plausibility and rejection of interpretation; in uncertainty; and of therapeutic containment itself as a necessary vehicle for therapeutic engagement. (Miller & Sweet, 2018, p. 58)

But it was only when I began to deconstruct Spinoza's multiple arrivals at well-known behaviors in Part III's *Definition of the Emotions*, under my own effort (Miller, 2021), encouraged by Joyce Tigner's careful examination of Spinozan pride and self-abasement (Tigner, 1985), that I recognized the extraordinary parallel between Spinoza's depiction of behavior and Bion's careful elaboration of Melanie Klein's shuttle between P/S and D. Each theorist, Spinoza and Bion, had mobilized his understanding of scientific method; and while separated by three hundred years, Bion's explicitly clinical algorithm, itself emergent roughly a century into the development of psychoanalysis, mirrored Spinoza's integration of affective experience and thinking, just as Bion's own psychoanalytic theory of thinking would recapitulate (unattributed), Spinoza's emphasis on the integrations of perception, feeling, imagination, and willing/desire, overseen by reason, preparatory to practical action (Bion, 1962).

Together with the similarity of Spinoza's conatus to D.W. Winnicott's self-preservative notion of being, Bion's unattributed Spinozism spoke to me directly, of Lou Andreas-Salomé's (1912) observation. Having anticipated themes in the development of psychoanalytic thought, the tacit embeddedness of *Ethics* within the fabric of evolving clinical method, however operating at a different level from the journal-based formal integration of Spinoza's thought within psychoanalysis, was my Spinozan-Deleuzian "flash" of illumination.

What was I to do with this understanding? Clinically, I found myself carefully attentive to patients' step-by-step pathways; and heard myself referring to distortions of experience, in Spinozan terms: perceiving, feeling, imagining, striving, and desiring. More critically, and supported too, by my own integrations of Bion's clinical algorithm, I took care to examine the conjunctions of mind's functionalities, and always through the patients' experiential lens. How did the confluence of forces recognized by my patient at time (n) become transformed through new iterations of cause and effect at time (n + 1)? In time, my conveyance of such questioning would be reciprocated by my patients, explaining to me their own observations of psychological process in terms of both affective and cognitive experiences, and their changing patterns and sequelae. I observed, whether as Bolognini's "European third" (Bolognini, 2011), or as Reid's value (1955), that the methodological algorithm by which I steered in clinical practice, was useful to my patients, in their orientation within what had been formerly confusing and alien.

I realized too, that just as Bion had understood his Kleinian terminology as an expressive language indicative of scientific process (Bion, 1992), my clinical translation of Spinozan categories in English from the original Latin, descended from the Hebrew and the earlier Arabic and Greek, through a fine integration, "as if through a cloud", of thinker, thought, and thought's object (II. Proposition 7, Scholium), oriented both me and my patient together in probing an inexhaustible possibility of unconscious recognitions. Further, that like Spinoza, I was focused upon the immediacy of behavioral effect, and the plausibility of proximate or efficient causation. The latter, of course, like changing cloud formations, would operate in continuous movement, caught only momentarily through either joint or single inquiry, in the context of clinical psychoanalysis.

Certainly, when contents tilted toward sexuality, we employed the same method, focusing on willing, striving, and desiring, the relational going on being of contemporary psychoanalytic understanding, as opposed to a libidinal construction preceding Spinoza's functionalities of mind. Such tension between Freud's sexualized formulation and Spinoza's focus on human being had been noted in the Anglophone literature as early as 1925 (Smith, 1925). Unspoken, it would also influence the American turn toward a humanistic psychoanalysis, with its European ambassadors of Spinoza including Karen Horney, Frederick Weiss, and Erich Fromm.

What continues its appeal to me in Spinoza's *cloudy mathematics* is the clarity of methodological direction at the general level of practice, the Levensonian clinical algorithm (1978), and the range of possibility in verbalized translation, transforming little-by-little, step by step, what has been inadequate, fragmentary, distorted and confused, to that ancient aspiration of greater perfection.[5] It is from such regularity of method and thought, expressed in subjective language and particularity, that the daily practice of psychoanalytic psychotherapy proceeds (Lewin, 1933; Sullivan, 1954).

Notes

1 Feuer (1958) would utilize a psychoanalytic interpretive lens in linking Spinoza to liberal humanism. Additionally, he would use the vehicle of a Spinozan dream fragment as the center of what he imputes to be Spinoza's psychological struggles (1957). In this latter arrogation of interpretive certainty, Feuer follows Smith (1925) and Tanner (1907a) in their claims about Spinoza's personality, reducing psychological thought to a critical, pejorative device, antagonistic to Spinozan openness. Later, Goetschel (2016) would pivot from Feuer's Spinozan dream analysis to a post-colonial critique, consistent with Spinoza's life experience in an Amsterdam deeply engaged in the new Atlantic Trade, inclusive of the brutalities of slavery, fundamental to profitable new industries, such as sugar production. However psychoanalytic as critique, neither Feuer's nor Goetschel's speculative dream analyses are clinical in nature, both lacking engagement with a reflective, self-interpreting subject.

2 A clinical example of such negation, depicted as emotional foreclosure, is provided in the vignette of the patient who, never having read Herman Melville, insists on knowledge of his oeuvre through what "everyone knows", Spinoza's *knowledge of the first kind* (Miller, 2021).

3 Spinoza provides a parallel statement of infinite regression in Ethics, in that

> every individual thing, i.e, anything whatever which is finite and has a determinate existence, cannot exist or be determined to act unless it be determined to exist and to act by another cause which is also finite and has a determinate existence, and this cause again cannot exist or be determined to act unless it be determined to exist and to act by another cause which is also finite and has a determinate existence, and so ad infinitum. (I. Proposition 28, p. 233)

4 Not only does Spinoza's geometrical format recapitulate ancient philosophical forms, but also, mirroring Descartes' use of geometrical proof, fits within the post-Baconian ethos of the "New Science", with its expressive aspirations in mathematical precision (Vickers, 1996).

5 The reader is also reminded of another hiatus in Spinozan reception, carried forward under the aegis of another philosopher, into American Interpersonal-Relational psychoanalysis. The dynamic, organic psychology, advanced by Sullivan, is rooted in the Spinozan philosophy of A.N. Whitehead (Sullivan, 1953; Whitehead, 1978), with Whitehead's process-related organic philosophy, a transformation of Spinozan monism (Whitehead, 1978, pp. 6–7).

Chapter 11

Tools of Clinical Inquiry

Considering two *worlds*, the body and the mind, Lou Andreas-Salomé observed that Baruch Spinoza had "developed throughout a method of its own for the one of these worlds which can be grasped psychologically" (Andreas-Salomé, 1964, p. 75). However complicated Spinoza's method, its intuitive, consistent, and plausible arguments allow for an immediacy of psychological grasp. In this, as Fromm reckons, Spinoza is the founder of modern psychology (Fromm, 1964a). Like psychoanalysis itself, Spinoza posited an overdetermined system of dependent concomitance relating mind to body. Yet, closer in thinking to John Dewey than to Freud in recognizing multiply iterated, efficiently caused chains of functional acts, differing through transformation from any predecessor fact itself, Spinoza's thinking found sufficient breadth and depth within the realm of the mind without resort to a biologized theory of drives (Fromm, 1964b; Smith, 1925). Instead, drives themselves, also caused by predecessor physical states, would themselves be products of efficient causal chains, rather than psychology's starting point. Formally, Spinoza notes that the cause of an effect

> cannot exist or be determined to act unless it be determined to exist and to act by another cause which is also finite and has a determinate existence, and this cause again cannot exist or be determined to act unless it be determined to exist and to act by another cause which is also finite and has a determinate existence, and so ad infinitum. (I. Proposition 28, p. 233)

DOI: 10.4324/9781003246404-16

Like his earlier, more narrative observation, disproving the impossibility of forging iron without the necessity of an iron hammer in the *Tractate on the Emendation of the Intellect*, Spinoza overturns facile argument with fact. Employing transformed functional categories in common use since Aristotle, Spinoza generates an intricate, dynamic psychology compounded of the elements: perception; feeling; imagination; desire; and reason. These are integrated through self-preservative action, itself extending across two psychic fields, from the internal world to human engagement with the external environment. Within each domain, Spinoza describes the operational transformation of human willing, striving, and endeavoring, implied by the Latin *conatus* and the Hebrew *hishtadlut*. For English speakers, the profundity of this idea is conveyed through its multiplicity of translated forms, much as Freud's *libido, trieb, ich*, and *es*, overflow their language of origin; and indeed, in the case of *ich* and *es*, acquire their own un-particle, the *unheimlich* London joke of Strachey and Jones, within their English transformations.

The unrecognized, unconscious willing of our internal world is conatus itself. Externalized into the environment, such *willing* becomes *appetite*; and *appetite* made conscious is transformed as *desire*. Necessarily, the internalization of desire undergoes integration again, with the unobservable thoughts and extensions of mind generating different levels of simultaneous, unconscious mental functioning.

Like Freud's later model, Spinoza's system of human psychology is moderated by the vicissitudes of pleasure and pain. Registered through the functions of perception and feeling, imbued with meaningful association and memory as well as creative imagination, titrations of registered pleasure and pain are the affective bridge between body and mind. Much as the psychoanalytic formulation of mind suggests the body's demand for work, Spinoza's concept of mind itself is a natural twinning of thought and extension: the discrete product of Nature's lawful, observable, causal chains. The idea of conatus, as received through a current of medieval Jewish philosophy derived from Islamic reception of ancient Greek philosophy, is a transformation of animal instinct through the advanced capabilities of the human mind relative to other species.

While the transformation of emotionally felt states of pleasure and pain are the result of mind's situated existence in the body, the functional work of mind is in thinking. Reminding the clinical reader of Bion's (1962) paper on the psychoanalytic theory of thinking, the function of thought, both for Spinoza as for Bion, is toward the refinement of externalized action. While Spinoza's aspirational value is toward making moral choices useful to self and society, these are not necessarily implied by his psychological theory. Rather because pathological functioning and non-pathological functioning operate by similar laws, the refinement of thinking toward pathological ends is as explainable by natural processes as are non-pathological acts.

Clinicians' recognitions of resistance and other defensive forms are intrinsic to Spinoza's model of mind, not as a function of Freudian repression, but rather of the unconsciously perceived sense that mind's self-preservative capabilities are threatened. Throughout life, both discrete and repetitive events, the traumas that philosophers term *accidents* in contrast with human *essence*, interact with the functional categories of mind both to preserve conatus and to shape it in limitation of capability. Because, like prior practical philosophies from which *Ethics* develops, the engagement of our reasoning capacity allows us to reflect upon mind itself, Spinoza's and Freud's method each challenge the hubris of complete human free will (Bernard, 1946; Fromm, 1964a, 1964b; Rathbun, 1934; Smith, 1925). Despite our limitations of free will, we do have the capability which for Spinoza is our moral imperative, for reflection upon what we do. As clinicians recognize, this is hardly a trivial task. Not only does mind intrinsically resist the assaults of doubting inquiry, but also, unconscious currents of pleasure and pain are unclear; and the products of inquiry suggest, as they do in psychoanalysis, that our unrecognized, unformulated, internal worlds are, for practical purpose, unlimited in conjoint union. Spinoza demonstrates this to the reader through an engaging, purposive method that cultivates the reader's own self-observation.

The Spinozan unconscious resembles today's broadening of the Freudian unconscious (Rathbun, 1934; Stern, 1987, 1997). Dredging such murky depths requires not only verbalization in naming contents but also successive approximations by the patient-analyst pair in tolerating changes of experience, much as Spinoza's model of conatus is transformed through its extensions in use from unconscious willing to unconscious appetite to conscious desire. *Ethics* speaks directly to this challenge. First is that our affective states proceed whether or not we productively engage our minds, in that

> the idea of the idea of any affection of the human body does not involve adequate knowledge of the human mind. (II. Proposition 29, p. 262)

Following from this is another level of uncertainty in that

> the idea that constitutes the nature of the human mind is likewise shown, when considered solely in itself, not to be clear and distinct, as is also the idea of the human mind and the ideas of affections of the human body insofar as they are related to the human mind, as everyone can easily see. (II. Proposition 28, Scholium, p. 262)

To strive for clarity, Spinoza provides a method embedded in the classical philosophic form of geometrical demonstration. However, simultaneously with the demands of a logic as precise as mathematics, his scholia function as disruptive commentaries, essays that push and pull at the linear presentation of the main text. Following Spinozan reference to Maimonides, I have similarly understood this as a hermeneutic move paralleling recognition of heretofore unformulated viewpoints, similar to the multi-layered interpretive stance of medieval philosophers. The analogy used by Maimonides is derived from a scriptural commentary on the word *apple*. Spinoza too, uses the word *apple*, although in its Latin translation, in his discussion of symbolism and associative processes (II. Proposition 18, Scholium). The Maimonidean apple, wrought in silver filigree, discloses through its intricate apertures, a golden core. In the same way, Spinoza discloses the underlying, dynamic forms of mental functioning.

The image of a filigreed apple's potential for disclosure is paralleled by another vividly Spinozan concept: of the changing, cloud-like integration of multiple psychological formations, each subject to different lawful relations of mind. Following an English translation of this idea (De Spinoza, 1996, II. Proposition 7, Scholium, p. 35), I recognize in this dynamic a *cloudy mathematics*, finding it psychologically present both in the writings of Lewin (Brown, 1936; Lewin, 1936) and Bion (Miller & Sweet, 2018). This strikingly modern position, linking the precision of scientific law with the imprecision of its particular human expression, is recapitulated by Kurt Lewin who writes

> What is the task of analysis? What should be the aim especially of a dynamical analysis? In my opinion the goal of analysis is to characterize the facts so that one can strictly derive the behavior, or any other kind of psychological event, in a logical way, or (to say the same from point of view) to be able to predict actual occurrences. The theoretical and practical goal of analysis is reached when such derivation is possible and then the task is completed.

> For such an "explanation: or prediction of events", we must know

> 1. The general laws of the particular events
> 2. The momentary constitution of the whole situation

> In order to analyze the situation, one must characterize the situation, that is, the psychological environment and the psychological person, through concepts that are logically, clearly and completely enough defined to allow logical derivations and which can be used as constants in place of the variable values of the equations which characterize the general laws. It is the task of prediction or derivation which will compel psychology to use more and more concepts of mathematical structure.

> The cause of the events is the relationship between the parts of the situation as dynamical facts., and a complete characterization of these dynamical facts would be a complete analysis. (Lewin, 1933, pp. 318–319)

Lewin's own mathematical ideal, like Bion's later mathematical algorithm describing clinical process (Bion, 1963; Miller & Sweet,

2018), both follow the *cloudy mathematical* form reflective of Spinozan precision and imprecision, especially when mediated through verbal communication. From this perspective, Spinoza extends to clinicians, practicing three hundred and fifty years after his death, a set of exacting and still useful, clinical tools. These include the following considerations:

1. That clear and distinct thinking often depends on addressing the *privation of knowledge* (II. Proposition 35, p. 265), itself clarified through exploration of three levels of knowledge: (1) the first, hearsay and opinion; (2) the second, consensual understandings (sometimes themselves distorted); and (3) the intuitive fact, similar to Bion's later idea of significance (Bion, 1992, p. 5). Bion writes of the respective roles of the analyst and patient in therapeutic engagement aimed to clarify perplexity,

   The peculiarity that distinguishes the psycho-analyst from his analysand is that the analyst is able to select the worthwhile fact, produce the deductive system and its associated calculus, experience the moment of union when the elements meet to give rise to a feeling that the cause has been found, and begin a process that issues in a change that produces a feeling that an effect and its cause has been linked. (Bion, 1992, p. 6)

Reciprocally,

   The analysand, on the other hand, is made aware of an hypothesis in a deductive system which he may or may not be able to use as a premise for further deductions. The deductive system thus formed may enable him in his turn to select one of these unifying facts. (Bion, 1992, p. 6)

Like *Ethics* as methodological tutorial, Bion here describes a procedural algorithm (Levenson, 1983), iterated time and again within the clinical relationship between analyst and patient. Through repetition, its experiential form itself supplements earlier, learned constriction of conatus with the new, necessarily generating doubt regarding previous distortions and privations of knowledge. Bion credits Henri Poincare with this idea, which is wholly congruent with Spinozan inquiry, detailed in *Ethics*. Indeed, the epigram to Bion's clinical diary, *Cogitations*, while directly linked to Poincare, is suggestive of Spinoza, through the "flash" discerned both by Deleuze and Romain Rolland (Deleuze, 1988; Vermorel, 2009). Quoting Poincare, Bion begins this clinical diary with the idea that "thought is only a flash between two long nights, but this flash[1] is everything" (Bion, 1992, vi).

2. The slow development of understanding emerges through repetitive unpacking of chains of efficient causation, much as in John Dewey's recognition of the reflex arc's action (Dewey, 1896). Clinically, as in Spinoza's presentation, these often clarify as a function of *nachtraglichkeit*, first established while working forward to a Deleuzian *middle* (Deleuze, 1988, p. 129) as we have observed in discerning the centrality of the Appendix to *Ethics* I; and then, having temporarily established a conceptual foothold, seeking intuitive understanding through the continuously changing perspectives of feeling, imagination, and desire.

3. The scope of inquiry concerns both intrapsychic and interpersonal fields, always object-related, and always generative of multiple levels of relation between elements in continuous dynamic activity. Spinoza's discrete naming of will, appetite and desire are indicative both of differing psychic fields and of the transformations in conatus, dependent on field.

4. Conatus itself, as our cardinal, self-preservative force, is approximately suggestive of Winnicott's *going on being* (1960). Its creative elaboration, underlined by Whitehead (1978), similarly suggests Winnicott's elevation of creativity to psychoanalytic consideration (Miller, 2015, pp. 31–44; Winnicott, 1953).

5. Spinoza's classical deployment of mathematics in philosophical demonstration leads to an algorithmic orientation, congruent with today's psychoanalytic understanding both of a general clinical practice method (Bion, 1992; Lewin, 1933; Levenson, 1983; Sullivan, 1954) and in recognizing specific moments of

clinical process conjoining the relation between psychic position, temporal moment, and observable behavioral expression (Bion, 1963; Miller & Sweet, 2018). That this generalized descriptive pathway of mental action discerned in the 17th century by Spinoza, is glimpsed only now, after years of 20th century psychoanalytic theoretical and clinical development, is nothing short of extraordinary. Through his extending of Melanie Klein's clinical thinking, Bion's (1963) mathematical algorithm recapitulates Spinoza's 17th century process descriptions of psychodynamic action in 20th century psychoanalytic language.

Spinoza's main algorithm, demonstrated in *Ethics* Part III, concerns (1) the interaction of conatus/willing, with (2) perception and feeling of pleasure/pain, (3) in conjoint union with imagination (the psychoanalytic *phantasy*, if unconscious; or *fantasy*, if conscious), toward object related action. Once (4) extended as behavior, Spinoza demarcates the transformation of conatus in appetite and conscious desire. This action forms the basis of (5) new internalized registrations of behavioral effects, active and interactive with other levels of ongoing mental action and inaction. The complicated, multi-leveled projection involves the conjunction of minds' functional domains, both internally and in external projection at different moments of time, together with introjection of mind's thought and extension, leading to confusions, ambivalences, and further lack of clarity. It also provides a fine field for reflective reason, itself pressed into a form of appetitive desire, focused narcissistically on mind.

Additionally, the observable effects emergent from this process are changeable from time (n) forward, such that time, association, and memory are folded into the Spinozan algorithm. Through different unions, different moments in time combined with different titrations of mind's basic functionalities, combine toward different forms of behavioral expression, consolidated in *Ethics* Part III. *Definition of the Emotions.*

6. Spinoza also articulates another conceptual matrix in *Ethics,* of intersection between an axis describing a continuum between the *speculative* and the *factual*, and the continuum between the *general* and the *particular* (Letter 9, pp. 781–782). An earlier

iteration of this intersection is presented by Spinoza in his *Treatise on the Emendation of the Intellect*. There, what will become transformed into *Ethics'* continuum between the *speculative* and *factual* is understood as a continuum between uncertainty and certainty. Intersecting this continuum is the continuum between *pleasure* and *unpleasure*.

Taken together, this Spinozan confluence of axes generates a three-dimensional model of intersections between the continua: (1) speculative/uncertain<>factual/certain; (2) general<>particular; and (3) pleasure<>pain, useful in locating both momentary positions of clinical difficulty and relative orientation within therapeutic impasse.

All of these forms are clinically applicable. We can appreciate this as related to a patient's communication: where does it stand on the dimension of speculation versus fact? How does it stand up either as a particular incident or as a general pattern? How does it reflect relative pleasure or pain, and in relation to what? Where are the confusions: is a particular sequence of events mistakenly taken as a general pattern? Is the shifting balance of pleasure and pain frozen in a single, remembered position? Is speculation distorted as fact, as in Spinoza's parallel to contemporary parataxis, in *knowledge of the first kind*?

7. Inquiry itself is recognized by the therapist as destabilizing psychic equilibrium, however transient or fixed. The mind's intrinsic resistance to intrusion upon its adaptive forms, suggests that anxiety is a continuous by-product of Spinozan inquiry, not unlike psychotherapy's "emotional storm", described by Bion, "when two personalities meet" and

   If they make sufficient contact to be aware of each other, or even sufficient to be *un*aware of each other, an emotional state is produced by the conjunction of these two individuals, and the resulting disturbance is hardly likely to be regarded as necessarily an improvement on the state of affairs had they never met at all. But since they *have* met, and since this emotional storm has occurred, the two parties to this storm may decide 'to make the best of a bad job'. (Bion, 1994, p. 321)

Here, Bion's own language of conjunction extends the conjunctive parallelism of Spinoza's model, beginning originally in Nature's two attributes of thought and extension, themselves descriptive of human psychology through a chain of efficient causation. Bion's clinical conjunction of two individuals related through the therapeutic field, extends Spinoza's individually observed engagement with the environmental world, situating it, like Sullivan (1954), within the clinical relationship, today's *analytic third* (Benjamin, 2004; Ogden, 1994).

8. The necessary disruptions of doubt upon fixed and defended thought, as well as in Bion's *emotional storm* entailed in clinical engagement, reflects the necessary containing of anxiety. Methodologically, Spinoza addresses this in relation to the reader, explaining at a confusing reading moment in *Ethics* II that at this point our readers will no doubt find themselves in some difficulty and will think of many things that will give them pause. So I ask them to proceed slowly step by step with me, and to postpone judgment until they have read to the end. (II. Proposition 11, Scholium, pp. 250–251)

Similarly, Bion advises his reader

> to read straight through this book, not to dwell too long upon difficulties, and in this way to gain a working knowledge of the book itself. But the book will have failed for the reader if it does not become an object of study, and the reading of it an emotional experience itself. My hope is that it will be an experience leading to an increased ability on the part of the analyst to mobilize his own resources of knowledge, clinical observation, theory construction (in the sense of propaedeutic to interpretation) and so to render this work out of date and hasten the day when what is perhaps the most distressing malady a patient and family will have to endure will be classed as 'curable'. (1992, p. 261)

Application of Spinoza's method of leads to the emendation of the intellect, a greater integrative psychological capability. Similarly, Bion's is intended to lead to a more rational, and therefore more certainly communicable, method of expression of psycho-analytic theory than obtains at present. (Bion, 1992, p. 261)

Unlike earlier commentators (Bernard, 1946; Rathbun, 1934; Smith, 1925, 1926; Tanner, 1907a), my comparative recognition is not that the earlier writer had anticipated the later. Rather, that through the trial and error of psychoanalytic development of theory and practice, Bion's reflections affirm the essential integrity of Spinoza's earlier speculations. The quiet, if eloquent proof is comparison of Bion's 20th-century clinical algorithm (Miller & Sweet, 2018), and the clinical algorithm we have discerned in Spinoza's 17th-century *Ethics*.

9. Spinoza's aspirational goal, reflected in Parts IV and V, is claimed to have been similar to a complete psychoanalysis (Smith, 1925). Yet more focused observation, congruent with our ongoing clinical work, is Spinoza's address of lacunae in understanding, not only in the privation of knowledge but also in the fixed omnipotence of "dreaming with eyes open"; and that consistently skeptical inquiry requires deploying the destabilizing tool of doubt. Spinoza affirms that

> The imaginations of the mind, looked at in themselves, contain no error; i.e., the mind does not err from the fact that it imagines, but only insofar as it is considered to lack the idea which excludes the existence of those things which it imagines to be present to itself. For, if the mind, in imagining nonexisting things to be present to it, knew at the same time that those things did not exist in fact, it would surely impute this power of imagining not to the defect but to the strength of its own nature. (II. Proposition 17, Scholium, p. 257)

Doubting, for Spinoza, like Freud's negation (Freud, 1925), is the first step in rational reflection. But desire is potent. Drawing the Latin poet Ovid close to the Hebrew preacher of Ecclesiastes traditionally attributed to King Solomon, Spinoza observes that

> men are motivated by uncritical belief more than by true reasoning, and why the true knowledge of good and evil stirs

up conflict in the mind and often yields to every kind of passion. (IV. Proposition 17, Scholium, pp. 329–330)

To choose one's proper course,

> It is necessary to know both the power of our nature and its lack of power, so that we can determine what reason can and cannot do in controlling the emotions. (IV. Proposition 17, Scholium, p. 330)

In affirming our going on being, "making the best of a bad job" every day, in weathering the emotional storms of psychotherapy toward more perfect understanding of self and the world, we both recognize and continue, Spinoza's clinical application.

10. The analyst's articulation, modification, and maintenance, of her value position is crucial in challenging fixed ideas and states of mind, step-by-step through Reason's imposition of skeptical doubt. Today, such consistent maintenance of psychoanalytic value, is clinically demonstrated by the *European third,*

> an authentic, internal, almost parental brotherhood between the analyst and the psychoanalysis- a brotherhood that preexits him, but one that is oriented in favor of his growth. (Bolognini, 2011, p. 42)[2]

The reader of *Ethics* discerns multiple qualities of literary expression, each reflective of Spinoza, however signaling different points of inflection and orientation. Such variations of Voice and Presence register upon the reader in intonation and passionate tenacity within Spinoza's own self-conscious subjectivity.[3] Despite the Freudian commonplace of evenly hovering attention, the analyst's subjectively singular Voice and Presence, from Breuer and Freud toward todays' vernacular representatives of psychoanalysis, Winnicott and Bion (Miller, 2016; Miller & Sweet, 2018), are immediately registered as unavoidable particulars in clinical contact. Not only through Spinoza's aspirational values esteemed by mid-20th century humanistic psychoanalysts, but also by his strong articulation of self, does

Spinoza represent a guide into our internal complexity, mindful of his own psychological strengths and challenges.

Like Bion, Winnicott, Sullivan, Ferenczi, Freud, and Breuer, like Lou Andreas-Salomé, Viktor Tausk, Karen Horney, Erich Fromm, Constance Rathbun, M. Hamblin Smith, Walter Bernard, and Amy Tanner, Baruch Spinoza both consciously and strategically, discloses himself to his readers in the pursuit of a more greatly discernable psychology: not a bad start to modern clinical practice.

Notes

1 Bion's recognition of conjunction is analogous to philosophy's experiential *flash*, itself articulated by Poincare and recognizable both in Spinoza (Andreas-Salomé, 1964; Deleuze, 1988; Vermorel, 2009) and in Maimonides (Stern, 2013).

2 The contemporary clinician, researching the reception history of psychoanalytic ideas, discovers that this attitude of brotherhood in inquiry is of longer duration than psychoanalysis. Seneca writes, "The first thing philosophy promises us is the feeling of fellowship, of belonging to mankind and being members of a community" (Seneca, 2014, p. 10).

3 Samuel Ibn-Tibbon, elaborating Maimonides' philosophical method of "whispering" in writing by allusion, similarly differentiates Voice and Presence, as rhetorical forms. He writes, that like the writer, his reader "must likewise be someone who can 'draw up the deep thing (reference is to Proverbs 20:5)', that is, someone who understands 'whispering'- who can understand the writer's intended meaning through only the slightest allusion" (Robinson, 2007, p. 159). Spinoza accomplishes such differentiation between (1) observational analysis of mental functioning and (2) aspirational desires of applied practice.

Part V

Chapter 12

The Multiple Polarities of Freud's Negative Particle

Discernment of a *clinical* Spinoza becomes possible only through the psychoanalytic reflective lens of deferred action, *nachtraglichkeit*. Just as our reading of *Ethics* follows this route from its origins in Spinoza's critique of anthropocentric faith, so too does Spinoza's method become clear and distinct in relation to early 21st-century psychoanalytic vernacular expression. Only in light of a century's psychoanalytic growth, commentary and supercommentary, tested by clinical practice, do we discern adequately in Spinoza's clinical hypotheses what could not be seen clearly yesterday.

However, a puzzle remains. Sometime in the 1960s, Baruch Spinoza vanishes from explicit psychoanalytic consideration.[1] Two dimensions of Spinoza's psychological thought are critical in solving this puzzle. The first addresses privations of knowledge. The second requires that we re-consider that end state called *oblivion* by W.R. Bion as the antithesis to repression and forgetting, in terms of Spinozan causality (Miller & Sweet, 2018, Ch 8). That is, what may seem impenetrable in its finality, may instead, be an effect traceable to efficient cause within a chain of proximate causes and events. Freud's Heine deployed such thinking in consideration of facts contributing to his quavering, poetic *shalshelet* (Goetschel, 2004, p. 271).

We have seen how, like the various translations of conatus as willing, endeavoring, and striving, imprecision accompanies our verbalized understandings. As if foreshadowing such multiplicity, Spinoza's three names, corresponding to three distinct realms of lived experience, mirror the complex transmission of ideas fundamental to

DOI: 10.4324/9781003246404-18

his thinking. Yet as observed both by Spinoza and by our psycho-analytic commentators upon Spinoza, it is easy to mistake partial understanding for a more complete integration of the whole. Mistaking the partial for the whole often leads to inadequacy, dis-tortion, and confusion. However, such piecemeal discovery re-capitulates the piecemeal process of development; and the continuous relations of conjunction and disjunction, affirmed and denied, re-flected in the actions of mind, contributing greatly to the wealth of our unconscious experience.

The receptive history of ideas suggests that ideas, both adequate and inadequate, are passed forward in pursuit of truth, whether of opinion, consensus, or by the flash of intuition. Necessarily, aspects of earlier, larger compounded ideas are split off or fragmented in future elaborations. Easily then, in the process of transmission and transformation, just as some ideas are clarified toward greater per-fection, others remain undeveloped, unquestioned, partial, and hidden. Such observation also reflects the continuous unconscious activities of mind in *Ethics'* psychology.

As within clinical inquiry, solution to the puzzle of Spinoza's psy-choanalytic absence begins farther afield. Yet the silence following Spinoza's half-century reduction from the *philosopher of psycho-analysis* (Andreas-Salomé, 1964) to exemplar of psychoanalytic hu-manism (Fromm, 1964a) provides an eloquent clue. Spinoza's valence, once representative of the Freudian "negative particle" in his identi-fication by Heine as a Jewish "fellow un-believer", changes to a po-sitive, if equally insufficient, representation. Carried in the luggage of 20th-century psychoanalyst refugees to the shores of the United States, personification of Amsterdam's 17th-century son of New Christian refugees from the Iberian Peninsula is transformed toward ex-emplifying the fundamental humanism of the psychoanalytic *gebildeter mensch*. Under such hypothesis, continuing iterations of cause and effect become clear. Within decades and the fading of an "old Berlin" psychoanalytic generation, having accompanied psychoanalysis from its theoretical origins to its advocacy of enlightened self-formation in the New World, the person of Spinoza disappears as the development of the clinical profession he anticipated powers ahead.

Psychologist Walter Bernard's (1934) introduction to a new American audience speaks to *Bildung*'s appropriation of Spinoza.

He writes not of *Ethics* itself, but of Spinoza's rediscovery "by that eager group of literary men on Germany with Lessing at their head" (Bernard, 1934, p. 11) toward the historical development of Spinoza's thought into later modernity (Goetschel, 2004). Waxing enthusiastic, Bernard writes that

> many philosophers, scientists, and literary men have freely confessed a more or less intimate devotion to, and dependence on Spinoza. (Bernard, 1934, p. 11)

Concluding his passionate statement by quoting Hegel, Bernard mistakes his audience in that his conclusion is in German, incomprehensible to Anglophone readers, *"Du hast entweder den Spinozismus oder gar keine Philosophie"* (ibid, p. 11).

However nostalgically, similar incomprehensibility is expressed by Richard Sterba (1982) in comparing the idealized psychoanalytic persona as the *gebildeter Mensch* relative to the American generations that followed, not only deficient in Greek and Latin, but also tragically separated from *Bildung*'s cultural breadth. Instead, as Martin Bergmann would observe later, psychoanalytic wisdom was to be entrusted to technically trained practitioners rather than intrepid explorers of the mind (Bergmann, 2017, p. 87).

A traumatic event scars the 20th-century development of psychoanalysis, also curtailing the enlightened philosophy of *Bildung*: the Nazi rise, necessitating European clinicians' midcentury reorientations in country, language, and the cultures of new host countries. At the same time, in parallel with the developmental progression of psychoanalysis, so too, did a century of progression in the human sciences, reconstitute cultural foundations in forms radically different from the philosophical and literary building blocks of *Bildung*. While Walter Bernard's reference points in Lessing and Hegel, may have been familiar to gymnasium educated individuals sharing his own fund of information (Bernard, 1934; Goetschel, 2004; Winter, 1999; Yovel, 1989b), Amy Tanner's early incomprehension of geometrical demonstration relative to her grounding in psychological laboratory science (Tanner, 1907a), is a representative early precursor of now contemporary American confusions, founded upon differing educational and cultural orientations. Viewed through the lens of oblivion as an end-state, the educational caesura between the German gymnasium and the American public school system is as large as the difference between the Catholic education of Orobio de Castro and Juan de Prado in Inquisitional Spain, and the Hebrew language education of Baruch Spinoza in the Amsterdam Jewish community (Fisher, 2020; Kaplan, 1989). Transition from one cultural system to another presents a caesura, as older individuals attempt accommodation to the new while mourning the passing of their assumptive worlds; and younger individuals arrogantly move forward, oblivious to what had been.

Reading historical psychoanalytic texts today, the contemporary clinical reader may be baffled by the degree of catch-up necessary to grasp psychoanalytic commentaries written from within funds of knowledge developed in different educational worlds. An example is in Erich Fromm's 1964 reception history of humanism in psychoanalysis (Fromm, 1964a) with its assumed reader recognition of: Nicholas de Cusa; Leibnitz; Spinoza; Hume; Herder; Lessing; Goethe; Joachim di Fiori; Schweitzer; Russell; Holderin; Gianozzo Manetti; Pico della Mirandola; Pope Innocent; Ernst Cassirer; Guillaume Postel; Augustine; Pelagius; Nietzsche; Freud; and Friedrich Heer; together with the reader's knowledge of European history since the Middle Ages.

Under the assimilative pressure to learn, but lacking the requisite funds of information, the contemporary clinician absorbs only the big picture. Subordinate to the more pressing personal demand of mastering clinical psychoanalytic thought and technique, such cloudy apprehension also extends its shadow of absence: one can never understand enough; however, the Winnicottian idea of the *good enough* now tinctures psychoanalytic thinking. That desire always meets insufficiency, especially an insufficiency that is also interpersonally conveyed, through the harsh gaze of the *gebildeter mensch* toward another, culturally different generation lacking in specific linguistic competencies (Sterba, 1982).

Just as absorbing the essential statements of vernacular psychoanalytic expression results in an overall general view rather than a crisply precise differentiation between writer and writer (Miller, 2016), so too does psychoanalytic learning itself involve the generation of one's own personalized, if cloudy, mathematics.

Not theory and technique alone, but also implicit continuity with the self-formative culture of *Bildung* is fundamental to psychoanalytic transmission, reflected in

> an authentic, internal, almost parental brotherhood between the analyst and the psychoanalysis- a brotherhood that preexits him, but one that is oriented in favor of his growth. (Bolognini, 2011, p. 42)

Freud's Privation of Knowledge

We began this journey to Spinoza in Freud's resonance with the troubled life of Heine's Hirsch-Hyacinth, the mouthpiece of a Jewish joke. Obscuring our way were two levels of idealization. The first was the cultural legacy of *Bildung* relative to future generations in delineating the psychoanalytic worldview. The second was in the authority of Freud both as the founder of the psychoanalytic movement and as an exemplar of self-development, the *gebildeter Mensch* (Sterba, 1982, p. 16). Subordinated to this doubled authority was that the educational culture of *Bildung* was itself, a pathway from society's prejudicial identification of the individual by religious orientation to the secularized primacy of the individual (Gilman, 1992; Mosse, 1985; Sorkin, 1983, 1987).

From this perspective, Baruch Spinoza, personified by Freud as an example of the humorous *un-particle*, was prominent not only in philosophy but, under *herem*, innovative in his surviving and thriving as an individual despite expulsion from the Jewish community. Freud's witty and reductive identification through Heine, with Spinoza as *fellow un-believer,* may be valid from the perspective of religious ritual practice, but as M. Hamblin Smith reflects, the question of Spinoza's belief in God, whether atheistic or God-intoxicated, remains open (Smith, 1925). That both Heine and Freud were engaged toward individual self-definition, striving for separation from attributed identity as Jews, an identity still presenting barriers to secular equality in both their lives, corresponds too, to external perceptions of Spinoza. Writing in Latin as Benedictus, linking his thought to Descartes, Hobbes, Seneca, Cicero, Cervantes, and Ovid as well as to Ecclesiastes, Hasdai

Crescas and in mufti, to Maimonides, it is easy to mistake Western European philosophy rather than Jewish philosophy as Spinoza's foundation. Complicating matters, beginning with the intercultural intellectual transmissions of the Renaissance, Jewish textual study had also become the province of

> an emerging community of Christian scholars who claimed expertise in Hebraic books and Jewish learning. Over the course of several centuries, this community insisted on translating Judaism into a language accessible and meaningful to Christians alone, independent and oblivious to Jewish sensibilities. (Ruderman, 2004, p. 12)

Harry Wolfson observes that by the time of Heine and Freud, Hebrew textual studies had devolved in Europe from a status equivalent to the study of Greek in having been "eliminated from European philosophy and relegated to the esoteric field of oriental wisdom" (Wolfson, 1934, p. 13). Indeed, observing the woeful state of classical Hebrew texts in European libraries before the First World War, Wolfson would comment

> I thought of these shabby tomes which incarnate the spirit of Saadia, Halevi, and Maimonides, of those unpublished works of Gersonides, Narboni, and the Shem-tobs, scattered all over the world and rotting in the holds of libraries; and I was overcome by that feeling of sadness and sorrow which to our forefathers was ever present throughout their exiled life amid the foreign splendors of European cities. (Wolfson, 1921, p. 32)

Scattered and rotting, Jewish texts themselves physically approximated Freud's characterization of Jewish civilization as if unlanguaged.

From this linguistic-textual context, Freud's late-life musings to his correspondent Romain Rolland, remembered from his earlier glimpsing of the Acropolis, suggest something more than a son's reflective sadness in Oedipal triumph. Freud, the unbelieving Jew, identifies with Rolland, the unbelieving Catholic, through the vehicle of Spinoza (Vermorel, 2009). Freud's embrace of Rolland, like our silver filigreed apple, suggests something else too: the triumph of the gymnasium with its task of educating competent, modern Europeans. Without question, both in his secular education and in the career opportunities that followed, Freud had surpassed Jakob Freud. But the visual cue of the Acropolis, like Spinoza's hoofprints on a beach, discloses another fierce if unstated battle, concluded only with the death of its participants. In an era when Hebrew language literacy among Jews had declined radically (Gillman, 2018), Jakob Freud had been capable of composing the complex Hebrew acrostic which he inscribed in Freud's childhood, illustrated bible, and presented to his son on Freud's thirty-fifth birthday (Ostow, 1989). From this perspective, unknown to Rolland, Freud's Acropolis recognition was also the triumph of the gymnasium's Latin and Greek literacies over Hebrew literacy. Just as the heretical Spinoza had written in Latin, so the courageous Freud would write psychoanalysis in German, informed by the classical languages of Latin and Greek.

For Freud, Jewish culture was "un-languaged", just as the Jew was Othered, *unheimlich*. Like our contemporary privations of knowledge, reflected in the gaps between our own educational cultures and those of our psychoanalytic forefathers, an educational caesura also separated Freud from Spinoza,[2] whose textual foundation was Hebrew.

Freud's linkage with Rolland through Spinozan individualism parallels Heine's earlier attempts to escape the ancient binary between "Athens and Jerusalem", first articulated by Tertullian in the 2nd century (Leonard, 2012, p. 1). Heine's transformation of this division occurs in his remarks pitting the "Hellene" with the "Nazarene" (Goetschel, 2013; Heine, 2006, pp. 36–37). Heine adeptly claims membership on the pagan side of his constructed divide, against the constricted religious thinking, both Jewish and Christian, represented by the Nazarene; and so folds the problem of being identified prejudicially as a Jew into the general problem of secularism versus faith.

It didn't work. The Heine statue on the Grand Concourse in the Bronx is a monument to the rejection by Dusseldorf, Heine's home-town, to its native son, as Jew. Purchased by a German-American choral society, it stands up the hill from Yankee Stadium, its provenance and reference to the poetical Lorelei impenetrable to present-day residents of the South Bronx (Miller & Sweet, 2018, Ch 8). But this statue's pathway to oblivion can become knowable, through tracing its history, step by step. Through a computer search engine, one finds adequate information on the New York City Parks website, https://www.nycgovparks.org/parks/joyce-kilmer-park/monuments/700. For Spinoza too, oblivions can be countered by knowledge; and knowledge affirmed step-by-step, through the linkages of proximate causality.

Heine, like Freud, in claiming his own individuality, attempted to escape from the fusion of two Spinozan knowledge types: knowledge of the first kind, opinion and hearsay; and knowledge of the second kind, consensus. Consolidation of 18th-century German culture had also claimed the legacy of Greek and Italian classical traditions (Berman, 1992). Such appropriation conveniently carried with it, the conceit of the cultural binary between "Athens" and "Jerusalem", the very trap from which Heine would attempt escape. Unacknowledged, perhaps unknown, this impenetrable division is incorrect both factually and textually.

Since antiquity, Hellenism has affected Jewish thought in content and form (Lieberman, 1950; Tcherikover, 1959). For example, the rabbinic text, *Pirke Avot,* which Maimonides harmonizes with Aristotelian philosophy in his *Eight Chapters*, is itself presented in the form of a Greek "doxography", beginning with a preliminary reception history similar in form to Diogenes Laertius', *Lives of the Eminent Philosophers* (Diogenes Laertius, 2018, I:12–17, pp. 8–11). From Philo (a contemporary of Seneca) in the 2nd century, through Spinoza in the 17th, active synthesis of Greek and Jewish thought had long preceded German claim to the classical tradition (Berman, 1992; Fraenkel, 2012). However, against popular opinion, Spinoza's *knowledge of the first kind,* together with *knowledge of the second kind* fixed in its erroneous certainty, Heine and Freud would struggle with their *un-believing* comrade, Spinoza, toward popular allowance to Jews of a secular individualism. What neither Heine nor Freud could recognize or know would become the province of 20th- and 21st-century textual study of classical Hebrew texts, clarifying the distorted conceptual binary between Athens and Jerusalem.[3]

Addressing Oblivion, Step by Step

Puzzlement about the psychoanalytic disappearance of Baruch Spinoza, Andreas-Salomé's *philosopher of psychoanalysis*, resolves through studying the contributory factors to such oblivion. These links, in turn, reveal a history in the reception of ideas, with large lacunae formed by changes in education and culture, such that former generational orientations become unknown to the future. Spinoza, who paired knowledge of Ovid and Ecclesiastes, would understand this problem of intergenerational memory and forgetting in the idea that

> the earlier ones are not remembered; so too those that will occur later will no more be remembered than those who will occur at the very end. (Ecclesiastes, 1:11, *Tanakh*, p. 1442)

We recognize that in the transmission and transformation of one idea into the next, parts of the earlier version fall away as others are elaborated. Psychoanalytic resonance with Spinoza affirms his holistic orientation: as we proceed step-by-step through the partialities of our understanding, the whole picture often eludes us. In this sense, psychoanalytic inquiry is interminable, with its continuous disclosure of the unformulated, the unrecognized, the distorted, and all the possible relations knowable only after recognitions of future development.

The present work depends not only upon psychoanalytic evolution toward its contemporary vernacular expression. It depends too, on the evolution beyond Wolfson's grim 1921 observation of classic Hebrew texts, toward the fruitful blossoming of academic Jewish Studies, especially scholarship related to Spinoza and medieval Jewish philosophy over the past century. That these are available in English, now the lingua franca of psychoanalysis itself, allows the researcher to address what seemed consigned to oblivion, by doubting our false understandings, including anti-Jewish sentiment bolstered by the erroneous binary of Athens/Jerusalem. Addressing such privation of knowledge step-by-step, through chains of efficient causation, we find that Spinoza remains today, the *philosopher of psychoanalysis*, just as he had in the early days of psychoanalytic discovery.

Coda

Speaking in 1950, at a memorial service for Paul Schilder, ego psychologist David Rapaport began his eulogy with a witty story. Both Rapaport and Schilder had begun their professional careers in Central Europe. They, and presumably much of Rapaport's audience that day, had been educated in Europe under the cultural assumptions of *Bildung*. Rapaport began,

> there was once a king who was entertaining another one. And since he was the king who had originated the idea that a king should have a cabinet he introduced his cabinet to his guest. The guest asked who was the most important member of the cabinet. The king pointed to one so far not introduced. "And what is his portfolio?" asked the guest. "Oh", he is the Minister without Portfolio"- and seeing the bewilderment of his guest, he added, "He knows what the rest of them are doing, and tells me about it". (Rapaport, 1967, pp. 368–369)

For Rapaport and his audience, there is no bewilderment at all. Told in English rather than in German or its original form in Yiddish or Hebrew, Rapaport's witticism is in the form of a *mashal*, a classical rabbinic parable (Hartmann & Budick, 1986, p. 365; Stern, 2013, p. 171). Like Jakob Freud's midrashic acrostic introducing Freud's Philipson bible, it would seem that Freud was in error about the unlanguaged nature of Jewish culture. However translated from Hebrew and Yiddish into English, like the earlier Greek philosophical ordering of the 2nd-century rabbinic *Pirke Avot*, this interpretive form of Jewish thought presented itself in the *Bildung* precincts of midcentury psychoanalysis. Glimpsed through Rapaport's encomium, the form of Freud's *unheimlich*, unlanguage positively sparkled to its audience through its negative particularity, like the gold within Maimonides' silver apple.

Notes

1 Explicit application of Spinozan concepts is the critical ingredient. For example, as shown above, Spinoza's psychological framework is present, unattributed, even in late 20th-century American psychoanalytic thought, through writers' long

theoretical familiarity with Spinozan thinking (Wolstein, 1953, 1987). Similarly, Sullivan (1953) references A.N. Whitehead's dynamic organic philosophy, unmindful of its Spinozan foundation (Whitehead, 1978).

2   Heine, however, plays on the borderline of such linguistic and ideational transmission with his allusions to the Passover seder, in "Arabic" (Chapter 3), his competitive striving with his predecessor, Moses Mendelssohn, via the poetic subject of Yehuda HaLevi, a late 11th-century Jewish philosopher (Goetschel, 2004), as well as reference through the characters in his travel stories, to historical persecutions of the Spanish Inquisition, with which Spinoza, too, was well-aware.

3   While David Bakan's posthumous work (Bakan, Merkur, & Weiss, 2009) claims Maimonidean parallels with psychoanalytic thought, the authors do not demonstrate a receptive chain of transmission. Our readings both of early psychoanalysts, absorbing the German development of Spinozan thought following Lessing, together with Spinoza's *Ethics* itself, expands Freud's limited characterization of Spinoza as secularized Jew; and returns Spinoza's thinking itself into psychoanalytic development. In so doing, a Spinozan link connects Bakan's Maimonides with Freud.

References

Abram, J. (1996) *The Language of Winnicott. A Dictionary of Winnicott's Use of Words.* London: Karnac.

Adler, J. (2014) Mortality of the soul from Alexander of Aphrodisias to Spinoza. In *Spinoza and Medieval Jewish Philosophy* (ed. S. Nadler). Cambridge: Cambridge University Press.

Adler, J. (2012) Joseph Solomon Delmedigo: student of Galileo, teacher of Spinoza. *Intellectual History Review*, 1: 1–17.

Alter, R. (2010) *The Wisdom Books. Job, Proverbs, and Ecclesiastes. A Translation with Commentary.* New York: W.W. Norton & Co.

Altmann, A. (1972) Eternality of punishment: a theological controversy within the Amsterdam rabbinate in the thirties of the seventeenth century. *Proceedings of the American Academy of Jewish Research*, 40: 1–88.

Andreas-Salomé, L. (1964) *The Freud Journal of Lou Andreas-Salome* (tr. Stanley A. Leavy). New York: Basic Books, Inc.

Aron, L. & Henik, L. (eds) (2010) *Answering a Question With a Question: Contemporary Psychoanalysis and Jewish Thought.* Brookline: Academic Studies Press.

Bakan, D., Merkur, D. & Weiss, D.S. (2009) *Maimonides' Cure of Souls. Medieval Precursor of Psychoanalysis.* Albany: SUNY Press.

Baranger, M. & Baranger, W. (2008) The analytic situation as a dynamic field. *International Journal of Psycho-Analysis*, 89: 795–826.

Barzilay, I. (1974) *Yoseph Shlomo Delmedigo (YASHAR of Candia). His Life and Works.* Leiden: E.J. Brill.

Beckett, S. (1964) *How It Is.* New York: Grove Press.

Benjamin, J. (2004) Beyond doer and done to: an intersubjective view of thirdness. *Psychoanalytic Quarterly*, 73: 5–46.

Bergmann, M.S. (2017) *The Origins and Organization of Unconscious Conflict. The Selected Works of Martin S. Bergmann.* London and New York: Routledge.

Berman, A. (1992) *The Experience of the Foreign. Culture and Translation in Romantic Germany* (tr. S. Heyvaert). Albany: SUNY Press.

Bernard, W. (1977) Psychotherapeutic principles in Spinoza's *Ethics. Speculum Spinozanum 1677-1977* (ed. S. Hessing). London: Routledge & Kegan Paul, pp. 63–80.

Bernard, W. (1972) Spinoza's influence on the rise of scientific psychology: a neglected chapter in the history of psychology. *Journal of the History of the Behavioral Sciences*, 8: 208–215.

Bernard, W. (1946) Freud and Spinoza. *Psychiatry*, 9: 99–108.

Bernard, W. (1934) *The Philosophy of Spinoza and Bruner*. New York: The Spinoza Institute of America, Inc.

Bion-Talamo, P. (2015) *Maps for Psychoanalytic Exploration*. (tr. S. Whiteside, ed. C. Mawson). London: Karnac.

Bion, W.R. (2005a) *The Tavistock Seminars* (ed. F. Bion). London: Karnac.

Bion, W. R. (2005b) *The Italian Seminars*. London: Karnac.

Bion, W.R. (1994) *Clinical Seminars and Other Works* (ed. F. Bion). London: Karnac.

Bion, W.R. (1992) *Cogitations*. London: Karnac.

Bion, W.R. (1990) *Brazilian Lectures. 1973 Sao Paolo, 1974 Rio de Janeiro/ Sao Paolo*. London: Karnac.

Bion, W.R. (1965) *Transformations: Change from Learning to Growth*. London: Tavistock.

Bion, W.R. (1963) *Elements of Psychoanalysis*. London: Karnac.

Bion, W.R. (1962) The psycho-analytic study of thinking. *International Journal of Psychoanalysis*, 43: 306–310.

Bion, W.R. (1959) Attacks on linking. *International Journal of Psychoanalysis*, 40: 308–315.

Bion, W. R. (1970) *Attention and Interpretation*. London: Karnac.

Bodian, M. (1999) *Hebrews of the Portuguese Nation: Conversos and Community in Early Modern Amsterdam*. Bloomington, IN: Indiana University Press.

Bollas, C. (2015) Psychoanalysis in the age of bewilderment: on the return of the oppressed. *International Journal of Psycho-Analysis*, 96: 535–551.

Bollas, C. (2006) Perceptive identification. *Psychoanalytic Review*, 93: 713–717.

Bolognini, S. (2011) *Secret Passages*. London: Routledge.

Borne, L. (1964) *How to Be an Original Writer in Three Days* (translated and with commentary by L. De La Durantaye), based on Ludwig Börne's *Sämtliche Schriften*, revised edition edited by Inge and Peter Rippmann (Dusseldorf: J. Melzer, 1964). Published in Harvard Review 31. http://www1.cmc.edu/pages/faculty/LdelaDurantaye/art_of_ignorance_harvard_review.pdf

Boulanger, G. (2015) Seeing double, being double: longing, belonging, recognition, and evasion in psychodynamic work with immigrants. *The American Journal of Psychoanalysis*, 75: 287–303.

Boyarin, D. (1997) *Unheroic Conduct. The Rise of Heterosexuality and the Invention of the Jewish Man*. Berkeley: University of California Press.

Brabant, E., Falzeder, E. & Giampieri-Deutsch, P. (eds) (1993) *The Correspondence of Sigmund Freud and Sandor Ferenczi, V 1, 1908–1914* (tr. P.T. Hopper). Cambridge and London: The Belknap Press of Harvard University Press.

Brentano, F. (1874) *Psychology from an Empirical Standpoint* (English translation, 1995 Routledge). Abingdon, Oxon: Routledge Classics, 2015.

Brill, A. (1931) Professor Freud and psychiatry. *Psychoanalytic Review*, 18: 241–246.

Brown, J.F. (1936) *Psychology and the Social Order. An Introduction to the Dynamic Study of Social Fields*. New York: McGraw-Hill Book Company.

Bruford, W.H. (1975) *The German Tradition of Self-Cultivation: 'Bildung'. From Humboldt to Thomas Mann*. Cambridge: Cambridge University Press.

Cervantes, M.d. (1615) *Don Quixote* (tr. E. Grossman). New York: Ecco. Re-published, 2005.

Civitarese, G. (2008) Immersion versus interactivity and analytic field. *International Journal of Psycho-Analysis*, 89: 279–298.

Colyer, C. (2015) W.I. Thomas and the forgotten four wishes: a case study in the sociology of ideas. *The American Sociologist*, 46: 248–268.

Davoine, F. & Gaudillière, J.-M. (2004) *History beyond Trauma*. New York: Other Books.

De La Vega, J. (1688) *Confusion De Confusiones* (tr. H. Kellenbenz). Republished 1957 as Kress Library of Business and Economics Publication No. 13. Cambridge: Harvard University Library.

De Spinoza, B. (1996) *Ethics* (edited and translated by Edwin Curley). New York: Penguin Books.

Defoe, D. (1719) *Robinson Crusoe*. London: Penguin Classics (Reprinted in 2001).

Deleuze, G. (1993) *The Fold. Leibniz and the Baroque* (tr. T. Conley). London: The Athlone Press.

Deleuze, G. (1988) *Spinoza. Practical Philosophy* (tr. Robert Hurley). San Francisco: City Lights Books.

Dewey, J. (1896) The reflex arc concept in psychology. *Psychological Review*, 3: 357–370.

Diehl, L.A. (2010) Theodate Smith and Amy Tanner: child savers of Clark University. *The Journal of Genetic Psychology: Research and Theory on Human Development*, 152: 273–287.

Diogenes Laertius (2018) *Lives of the Eminent Philosophers* (tr. P. Mensch; ed. J. Miller). Oxford: Oxford University Press.

Disney, W. (1940) *Fantasia*. Anaheim: Walt Disney Productions.

Draper, H. (1982) *The Complete Poems of Heinrich Heine. A Modern English Version*. Boston: Suhrkamp/Insel.

Ebreo, L. (2016) *Dialogues of Love* (tr. D. Bacich & R. Pescatori). Toronto, Buffalo, London: University of Toronto Press.

Ehrenreich, B. (2001) *Nickle and Dimed. On (Not) Getting by in America*. New York: Metropolitan Books.

Epictetus (1995) *The Discourses as Reported by Arrian, The Manual, and Fragments. V1* (tr. W.A. Oldfeather). Cambridge and London: Harvard University Press.

Erikson, E. (1956) The problem of ego identity. *Journal of the American Psychoanalytic Association*, 4: 56–121.

Farrell, J. (2007) Lucretian architecture: the structure and argument of *De rerum natura*. In *The Cambridge Companion to Lucretius* (eds S. Gillespie & P. Hardie). Cambridge: Cambridge University Press, pp. 76–110.

Federn, P. (1940) Psychoanalysis as a therapy of society. *American Imago*, 5: 65–80.

Federn, P. (1926) Some variations in ego-feeling. *International Journal of Psycho-Analysis*, 7: 434–444.

Federn, P. (1915) Some general remarks on the principles of pain-pleasure and of reality. *Psychoanalytic Review*, 2: 1–11.

Ferenczi, S. (1933) Confusion of tongues between adults and the child. The language of tenderness and of passion. In *Final Contributions to the Problems and Methods of Psycho-Analysis*. London: Karnac Books, 1980, pp. 156–167.

Ferenczi, S. (1932) *The Clinical Diary of Sandor Ferenczi* (ed. J. Dupont; tr. M. Balint & M.Z. Jackson). Cambridge: Harvard University Press, 1988.

Ferenczi, S. (1909) Introjection and transference. In *Sex in Psychoanalysis* (tr. E. Jones). New York: Basic Books (published in 1950).

Ferenczi, S. & Rank, O. (1923) *The Development of Psychoanalysis* (tr. C. Newton). Madison, CT: International Universities Press (Reprinted in 1986).

Feuer, L.S. (1958) *Spinoza and the Rise of Liberalism*. New Brunswick and Oxford: Transaction Books.

Feuer, L.S. (1957) The dream of benedict de Spinoza. *American Imago*, 14: 225–242.

Fisher, B.E. (2020) *Amsterdam's People of the Book. Jewish Society and the Turn to Scripture in the Seventeenth Century*. Cincinnati: Hebrew Union College Press.

Fleck, L. (1979) *Genesis and Development of a Scientific Fact* (tr. F. Bradley & T.J. Trenn). Chicago: University of Chicago Press (Originally published in German, 1935).

Ford, P. (2007) Lucretius in early modern France. In *The Cambridge Companion to Lucretius* (eds S. Gillespie & P. Hardie). Cambridge: Cambridge University Press, pp. 227–241.

Fraenkel, C. (2012) *Philosophical Religions from Plato to Spinoza. Reason, Religion and Autonomy*. Cambridge: Cambridge University Press.

Fraenkel, C. (2009a) Hasdai Crescas on god as the place of the world and Spinoza's notion or god as "Res Extensa". *Aleph*, 9: 77–111.

Fraenkel, C. (2009b) From Maimonides to Samuel ibn Tibbon: interpreting judaism as a philosophical religion. In *Traditions of Maimonideanism* (ed. C. Fraenkel). Leiden & Boston: Brill, pp. 177–212.

Freud, A. (1936) *The Ego and the Mechanisms of Defense* (tr. C. Baines). London: Hogarth Press (Reprinted in 1966).

Freud, S. (1953) *On Aphasia*. New York: International Universities Press (Originally published in 1891).

Freud, S. (1939) *Moses and Monotheism. The Standard Edition of the Complete Works of Sigmund Freud*, vol. 23. London: Hogarth, pp. 1–138.

Freud, S. (1938) An outline of psycho-analysis. *S.E.* 23: 139–208.

Freud, S. (1927) Humour. *The Standard Edition of the Complete Works of Sigmund Freud*, vol. 21. London: Hogarth, pp. 159–166.

Freud, S. (1926) Address to the society of B'nai Brith. *S.E.* 20: 271–274.

Freud, S. (1925) Negation. *S.E.*, 19: 233–240. London: Hogarth.

Freud, S. (1923) The Ego and the Id. *S.E.*, 19: 1–66. London: Hogarth.

Freud, S. (1919) *Lines of Advance in Psycho-analytic Therapy*. Standard edition (Vol. 17, pp. 157–168). London: Hogarth.

Freud, S. (1917) Mourning and melancholia. *S.E.*, 14: 237–258. London: Hogarth.

Freud, S. (1915) Thoughts for the times on war and death. *S.E.*, 14: 273–300. London: Hogarth.

Freud, S. (1913) *Totem and Taboo: Some Points of Agreement between the Mental Lives of Savages and Neurotics*, vol. 13. London: Hogarth, pp. vii–162.

Freud, S. (1910a) Five lectures on psycho-analysis. *S.E.*, 11: 1–56. London: Hogarth.

Freud, S. (1910b) Leonardo da Vinci and a memory of his childhood. *S.E.*, 11: 57–138. London: Hogarth.

Freud, S. (1905) Jokes and their relation to the unconscious. *S.E.*, 8: 1–247. London: Hogarth.

Freud, S. (1901) *The Psychopathology of Everyday Life: Forgetting, Slips of the Tongue, Bungled Actions, Superstitions and Errors. The Standard Edition of the Complete Works of Sigmund Freud*, vol. 6. London: Hogarth, pp. vii–296.

Freud, S. (1900) *The Interpretation of Dreams. The Standard Edition of the Complete Works of Sigmund Freud*, vol. 4. London: Hogarth, pp. ix–627.

Freud, S. (1890) Psychical(or mental) treatment. *S.E.*, 7: 281–302.

Fromm, E. (1973) *The Anatomy of Human Destructiveness*. London: Pimlico.

Fromm, E. (1964a) Humanism and psychoanalysis. *Contemporary Psychoanalysis*, 1: 69–79.

Fromm, E. (1964b) *The Heart of Man*. New York: Harper & Row Publishers.

Frosh, J. (2013) *Hauntings: Psychoanalysis and Ghostly Transmissions*. Houndsmill, Basingstoke, Hampshire: Palgrave Macmillan.

Galdi, Giselle. (2019) Personal communication.

Gay, P. (1988) *Freud. A Life for our Times*. New York: W.W. Norton.

Geller, J. (2004) The psychopathology of everyday Vienna: psychoanalysis and Freud's familiars. *International Journal of Psycho-Analysis*, 85: 1209–1223.

Gillespie, S. (2007) Lucretius in the English renaissance. In *The Cambridge Companion to Lucretius* (eds S. Gillespie & P. Hardie). Cambridge: Cambridge University Press, pp. 242–253.

Gillman, A. (2018) *A History of German Bible Translation*. Chicago and London: The University of Chicago Press.

Gilman, S.L. (1990) Freud Reads Heine Reads Freud. In *The Jewish Reception of Heinrich Heine* (ed. M.H. Gelber). Tubingen: Max Niemayer Verlag, 1992.

Gilman, S.L. (1992) Freud, race and gender. *American Imago*, 49: 155–183.

Gilman, S. (1972) *The Spain of Fernando de Rojas. The Intellectual and Social Landscape of La Celestina*. Princeton: Princeton University Press.

Goetschel, W. (2016) Spinoza's dream. *The Cambridge Journal of Postcolonial Literary Inquiry*, 3: 39–54.

Goetschel, W. (2013) *The Discipline of Philosophy and the Invention of Modern Jewish Thought*. New York: Fordham University Press.

Goetschel, W. (2004) *Spinoza's Modernity. Mendelssohn, Lessing, and Heine.* Madison: University of Wisconsin Press.

Gomez-Aranda, M. (2006) The meaning of Qohelet according to Ibn Ezra's scientific explanations. *Aleph Historical Studies in Science and Judaism,* 6: 6339–6370.

Gonzalez-Torres, M.A. (2017) Personal communication. Florence, May 2017.

Gorfinkle, J.M. (1912) *The Eight Chapters of Maimonides on Ethivs (Shemonah Perakim). A Psychological and Ethical Treatise* (ed. and tr. J.M. Gorfinkle). New York: Columbia University Press.

Green, A. (2015) A portait of Spinoza as a Maimonidean reconsidered. *Shofar: An Interdisciplinary Journal of Jewish Studies,* 34: 81–106.

Green, A. (1997) The intuition of the negative in playing and reality. *International Journal of Psycho-analysis,* 78: 1071–1084.

Green, A. (1975) The analyst, symbolization and absence in the analytic setting (on changes in analytic practice and analytic experience. *International Journal of Psycho-Analysis,* 56: 1–22.

Greenblatt, S. (2011) *The Swerve. How the Renaissance Began.* London: Vintage Books.

Groddeck, G. (1923) *The Book of the It* (tr. V.M.E. Collins). New York: International Universities Press (Republished in 1976).

Grossman, W.I. (1992) Hierarchies, boundaries, and representation in a Freudian model of mental organization. *Journal of the American Psychoanalytic Association,* 40: 27–62.

Grossman, W.I. & Simon, B. (1969) Anthropomorphism-motive, meaning, and causality in psychoanalytic theory. *Psychoanalytic Study of the Child,* 24: 78–111.

Grotstein, J.S. (2007) *A Beam of Intense Darkness: Wilfred Bion's Legacy to Psychoanalysis.* London: Karnac.

Halbertal, M. (2014) *Maimonides: Life and Thought* (tr. J. Linsider). Princeton: Princeton University Press.

Hartman, G.H. & Bucdick, S. (eds) (1986) *Midrash and Literature.* New Haven and London: Yale University Press.

Harvey, W.Z. (2012) Gersonides and Spinoza on conatus. *Aleph,* 12: 273–297.

Harvey, W.Z. (1998) *Physics and Metaphysics in Hasdai Crescas.* Amsterdam: J.C. Gieben.

Harvey, W.Z. (1981) A portrait of Spinoza as a Maimonidean. *Journal of the History of Philosophy,* 19: 151–172.

Heine, H. (2008) *Travel Pictures* (tr. P. Wortsman). Brooklyn: Archipelago Books (Originally published in 1826).

Heine, H. (2006) *Ludwig Borne: A Memorial* (tr. J.L. Sammons). Rochester, New York: Camden House (Originally published 1840).

Holowchak, M. (2013) Freud on philosophy and philosophers: patching the gaps in the universe with nightcaps and dressing-gown tatters. *International Forum of Psychoanalysis*, 22: 149–160.

Horney, K. (1980) *The Adolescent Diaries of Karen Horney*. New York: Basic Books.

Howell, E.F. (2014) Ferenczi's concept of identification with the aggressor-understanding dissociative structure with interacting victim and abuser self states. *The American Journal of Psychoanalysis*, 74: 48–59.

Ibn Ezra, A. (1988) *Ibn Ezra's commentary on the Pentateuch* (tr. H.N. Strickman & A.M. Silver) New York: Menorah Publishing (Originally written, 12th century).

Israel, J. (2002) *Diasporas within a Diaspora: Jews, Crypto-Jews, and the World Maritime Empires (1540-1740)*. Leiden and Boston: Brill.

Israel, J. (2001) *Radical Enlightenment. Philosophy and the Making of Modernity 1650-1750*. Oxford: Oxford University Press.

James, W. (1981) The Principles of Psychology Volume 1. In *The Works of William James* (eds F.H. Burkhardt, F. Bowers & I.K. Skrupelis). Cambridge & London: Harvard University Press (Originally published in 1890).

James, W. (1904) The Chicago School. *Psychological Bulletin*, 1: 1–5.

Kaplan, Y. (1989) *From Christianity to Judaism. The Story of Isaac Orobio de Castro*. Oxford and Portland, Oregon: The Littman Library of Jewish Civilization.

Kilborne, B. (2014) Trauma and the unconscious: double conscience, the uncanny and cruelty. *The American Journal of Psychoanalysis*, 74: 4–20.

Klein, D. (1981) *Jewish Origins of the Psychoanalytic Movement*. New York: Praeger.

Klein, M. (1946). Notes on some schizoid mechanisms. *International Journal of Psycho-Analysis*, 27: 99–110.

Koch, S.(1999) *Psychology in Human Context. Essays in Dissidence and Reconstruction* (eds D. Finkelman & F. Kessel). Chicago and London: The University of Chicago Press.

Kogan, I. (2017) Anti-semitism and xenophobia. *The American Journal of Psychoanalysis*, 77: 378–391.

Kuhn, T.S. (1970) *The Structure of Scientific Revolutions*. Second Edition, Enlarged. Chicago: University of Chicago Press.

La Vopa, A.J. (1990) Specialists against specialization: hellenism as professional ideology in German classical studies. In *German Professions*

1800–1950 (eds G. Cocks & Jarausch). New York, Oxford: Oxford University Press, pp. 27–45.

Lapovsky, I. (March 17, 2019) How Cambridge Analytica sparked the great privacy awakening. *Wired.* https://www.wired.com/story/cambridge-analytica-facebook-privacy-awakening/

Leonard, M. (2012) *Socrates and the Jews. Hellenism and Hebraism from Moses Mendelssohn to Sigmund Freud.* Chicago: The University of Chicago Press.

Levenson, E.A. (1983) *The Ambiguity of Change.* New York: Basic Books.

Levenson, E.A. (1978) II. General systems theory: model or muddle. *Contemporary Psychoanalysis,* 14: 18–30.

Lewin, K. (1936) *Principles of Topological Psychology.* New York: McGraw-Hill Book Company, Inc.

Lewin, K. (1933) Vectors, cognitive processes, and Mr Tolman's criticism. *Journal of General Psychology,* 9: 318–345.

Lieberman, S. (1950) *Hellenism in Jewish Palestine. Studies in the Literary Transmission, Beliefs, and Manners of Palestine in the I Century B.C.E-IV Century C.E.* New York: The Jewish Theological Seminary of America.

Lobel, D. (2007) *A Sufi-Jewish Dialogue. Philosophy and Mysticism in Bahya Ibn Paquda's Duties of the Heart.* Philadelphia: University of Pennsylvania Press.

Lucretius (2008) *On the Nature of Things* (tr. W.E. Leonard). Project Gutenberg. eBook #785. Retrieved from https://www.gutenberg.org/cache/epub/785/pg785-images.html#link2H_4_0017. This eBook is for the use of anyone anywhere at no cost and with almost no restrictions whatsoever. You may copy it, give it away or re-use it under the terms of the Project Gutenberg License included with this eBook or online at www.gutenberg.org.

Maimonides, M. (1963) *The Guide of the Perplexed, v.1* (tr. S. Pines). Chicago: The University of Chicago Press.

Makari, G. (2008) *Revolution in Mind.* New York: HarperCollins.

Malter, H. (1912) Personifications of soul and body. *Jewish Quarterly Review,* 2: 453–479.

Mansoor, M. (tr) (1973) *Book of Direction to the Duties of the Heart.* London: Routledge and Kegan Paul.

Mason, A. (2000) Bion and binocular vision. *International Journal of Psychoanalysis,* 81: 983–989.

Mead, G.H. (1922) A behavioristic account of the significant symbol. *Journal of Philosophy,* 19: 157–163.

Mead, G.H. (1904) The relations of psychology and philology. *Psychological Bulletin*, 1:375–391.

Menoca, M.R., Scheindlin, R.P. & Sells, M. (eds) (2000) *The Literature of Al-Andalus*. Cambridge: Cambridge University Press.

Meyer, L. (2002) Preface. To the host reader, Lodewijk Meyer gives greetings. *Preface to Principles of Cartesian Philosophy and Metaphysical Thoughts*. In Spinoza (2002), pp. 116–120.

Miller, G. (1956) The magical number seven, plus or minus two: some limits on our capacity for processing information. *Psychological Review*, 63: 81–97.

Miller, I. (2021) Histories, traumas and emotional foreclosure from Manhattan to Dublin and back. *American Journal of Psychoanalysis*, 81. 10.1057/s11231-021-09282-2

Miller, I. (2019) Doublings between bewilderment and enlightenment: Reading Freud with Heine on the troubled identity of Hirsch–Hyacinth. *American Journal of Psychoanalysis*, 79: 17–39.

Miller, I. (2018a) Reading Willy Wonka in the era of anti-thinking. *American Journal of Psychoanalysis*, 78: 113–125.

Miller, I. (2018b) Beyond anti-thinking: psychoanalysis as politics. *American Journal of Psychoanalysis*, 78: 463–477.

Miller, I. (2017) Reading Beckett in the context of psychoanalysis: a literary bridge between one-person and two-person psychology. *British Journal of Psychotherapy*, 33: 456–469.

Miller, I. (2016) *Defining Psychoanalysis: Achieving a Vernacular Expression*. London: Karnac.

Miller, I. (2015) *On Minding and Being Minded*. London: Karnac.

Miller, I. (1987) William James and the psychology of consciousness- beginnings of the American school. *Contemporary Psychoanalysis*, 23: 299–313.

Miller, I. & Sweet, A. (2018) *On the Daily Work of Psychodynamic Psychotherapy*. Abington Park, Oxon: Routledge.

Moore, T.V. (1921) The parataxes: a study and analysis of certain borderline mental states. *Psychoanalytic Review*, 8: 252–283.

Mosse, G.L. (1985) *German Jews Beyond Judaism*. Bloomington: Indiana University Press; Cincinnati: Hebrew Union College Press.

Mucci, C. (2014) Trauma, healing, and the reconstruction of truth. *The American Journal of Psychoanalysis*, 74: 31–47.

Nadler, S. (2011) *A Book Forged in Hell. Spinoza's Scandalous Treatise and the Birth of the Secular Age*. Princeton: Princeton University Press.

Nadler, S. (2001) *Spinoza's Heresy. Immortality and the Jewish Mind.* Oxford: Clarendon Press.

Nadler, S. (1999) *Spinoza. A Life.* Cambridge: Cambridge University Press.

Nirenberg, D. (2013) *Anti-Judaism. The History of a Way of Thinking.* New York: W.W. Norton.

Nussbaum, M.C. (1994) *The Therapy of Desire. Theory and Practice in Hellenistic Ethics.* Princeton: Princeton University Press.

Offenberg, A. (1973) Spinoza's library. The story of a reconstruction. *Quaerendo*, 3: 309–321.

Ogden, T.H. (2004) On holding and containing, being and dreaming. *International Journal of Psycho-Analysis*, 85: 1349–1364.

Ogden, T.H. (1994) The analytic third: working with inter-subjective clinical facts. *International Journal of Psycho-Analysis*, 75: 3–19.

Ostow, M. (1989) Sigmund and Jakob Freud and the Philippson Bible- (with an analysis of the birthday inscription). *International Review of Psycho-Analysis*, 26: 483–492.

Perry, H.S. (1982) *Psychiatrist of America. The Life of Harry Stack Sullivan.* Cambridge and London: The Belknap Press of Harvard University.

Petit, M. (2008) The new woman as 'tied-up dog". Amy E Tanner's situated knowledges. *History of Psychology*, 11: 145–163.

Pinsker, L. (1882) *Auto-Emancipation. An Appeal to His People.* Published online on http://www.jewishvirtuallibrary.org/quot-auto-emancipation-quot-leon-pinsker

Rank, O. (1914) *Double. A Psychoanalytic Study* (tr. and ed. H. Tucker, Jr.). Chapel Hill: UNC Press (Published in 1971).

Rapaport, D. (1967) Paul Schilder's contribution to the theory of thought process. In *The Collected Papers of David Rapaport* (ed. M. Gill). New York: Basic Books, pp. 368–384.

Rathbun, C. (1934) On certain similarities between Spinoza and psycho-analysis. *The Psychoanalytic Review*, 21: 1–14.

Reid, J.A. (1955) The problem of values in psychoanalysis. *American Journal of Psychoanalysis*, 15: 115–122.

Reiner, A. (2021) What language are we speaking? Bion and early emotional life. *American Journal of Psychoanalysis*, 81. 10.1057/s11231-021-09281-3

Robinson, J.T. (2007) *Samuel Ibn Tibbon's Commentary on Ecclesiastes.* Tubingen: Mohr Siebeck.

Ross, D. (1991) *The Origins of American Social Science.* Cambridge: Cambridge University Press.

Rudavsky, T.M. (2018) *Jewish Philosophy in the Middle Ages. Science, Rationalism, and Religion.* Oxford: Oxford University Press.

Rudavsky, T. (2015) The science of scripture: Abraham Ibn Ezra and Spinoza on biblical hermeneutics. In *Spinoza and Medieval Jewish Philosophy* (ed. S. Nadler). Cambridge: Cambridge University Press.

Rudavsky, T.M. (2001) Galileo and Spinoza: heroes, heretics, and hermeneutics. *Journal of the History of Ideas*, 62: 611–631.

Ruderman, D.B. (2004) Introduction. In *Cultural Intermediaries. Jewish Intellectuals in Early Modern Italy* (eds D.B. Ruderman & G. Veltri). Philadelphia: University of Pennsylvania Press, pp. 1–23.

Saperstein, M. (2005) *Exile in Amsterdam. Saul Levi Morteira's Sermons to a Congregation of 'New Jews'*. Cincinnati: Hebrew Union College Press.

Sarason, S.B. (1981) *Psychology Misdirected*. New York: The Free Press.

Schafer, R. (1999) Recentering psychoanalysis. *Psychoanalytic Psychology*, 16: 339–354.

Schafer, R. (1976) *A New Language for Psychoanalysis*. New Haven and London: Yale University Press.

Schafer, R. (1968) *Aspects of Internalization*. New York: International Universities Press.

Schlesier, R. (1990) Homeric laughter by the rivers of Babylon: Heinrich Heine and Karl Marx. In *The Jewish Reception of Heinrich Heine* (1992) (ed. M.H. Gelber). Tubingen: Max Niemayer Verlag.

Seneca, L.A. (2015) *Letters in Ethics* (tr. M. Graver & A.A. Long). Chicago: University of Chicago Press.

Seneca (2014) *Letters from a Stoic* (tr. and ed. R. Campbell). Milton Keyes: Penguin Classics.

Simon, U. (1993) Interpreting the interpreter: supercommentaries on Ibn Ezra's commentaries. In *Rabbi Abraham Ibn Ezra: Studies in the Writings of a Twelfth-Century Jewish Polymath* (eds I. Twersky & J. Harris). Cambridge and London: Harvard University Press, pp. 86–121.

Smith, M.H. (1926) General: M. Hamblin Smith. Spinoza's anticipation of recent psychological developments. British Journal of Medical Psychology, Part 4, 1925, pp 257–278. *International Journal of Psycho-Analysis*, 7: 492.

Smith, M.H. (1925) Spinoza's anticipation of recent psychological developments. *The British Journal of Medical Psychology*, 5(4): 257–278.

Sorkin, D. (1987) *The Transformation of German Jewry, 1780–1840*. New York and Oxford: Oxford University Press.

Sorkin, D. (1983) Wilhelm von Humboldt: the theory and practice of self-formation (*Bildung*), 1791–1810. *Journal of the History of Ideas*, 4: 55–73.

Spinoza, B. (1670) Theological-political treatise. In Morgan, M. (Ed.), *Spinoza: Complete Works*. S. Shirley (Trans.) (pp. 383–583). Indianapolis, IN: Hackett Publishing.

Spinoza, B. (2002) *Spinoza Complete Works* (ed. M.L. Morgan; tr. S. Shirley). Indianapolis: Hackett Publishing Company.

Spinoza, B. (2007) *Theological-Political treatise* (ed. J. Israel; tr. M. Silverthorne & J. Israel). Cambridge: Cambridge University Press.

Stein, G. (1913) Sacred Emily. https://www.poetrynook.com/poem/sacred-emily

Sterba, R. (1982) *Reminiscences of a Viennese Psychoanalyst*. Detroit: Wayne State University Press.

Stern, D.B. (2017) Introduction. Interpersonal psychoanalysis: history and current status. In *The Interpersonal Perspective In Psychoanalysis, 1960's–1990's. Rethinking Transference and Countertransference* (eds D.B. Stern & I. Hirsch). Abingdon and New York: Routledge, pp. 1–28.

Stern, D.B. (2013a) Field theory in psychoanalysis, part I: Harry Stack Sullivan and Madeleine and Willy Baranger. *Psychoanalytic Dialogues*, 23: 487–501.

Stern, D.B. (2013b) Field theory in psychoanalysis, part 2: Bionian field theory and contemporary interpersonal/relational psychoanalysis. *Psychoanalytic Dialogues*, 23: 630–645.

Stern, D.B. (1997) *Unformulated Experience. From Dissociation to Imagination in Psychoanalysis*. Hillsdale, NJ: The Analytic Press.

Stern, D.B. (1987) Unformulated experience and transference. *Contemporary Psychoanalysis*, 23: 484–490.

Stern, D. N. (1985) *The Interpersonal World of the Infant. A View from Psychoanalysis and Developmental Psychology*. New York: Basic Books.

Stern, J. (2013) *The Matter and Form of Maimonides' Guide*. Cambridge: Harvard University Press.

Stitskin, L. (1962) Abraham Ibn Ezra's concept of man. *Tradition*, 4: 252–256.

Stonequist, E.V. (1937) *The Marginal Man: A Study in Personality and Culture Conflict*. New York: Russell and Russell, 1961 (originally published by Charles Scribners' Sons, 1937).

Strachey, J. & Strachey, A. (1985) *Bloomsbury/Freud. The Letters of James and Alix Strachey, 1924–1925* (eds P. Meisel & W. Kendrick). New York: Basic Books.

Strauss, L. (1952) *Persecution and the Art of Writing*. Glencoe: Free Press.

Studnicki-Gizbert, D. (2009) *La Nacion* among the nations: Portuguese and other maritime trading diasporas in the Atlantic, sixteenth to eighteenth centuries. In *Atlantic Diasporas. Jews, Conversos, and Crypto-Jews in the Age of Mercantilism, 1500–1800* (eds R.L. Kagan & P.D. Morgan). Baltimore: Johns Hopkins University Press.

Sullivan, H.S. (1954) *The Psychiatric Interview* (eds H.S. Perry & M.L. Gawel). New York: W.W. Norton & Company.

Sullivan, H.S. (1953) *The Interpersonal Theory of Psychiatry* (eds H.S. Perry & M.L. Gawel). New York: W.W. Norton & Company.

Sutliffe, A. (2009) Jewish history in an age of atlanticism. In *Atlantic Diasporas. Jews, Conversos, and Crypto-Jews in the Age of Mercantilism, 1500–1800* (eds E. Kagan & P.D. Morgan). Baltimore: The Johns Hopkins University Press.

Swetschinski, D.M. (2000) *Reluctant Cosmopolitans. The Portuguese Jews of Seventeenth-Century Amsterdam*. Oxford and Portland, Oregon: The Littman Library of Jewish Civilization.

Tanakh (1985) *A New Translation of the Holy Scriptures According to the Traditional Hebrew Text*. Philadelphia and Jerusalem: Jewish Publication Society.

Tanner, A. (1907a) Spinoza and modern psychology. *The American Journal of Psychology*, 18: 514–518.

Tanner, A. (1907b) Glimpses at the mind of a waitress. *American Journal of Sociology*, 13: 48–55.

Tauber, A.I. (2010) *Freud, The Reluctant Philosopher*. Princeton and Oxford: Princeton University Press.

Tausk, V. (1934) Ibsen the druggist. *Psychoanalytic Quarterly*, 3: 137–141.

Tausk, V. (1969) Diagnostic considerations concerning the symptomatology of the so-called war psychoses. *Psychoanalytic Quarterly*, 38: 382–404.

Tcherikover, S. (1959) *Hellenistic Civilization and the Jews* (tr. S. Applebaum). Philadelphia: Jewish Publication Society of America.

Thomas, W.I. (1917) The four wishes. *Social Behavior and Personality. Contributions of WI Thomas to Theory and Social Research* (ed. G. Volkart). Westport: Greenwood Press, pp. 111–144 (Reprinted in 1981).

Tigner, J.A. (1985) An analysis of Spinoza's pride and self-abasement. *American Journal of Psychoanalysis*, 45: 208–220.

Tolman, E.C. (1932) *Purposive Behavior in Animals and Men*. New York and London: The Century Company.

Veltri, G. (2004) *Philo* and *Sophia*: Leone Ebreo's concept of Jewish philosophy. In *Cultural Intermediaries. Jewish Intellectuals in Early Modern Italy* (eds D.B. Ruderman & G. Veltri). Philadelphia: University of Pennsylvania Press, pp. 55–66.

Vermorel, H. (2009) The presence of Spinoza in the exchanges between Freud and Rolland Romain. *International Journal of Psycho-Analysis*, 90: 1235–1254.

Vickers, I. (1996) *Defoe and the New Sciences*. Cambridge: Cambridge University Press.

Volkan, V. (2017) *Immigrants and Refugees: Trauma, Personal Mourning, and Border Psychology*. London: Karnac.

Wachtel, N. (2013) *The Faith of Remembrance. Marrano Labyrinths.* Philadelphia: University of Pennsylvania Press.

Waelder, R. (1951) The structure of paranoid ideas: a critical survey of various theories. *International Journal of Psycho-Analysis*, 32: 167–177.

Waelder, R. (2007) The principle of multiple function: observations on over-determination. *Psychoanalytic Quarterly*, 76: 75–92 (Originally published in 1936).

Weiss, F.A. (1952) Psychoanalysis and moral values. *American Journal of Psychoanalysis*, 12: 39–49.

Whitehead, A.N. (1978) *Process and Reality. Corrected Edition* (eds D.R. Griffin & D.W. Sherburne). New York: The Free Press (Originally published in 1929).

Winnicott, D.W. (1960) The theory of the parent-infant relationship. *International Journal of Psychoanalysis*, 41: 585–595.

Winnicott, D.W. (1953) Transitional objects and transitional phenomena: a study of the first not-me possession. *International Journal of Psychoanalysis*, 34: 89–97.

Winter, S. (1999) *Freud and the Institution of Psychoanalytic Knowledge*. Stanford: Stanford University Press.

Winter, S. (1997–1998) "Schoolboy Psychology": Freud's classical education and the institutionalization of psychoanalytic knowledge. *Cultural Critique*, 38: 137–175.

Wisse, R. (2013) *No Joke. Making Jewish Humor.* Princeton: Princeton University Press.

Wolfson, H.A. (1934) *The Philosophy of Spinoza. Unfolding the Latent Processes of His Reasoning.* Cambridge, MA: Harvard University Press.

Wolfson, H. (1921) The needs of Jewish scholarship in America. *The Menorah Journal*, 7: 28–35.

Wolfson, H.A. (1916) Crescas on the problem of divine attributes. *The Jewish Quarterly Review, New Series*, 7: 1–44.

Wolstein, B. (1987) Anxiety and the psychic center of the psychoanalytic self. *Contemporary Psychoanalysis*, 23: 631–658.

Wolstein, B. (1953) The romantic Spinoza in America. *Journal of the History of Ideas*, 14: 439–450.

Yerushalmi, Y.H. (1991) *Freud's Moses: Judaism Terminable and Interminable.* New Haven: Yale University Press.

Yerushalmi, Y.H. (1982) *Zakhor: Jewish History and Jewish Memory.* Seattle: University of Washington Press.

Yerushalmi, Y.H. (1980) The re-education of Marranos in the seventeenth century. In *The Faith of Fallen Jews. Yosef Haim Yerushalmi and the Writing of Jewish History* (eds D. Myers & A. Kaye). Waltham, MA: Brandeis University Press, pp. 157–174 (Published in 2014).

Yerushalmi, Y.H. (1976) *The Lisbon Massacre of 1506 and the Royal Image in the Shebet Yehudah.* Cincinnati: Hebrew Union College Annual Supplements.

Yerushalmi, Y.H. (1971) *From Spanish Court to Italian Ghetto. Isaac Cardoso: A Study in Seventeenth Century Marranism and Jewish Apologetics.* New York: Columbia University Press.

Yovel, Y. (2009) *The Other Within. The Marranos. Split Identity and Emerging Modernity.* Princeton: Princeton University Press.

Yovel, Y. (1989a) *Spinoza and Other Heretics (V1). The Marrano of Reason.* Princeton: Princeton University Press.

Yovel, Y. (1989b) *Spinoza and Other Heretics (V2). The Adventures of Immanence.* Princeton: Princeton University Press.

Zagorin, P. (1990) *Ways of Lying: Dissimulation, Persecution, and Conformity in Early Modern Europe.* Cambridge: Harvard University Press.

Zuboff, S. (January 29, 2021) The coup we are not talking about. We can have democracy, or we can have a surveillance society, but we cannot have both. *The New York Times.* https://www.nytimes.com/2021/01/29/opinion/sunday/facebook-surveillance-society-technology.html

Index

Page numbers followed by "n" indicate a note on the corresponding page.